Marketing, Sales and Cu

institute of
financial services

Marketing, Sales and Customer Service

2nd edition

Neil Russell-Jones

Institute of Financial Services
4-9 Burgate Lane
Canterbury
Kent
CT1 2XJ

T 01227 818649
F 01227 479641
E editorial@ifslearning.com

Institute of Financial Services publications are published by The Chartered Institute of Bankers, a non-profit making registered educational charity.

Typeset by Kevin O'Connor
Printed by Antony Rowe Ltd, Wiltshire

© The Chartered Institute of Bankers 2003
Reprinted 2004

ISBN 0-85297-690-9

Contents

One

Introduction

Introduction to the section

Topics in this chapter

About this book

Objectives of the book

Structure

How to use the book

Some definitions

About this book

This book is about understanding how to get customers to buy or take up your products and services – ie it is about **Marketing** and **Sales** in financial services. It looks at all aspects of these topics from the initial theoretical and philosophical thinking behind them as management disciplines, through the practicalities of dealing with customers and on to building continuing relationships with the customers after acquisition – **Customer Service**.

Figure 1.1: Marketing, sales and customer service: the continuum

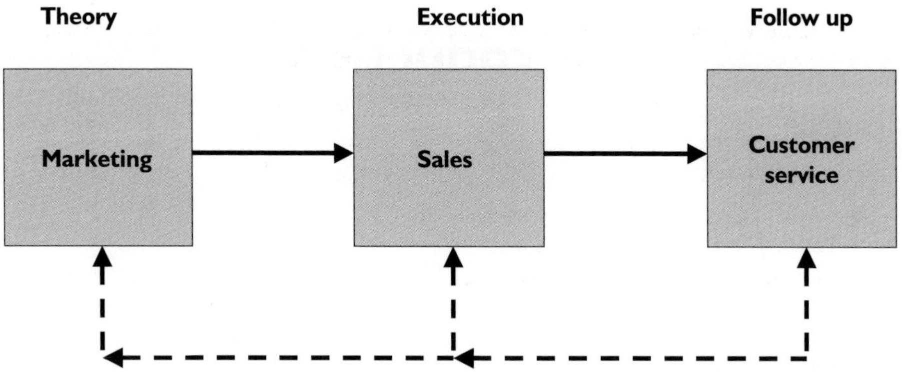

Theory	Execution	Follow up

The subject can be divided into three stages:

- The first – **marketing** – looks at the thinking and understanding necessary to facilitate the development of the environment, at a *macro* level, for you to encourage your customers to take your offerings. It represents the *theoretical* component or aspect of the relationship. This could also be called the **positioning** of your offerings in the marketplace.
- The next stage – **sales** – is concerned with the interaction with the customers, at a *micro* level, where they discuss their individual needs and (you hope) actually buy your services; and is about explaining the benefits that they get from them. It is the *execution* of the theory. This can also be called the **acquisition** of new customers.
- The final or third stage – **customer service** – deals with the way you manage your customers once they have moved from prospects to customers and have a commercial relationship with you – which you wish to maintain and enhance (sell more – product penetration) and is the *follow-up* to the execution. This stage not only provides links into future and additional sales but also provides feedback for marketing initiatives based on reactions and comments made by customers to assist in making the marketing and subsequently sales more targeted, better focused on needs and ultimately, of course, from the organization's point of view, more successful. This can also be referred to as the **retention** of existing customers.

1.1   Objectives of the book

This book has been written with two objectives in mind.

Firstly: to serve as a textbook for the **Institute of Financial Services**. It covers part of the syllabus – specifically the **Marketing, Sales and Customer Service** module. Each chapter denotes which parts of the syllabus it covers and the main topics therein.

Note, however, that some chapters cover more than one part of the syllabus; and equally some parts are covered in more than one chapter.

Secondly: it has been written to serve as an introduction to marketing and sales and as a readable and useful book for students of the subject generally or for interested readers. It is therefore structured in the logical sequence for:

◆ understanding **Marketing** – the theory;
◆ **Selling** – the execution; and then
◆ **Customer service** – the follow up.

1.2   Structure

To meet these objectives the book is divided into an introduction and then three other main parts:

The first section – **marketing** – lays the foundations for an understanding of marketing. This covers the definition of marketing, the key elements of the marketing mix, marketing segmentation, market research (how to collect information about your customers [and competitors]), competition analysis as well as where marketing fits in with strategy, plans, targets and goals.

The second section – **sales** – explores the practicalities of actually persuading customers to accept your offerings. It focuses on understanding why your customers buy and then how to use that information and that understanding to sell to them, communication and the importance of branding and pricing.

The final section – **customer service** – focuses on keeping your (existing as well as newly acquired) customers. It explores the information you need on your customers, dealing with customers, 'knowing your customers' and their future needs and wants, and the 'ethics' of selling.

At the end of the book you can find a glossary of terms, an index and other useful items.

How to use the book

To assist you in making the most from the book each chapter contains the following items:

◆ a summary of the contents;
◆ what you should be able to understand at the end of the chapter;
◆ further reading on the subject (as relevant).

This is to enable you to understand the key items covered in a chapter – if you are 'dipping' into it, the key things that you should understand after reading it and for those interested in deeper analysis or broader reading, a list of further reading.

1.3   Some definitions

Throughout this book there are some terms that have special meanings, or usage. A full glossary can be found in the appendices. For avoidance of confusion you should note the following:

any reference to *him* or *her* includes both genders and often the plural.

Other terms include:

Buyers

Those people, groups of people or organizations that purchase the offerings made in a market. Sometimes they are referred to as clients or customers and often, in retail, called consumers. Note however that not all buyers are end consumers of the offering and may include warehouses, re-sellers, agents and retailers. Manufacturers often buy both raw materials and components and sometimes finished goods.

Sellers

Those people, groups of people and organizations that offer a product or service to the market and attempt to meet needs and wants and to match demand with supply.

Unless you have both buyers and sellers there is no market.

Market

The mechanism whereby buyers and sellers are brought together. This may be a physical location – eg Lloyds of London or a stock exchange or just the intangible set of transactions that effect buying and selling – eg the London Foreign Exchange (F/X) market which is just a collection of telephone lines and limits in banks, brokers and other players.

Within a market there can be many sub-markets. For example you could split financial services into banking, insurance, asset management, securities, treasury and other services. In turn banking could be split into retail banking, wholesale, international, corporate, institutional, and investment and merchant banking. Similarly insurance includes personal lines, re-insurance, marine, life, energy, special risks and so on. These splits are of course not set in stone and with the blurring of boundaries driven by change often overlap – eg bancassurance, allfinanz, etc.

Marketing

There are many definitions of marketing. Kotler uses the following:

> '**Marketing** is a social and managerial process by which groups and individuals obtain what they need and want through creating and exchanging products and value with others'.

This definition subsumes both selling and customer service as a part of the whole concept of marketing. Other definitions will be explored in section II.

Product

A manufactured item such as an aeroplane, a DVD player, a bottle of whisky, a box of toy bricks or a four-wheel drive car – where there is a *physical* delivery (or the opportunity for it, which might not be exercised).

Service

The supply of (often) people-based services – eg professional advice, architecture, dry cleaning; or less tangible items such as an overdraft, insurance or IT management of systems through facilities management.

The terms 'products' and 'services' are often used interchangeably to mean both, and this book is no exception.

Intangible items

This includes such things as brands and ideas, which cannot be touched but can have real value.

Brand

The actual name that items are sold or marketed under:

- ◆ Galaxy, Dairy Milk, Bourneville plain, Milky Bar are all types of chocolate made by Mars, Cadbury, Cadbury and Nestle respectively;
- ◆ Boddingtons, Carling, Guinness, 'Old Peculiar' are all types of beer;
- ◆ Barclays, HSBC, Nationwide, Abbey National, Royal Bank of Scotland, Coutts (even though a part of the latter) are all banks of one type or another;
- ◆ Norwich Union, Prudential, Swiss Re, Scottish Widows, Jardines, Willis Coroon are all types of insurance company – but including life, general, reinsurance and broking;
- ◆ Visa, Mastercard, American Express and Diners are all charge or credit cards.

The names of products and services may include the names of the company offering them, or equally may not, and this can be quite confusing. For example your American Express card may have been issued by American Express, or equally by another bank such as Royal Bank of Scotland or by a non-bank. The holding company for Norwich Union is now called Aviva, but known in Ireland as Hibernian. The main credit card issued by Barclays Bank – Barclaycard – is co-branded VISA – which is an internationally accepted brand for credit cards. Barclays also issues Visa cards for other companies.

Many firms now manufacture products and services which are then sold by others known as **white labelling** (not to be confused with kitchen items such as fridges or cookers known as **white goods** because of the typical colour in which they were supplied) and is an increasing phenomenon in financial services as more competitors join in and do not wish to 'manufacture' services themselves.

Two

The foundations of marketing

Marketing theory largely grew out of *economics*, which is concerned with such ideas as production, consumption, distribution and exchange of goods and services, and it is principally the latter that gave birth to marketing. This came from a desire to understand in more detail the issues surrounding **supply** and **demand** and to probe the driving forces that cause changes and thence to develop theoretical concepts to allow firms to try to influence them – in fact the study of markets and behaviour.

Further works in these areas can be found in the reading lists.

Marketing is not an activity that is carried on a day-to-day basis on its own in isolation from the rest of the firm. As a management discipline it sits within an organization's general strategies and plans and is influenced very much by other disciplines such as finance, production or development. Planning and budgeting are also key aspects of marketing, as is research into both competition/markets and customers.

Further definitions of marketing

The definition of marketing quoted in the introduction, from Kotler, focused on meeting needs of individuals and groups; but a fuller definition is as follows:

> 'The function of sales, distribution, advertising and sales promotion, product planning and market research. That is, those functions in a business that directly involve contact with the consumer and assessment of his needs, and the translation of this information into outputs for sale, consistent with the firm's objectives.'

Penguin Dictionary of Economics

This definition is very full and precise and brings in all the key elements of getting your outputs to customers:

- ◆ research to find out what is required;
- ◆ product planning to develop an offering to meet those needs;
- ◆ informing the customer what it is you offer – advertising and promotion; and then
- ◆ getting it to the customers – distribution.

It also links the marketing process into the firm's objectives – ie its strategy – a concept that underpins marketing as it must be aligned with the strategic intent of the organization.

Another definition is:

> 'Marketing is the management process responsible for identifying, anticipating and satisfying customer requirements profitably.'

> *Chartered Institute of Marketing (UK)*

This particular definition brings in a concept that is important and implicit in the previous definition, but explicit here - that of profit. If you cannot sell your outputs for a profit then you are giving them away and will soon go out of business.

Finally cynics say:

> 'Marketing is common sense with buzzwords'

ie no rocket science, just knowledge of what customers want and how to get it there.

The concepts with which marketing is concerned are both simple at one level and extremely complex at the other. The basic supply and demand graph, so familiar to everyone, demonstrates the theory and concept in a very simple manner. When analysing the real world, however, the model is not nearly so straightforward because there are almost always very many interacting and complex variables, which make analysis difficult and often devolving down into best 'guesstimates'. Take a simple supply chain as shown in Figure 2.1.

Figure 2.1: Supply chain

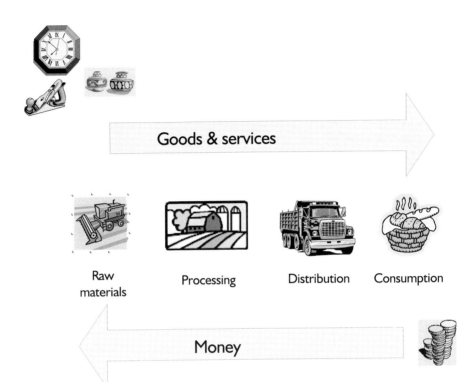

Raw materials

Processing

Distribution

Consumption

In general, products flow one way and money flows the other way; but the supply chain, however, can be extremely complex. In this case it starts with grain, which is harvested when it is ripe, then processed to make flour and thence bread then distributed to outlets and finally bought by consumers and eaten. Each step has many complex interactions and may vary in scope and scale from a small-scale interaction between one farmer, one baker and the local village (say 400 people); to major retail outlets buying millions of loaves a year for millions of customers.

Even in the simple model there are several variables for supply and demand. To whom does the farmer sell – to a local or distant miller? direct to the baker who will mill it? to people? or to a large consortium that will process grain and then on-sell to bakers and consumers? The latter can, of course, usually buy finished goods – bread rolls etc – but often also raw materials – flour, yeast etc – for making their own bread. Similarly before the grain is harvested it has to be sown and that, in itself, involves many steps as the farmer may have to buy tractors, fertilizer, casual labour, seed etc. Demand and supply will fluctuate at each stage in the chain – and not always in step, because each stage is influenced by different issues or by the same issues but in different strengths. As a result it can be very difficult to analyse markets and to forecast relative demand and then produce goods accordingly.

2.1 Markets

Although at a basic level a market has been defined as a place where buyers and sellers interact, they are not uniform and there are several recognized special types of market:

Sellers market – where the power lies with those selling their offering – usually in monopoly or oligopoly situations or where demand is fast exceeding supply and goods simply walk off the shelves – for example when 'Cabbage Patch Dolls' or 'Thunderbirds – Tracy Islands' were the toys to have, or when the *dot.com* boom started and share prices for those companies went through the roof, as buyers have to bid up for offerings which equalizes the demand/supply relationship.

Buyers market – where the power is with buyers, and sellers have to be very innovative and imaginative in persuading the buyers to take their offerings. This is the case with many markets now because they are 'mature', with flat demand and many competing and substitute goods. Also when demand falls – after the dot.com boom collapsed the prices dropped through the floor and shares could not be given away. When the market is flat outlets often resort to 'sales' to stimulate demand, because by reducing the price consumers are encouraged to come in and buy.

Price-taking market – is a market where near perfect competition exists. The key components for this include:

- ◆ Transparency of transactions
- ◆ Homogeneity of goods
- ◆ Universal availability of knowledge
- ◆ Highly mobile resource

Where these conditions exist suppliers are forced to charge the same price. Although this market never exists perfectly, many markets operate very close to this, and as a result there is downward price pressure – eg the mortgage market where prices (the interest rates payable on the mortgage) are advertised and often put into 'best buy' league tables. These tables in turn are considered as key marketing tools by, for example, Building Societies because they are widely publicized and read and give great market coverage to them.

Key market variables

There are some key variables that it is necessary to understand because they form part of the framework or backdrop to marketing. They are:

- ◆ Size and elasticity of the market
- ◆ Demand
- ◆ Utility
- ◆ Life cycles

Size and elasticity of the market

When considering a market it is critical to understand two concepts – the **size** of the market – ie the spend currently available and how it might change in the future and the **elasticity** of the market – how it will react to changes in prices because price is a key element in selling anything (see marketing mix below). This in turn has four key components:

- ◆ Whether the offering is a 'necessity' (something that you must buy eg food, clothing, heat etc) or a luxury – a nice-to-have;
- ◆ How important the item is to a budget – for some, perhaps on low or fixed incomes while food may be a necessary, price may also be a factor because they have to allocate a very limited income across many items. For others it may be irrelevant;
- ◆ The availability of substitutes and the quality. For example rice, potatoes and pasta are all bread substitutes (but not if you want a sandwich) and in the UK are all readily available. Similarly there are many differing monetary products around to tempt customers into using them;
- ◆ How quickly you can adjust to price changes – ie if you supply a component for someone else and it is difficult for them to replace it in the short term they essentially have to pay the new price. The longer-term effects may of course be totally different, because they may seek out alternative suppliers or goods and cease buying from you if the price change is particularly adverse, or they cannot pass it on to their customers. Note that customers usually have little or no difficulty in adjusting down to lower prices – but it may be virtually impossible to put them up again.

Demand

This is a critical factor in determining what to sell – and also how much to charge for it. Price is the most effective way of rationing scarce goods. When demand exceeds supply the price will rise to reduce demand. The inverse applies – when demand is low the price will fall to increase demand. Competition by and large operates to reduce prices. Demand is a function of the following variables:

- ◆ **Consumer fashion/tastes** – which can change often arbitrarily and in an irrational manner. Equally they can be manipulated by firms and, sometimes, even governments if it suits them. In fashion there is truly little that is new – fashion houses roll old designs around on a periodic basis and we are seeing many previous fashions which were 'out' that are now back 'in' – eg stack-soled/heeled shoes, miniskirts and flares/bellbottoms. DVD players are a good example where manufacturers want people to buy them to replace/augment their video recorder and as everyone has a TV and would not normally replace it that often – but a DVD player demands a new TV screen to achieve that 'perfect DVD resolution'. Changes in food 'science' also have an effect on sales. The increased awareness of sugar in foods has lead to a phenomenal growth in sugar-free or reduced-sugar drinks – similarly with caffeine-free products.

◆ **Market size** – which can fluctuate for short periods – eg where a new product is available and a market grows rapidly until it becomes 'saturated' – as is the case with PCs because most homes have one or more and growth has fallen. They can also change over the longer term. For example the demographic changes in the West (as births fall) have resulted in reduced need for babywear and greater emphasis on health care and pension provision. This is also the case with mortgages where most mortgage sales are re-mortgages or, at the top-end, second-home purchases as few younger people are around to enter the market. As a result there is increasing emphasis on keeping current customers because there are fewer 'newer' ones around and therefore it is much harder to replace those leaving.

◆ **Future expectations** – does the buyer perceive that the market economy will grow or shrink – and as result will they borrow more to fund purchases in the expectation that it can be repaid through earnings or will they cut back on spending and save or pay off debts just in case things turn down?

◆ **Price of the product** – as prices fall there is a tendency to buy more although it is not a 'straight-line' relationship but tends to be stimulated at what are known as 'price points' where small changes in price result on large increases in demand (the inverse of the straw that breaks the camels back). This is often caused where the price change alters the perception of a good/service (if it is more expensive it must be better).

◆ **Price of competing products** – where consumers perceive that another product is similar to your product and it is cheaper they will buy that one in preference to yours as they will feel that they are getting the same product for a lower price.

◆ **Price of substitutes** – these share the same relationship as that with competing products although not quite as close because there is a definite trade-off between, say, pasta and potatoes in terms of what you get, whereas there is little difference between the many different brands of petrol (competing goods).

◆ **Price of complementary goods and services** – can affect the demand because a reduction in the price of eggs may encourage you to buy more bacon to make a traditional breakfast. Conversely if the price of milk trebled overnight then it is highly probable that sales of breakfast cereals and possibly tea and coffee would fall (or perhaps that of a coffee whitener or milk substitute would rise).

◆ **Advertising and/or marketing effort** – clever and sophisticated marketing can create a 'new' market quite quickly. For example there was no real market for 'music on the move' before the Sony Walkman was invented and marketed – similarly with faxes – they took off virtually overnight only in turn to be eclipsed largely by the Internet. Currently there is a campaign to sell digital radio (and therefore new sets) – but it is not really succeeding because the market does not perceive a great value or benefit in changing from current radios at the moment.

◆ **Disposable income or discretionary spend** – most buyers divide income (albeit subconsciously) into that required to meet 'necessary' spending (as defined by Maslow in his hierarchy of needs qv) such as food, shelter, clothes light and heat etc and other or 'discretionary' spending – often for luxuries (and equally often for 'rubbish'). Goods and services can change category – in the UK vacuum cleaners, refrigerators, televisions, telephones and cookers, once luxuries, would now be considered necessaries by most people – similarly with dishwashers, PCs, CD players and holidays, which are rapidly moving into this category

◆ **Other issues** – for example seasonality – most firework manufacturers will sell most of their output (in the UK) in the run-up to bonfire night – and a lot of chocolate is sold at two key periods – Easter and Christmas. This sort of demand gives 'lumpy' cashflows because costs are incurred over the year but income is gained during short intense periods. Suppliers therefore often try to change the patterns by marketing such things as 'summer sales' for goods not usually bought at that time, or 'winter breaks' for what might normally be categorized as summer destinations for holidays – usually at lower prices. Another way to try to manage demand is by selling 'off-peak' services to encourage people to use clubs or trains during periods other than the high-demand times (on the train rush hours or lunch times for health clubs in cities). Boycotts or a perception can also change demand. For example few people in the USA or the UK wear fur due to (often very violent) campaigns by animal rights activists coupled with a change in the climate to warmer winters (whereas in other countries the markets have hardly been altered (eg France, Central Europe).

Utility

This is an economic concept that expresses **the value** that a purchaser perceives that they will receive from buying your goods or using your services. Typically buyers will try to maximize the utility from their expenditure – whether they are consumers or businesses – because they all have limited spending power. As a result you are only as good as the last interaction with a customer – if you wish to sell more. They will also pay more where they perceive that there is a greater utility or value. It is often influenced by reference to intangible things such as culture and social issues or mores. When selling to French people or firms they value the 'Frenchness' of an item very highly – often to the detriment of other benefits, and there is a great bias against US, Japanese and often UK goods. Japanese consumers are very sensitive to global brands and will often pay premiums for the name (see branding). For some people – particularly those with low disposable income – price iş a key factor. This utility/value concept is explored in great depth under **Customer Value Proposition** and is a central tenet of good and effective marketing and selling.

Life cycles

All goods and services are subject to what is known as the product life cycle. This is how demand for a particular thing changes as it 'matures'. In general the cycle is the same – but the time horizons vary dramatically.

The stage of the life cycle also affects the sales, profits and strategies adopted by players. A typical cycle is shown in Figure 2.2.

Figure 2.2: Life cycle

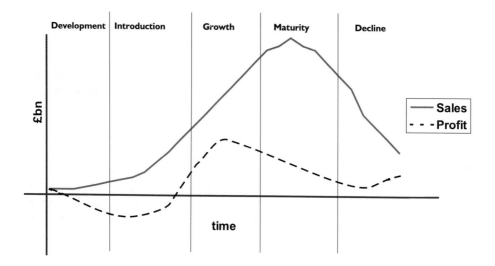

The stages are:

Development – where the product is developed and incurs cost of R&D with no income.

Introduction – where the product first 'hits the streets' – usually no profits because there is a high product-marketing cost.

Growth – where the product's sales take off, and revenue and profit climb.

Maturity – where the product has achieved high penetration into the market and therefore sales flatten off – also requires increased marketing spend to fight off competition or to stimulate sales.

Decline – where sales and profits drop although profits can be increased as other sellers pull out.

A life cycle can cover:

◆ a product **class** – eg diesel vehicles
◆ a particular **product form** – eg diesel vans
◆ a **branded product** – eg Vauxhall vans.

Not all cycles are the same because the generic pattern shown and the time spent in stages can vary. Product classes tend to have a longer lifespan than brands in many markets – eg training shoes or mobile phones – where the basic idea still exists but the brands/types have changed many times following fashion and developments. Most mortgage products are now offered only for a limited period – and then the next 'new product' is developed – incorporating different rates and a few other changes.

Fads

Fads also play a major part in determining life cycles of some products because, as the initial furore dies away, the sales drop to virtually zero as the products become yesterday's things – with which nobody wants to be seen – eg hula-hoops (the child's plastic hoop not the snack) in the 1950s, Rubic's cube in the 1980s, and (fortunately) 'clackers' in the 1970s. A fad normally has a very steep rise and a very steep drop in life cycle over a short time period. Fad sales have no lasting base because they do not satisfy long term *needs* – merely short term *wants* (usually to be seen with the particular thing). In 2000 the key item for Christmas seemed to be scooters and just about every child had one. The next year they were sold in only small quantities. In 2001 and 2002 it was merchandizing of both *Harry Potter* and the *Lord of the Rings* goods linked to film releases, and because of the serial nature of those particular films such fad products will continue for at least the next two years.

Summary

1 Products and services are different – the former real the latter intangible.
2 The names under which services are offered (brands) and names of the companies offering them may differ.
3 Both buyers and sellers are required to create a market.
4 Demand is very complex and is affected by a wide range of variables (price, substitute goods, future expectations etc).
5 Not all cycles are the same because the generic pattern shown and the time spent in stages can vary.

Select bibliography

Marketing pocketbook: Russell-Jones & Fletcher

Principles of Marketing (Chapters 1 and 2): Kotler

Three

Why the financial services sector is different

Topics in this chapter

Service *v* product

Financial services

Delivery channels

3.1   Introduction

This book is not a legal textbook and it is essential, therefore, that you are familiar with the relevant legislation that affects your operations, as well as any internal rules (handbook) and any informal rules such as association rules – eg banking code of conduct.

There are several issues that make financial services different:

- ◆ In most industries items are sold for money – but in the case of financial services institutions their offerings actually are money and related items;
- ◆ Regulation is far more intense in financial services than in any others and more far-reaching;
- ◆ It deals with services not products and the offerings are intangible – not physical or 'real' – which causes issues for sellers and buyers;
- ◆ Customers often sit on both sides of the value chain – ie as depositors and borrowers;
- ◆ Distribution is complex, regulated and changing continually.

Milton and Rose Friedman *(Free to Choose – 1980)* define how you can spend money.

There are only four ways in which you can spend money:

'Your own money on yourself

Your own money on someone else

Another person's money on yourself

Another person's money on another person'

The latter two ways are of course of great interest to lenders and the first two in many ways to those concerned with savings and investments.

Money

Money is a very emotional thing. Generally, coinage in use has little intrinsic value any more, because it is no longer made of precious metals such as gold or silver; and paper notes in general use have no value at all. Basic economics, however, tells us that, *inter alia*, money acts as a store of wealth and as a medium of exchange. In our modern economies money is used to buy goods and services rather than having to resort to barter, which is inefficient and can be difficult (how many pigs and sheep will it cost me to buy a tractor, but actually I wanted a CD player and a house and you want cows and salt?). It is also 'saved' or invested, in which capacity it is functioning as a store of wealth.

Financial services, and in particular banking, is different from other business sectors because its product is money itself – whether as a place to keep it; or a place to borrow it; and in insurance terms as a means of making sure you recoup monetary losses that might arise or invest for the future. Banks can, through items such as loans and overdrafts, create money 'at a stroke' and supervisory authorities and governments worry about the amount of money that might be created and accordingly legislate to control it. The stability of the monetary system is a critical issue for governments because a loss of confidence in the value or worth of a nation's currency (which, as mentioned before, has no intrinsic value) can have devastating affects on the economy.

Regulation

As a result financial services, in an age that could be described as the 'bureaucratic age' and seems to generate increasing and more pervasive regulation generally, is more heavily regulated than any other sector in order to protect the public from possible sharp practice, fraud and other types of theft. There are also lots of rules covering the ability of companies to manage themselves and these tend to concentrate on how **'solvent'** a company is – ie can it meet its short-term obligations – and how well **capitalized** it is – ie can it meet potential losses that may arise from its operations.

With the increasing global nature of operations and the likelihood that some of the money placed across the world may be 'suspect' there are also a lot of regulations dealing with 'hot' money – money laundering – which have given rise to some quite bizarre interpretations such as firms that have had relationships with people for many years now having to ask for proof that they are who they purport to be.

The history of regulation in financial services is long. Some of the more relevant acts, directives and milestones etc include:

- ◆ **1971 – Competition and Credit Control** – designed to increase competition among what was widely regarded as a cartel in banks.
- ◆ **1986 – Building Societies Act** – designed to liberalize the building society movement – which lead directly to demutualization.
- ◆ **1986 – 'Big bang'** – the liberalization of securities and abolition of fixed commissions resulting in a scramble to buy securities brokers and jobbers – changing the face of securities trading and ultimately leading to the disappearance of most firms/names that had previously existed.
- ◆ **1990 Second Banking Directive** – designed to ensure a level playing field across the European Common Market (now EU).
- ◆ **1998 – Financial Services Authority (FSA)** took over responsibility for supervision of UK banks from the Bank of England.
- ◆ **1999 – FSA** took over responsibility for everything else in financial services becoming a unitary supervising authority[1].
- ◆ **Enterprise Act** (due to come into force mid-2003) will change the position and powers/rights of secured lenders in bankruptcy/liquidation/receivership.

Why regulate?

There are many reasons why regulations are passed in financial services and they include:

- ◆ To protect consumers
- ◆ To maintain the soundness of financial institutions
- ◆ To maintain stability of the financial system
- ◆ To obviate/reduce criminal activity concerning money

These are explored in more detail below.

To protect consumers

In general there has been a steady move from the traditional British legal precept of *'caveat emptor'* (buyer beware) to the more paternalistic and protectionist continental European view that consumers must be protected from the 'unscrupulous criminals' that run financial institutions. Because these institutions generally take money from the public and because products can often be very complex (in operation if not in design), coupled with the fact that most people are financially unsophisticated, there are often opportunities for fraud or deception although these instances are fairly rare in the UK. Life insurance is currently suffering from a major fall-out caused by perceived mis-selling in the 1980s and 1990s when many people were apparently persuaded to change their policies or to take out new policies – often endowments linked with mortgages which were represented as good deals. For many the opposite turned out to be the case and many millions of pounds of compensation are now being paid out. Some of the key issues driving this are:

- Many products are just too technical for the consumer to grasp properly (small print);
- Contracts are often one-sided in favour of the supplier (eg guarantees that also function unbeknown to guarantors as indemnities – thus changing third-party liability into first-party liability);
- Information is usually asymmetric – ie suppliers often have much more than consumers;
- Such information that is available to consumers is often inadequate or too difficult to understand in entirety;
- Comparisons of true price or quality are extremely difficult (it is easy to compare different brands or types of baked beans or lemonades – but much harder to compare investment trusts or life policies) – but see the FSA official website which attempts to offer such comparisons.

This therefore has lead to calls for legislation to attempt to provide more transparency – eg in APR quotes for loans or credit cards.

To maintain soundness of financial institutions

Confidence in organizations is ephemeral and can disappear overnight (eg Andersen following the Enron/Worldcom debacle) and banks are no exceptions to this. A loss of confidence in an institution can cause a run on its deposits and, given the low levels of liquidity to deposits that banks hold for commercial reasons, cause it to fail. This in turn can have a knock-on effect on the whole monetary system which authorities are naturally enough keen not to have happen.

In addition financial institutions also hold monies in a fiduciary capacity and therefore require supervision to ensure customer welfare. (There have been some spectacular failures although not in the UK in recent times – such as BCCI, the USA Savings and

Loans crisis and the seemingly never-ending requirement by continental European banks for re-capitalization).

To maintain stability of the financial system

Banks by the nature of their operations play a pivotal role in the disbursement and smooth handling of money – the oil of the economic and financial engine – eg payments. Any issues here can have very quick knock-on effects in the economy and therefore supervising authorities are keen to ensure that liquidity is maintained and accordingly confidence on the system.

To obviate/reduce criminal activity concerning money

The need to catch criminals and to ensure that they are unable to hide or transfer their ill-gotten gains easily around the world is a key issue for financial supervisors. They are keen to ensure that banks and insurance companies do not facilitate money laundering by such criminal types and that adequate precautions are in place when dealing with large sums of money.

For a practitioner in financial services it is vital that he or she is up to date with all the relevant legislation because many activities that take place within financial organizations are covered by, often quite onerous, legislation (regulated environment).

In view of the foregoing then regulation is an ever-present factor when working in financial services. By contrast much of the legislation is passed to encourage deregulation – ie the loosening of controls on activities.

Deregulation

In this context the term deregulation does not alas mean a reduction in legislation but rather an attempt by authorities and governments to encourage a more liberal approach to financial services such as a reduction in some entry requirements, or the sweeping away of outmoded or 'Spanish practices' and cartel operations. This is to encourage more players and therefore more competition – leading to (it is hoped) a reduction in prices from this more competitive marketplace.

Accordingly the financial services market has changed enormously with demutualization (Abbey National, Northern Rock, Halifax, Friends'), many Mergers and Acquisitions (RBS/NatWest; HSBC/Midland, Barclays/Woolwich, Lloyds/TSB/C&G etc) and a lot of rationalization (usually resulting in branch closures and redundancies). At the same time many new players from outside financial services have entered the fray (M&S, Virgin, Tesco, Sainsbury's, the AA and so on) selling a range of products including banking, investment and credit cards, while most large department stores and chains now offer in-house store cards with credit facilities. In addition, the lines between different sub-sectors blur as banks buy insurance companies and vice versa. Virtually everyone imaginable offers credit cards (AA, WWF, British Gas etc) and not a day passes it seems without a letter from someone offering you yet another credit card – which is a sign of a saturated market, where most new business comes from persuading customers to switch, usually by way of introductory cheap rates.

These changes have also been fuelled by radical changes to distribution channels such as ATMs, remote processing centres (such as call centres) and the Internet, which have swept away much of the need, perceived or otherwise, for a bricks-and-mortar network. Most of these are offered as joint ventures with established players and some as 'white labelled goods' qv. For many stores that had ATMs on site and also offered cashback at the till it seemed a logical step to offer other products as well – either indirectly through literature available in-store or as in Morrisons' case (a food retailer) directly through the branches via Midland Bank (HSBC). With similar trends in garages will it be long before we see BP Bank?

The third factor has been the change in usage of networks as people have stopped going to branches, because it is no longer necessary. This has affected throughput, or footfall, and coupled with competition to change to direct banking or insurance, put further pressure on bricks and mortar.

3.2   Services versus products

Within the financial services market *products* are not actually offered although they are often referred to as such. What are offered are services. By the same token many offerings are very complex due to the inherent nature of the offering, which contains many variables – eg pension provision or investment – due to the time horizons involved or where security is required eg mortgages.

An apple is a simple product – it is bought and consumed rapidly in succession. A car is a more complex item and its purchase may involve comparisons of different makes etc and test drives but nonetheless is relatively easy to understand. You buy the car and drive it and after you consider it to be of no more value to you – you sell it for its residual value or scrap and possibly purchase another one, and this gives little cause for problems with understanding the transaction and its implications.

An investment, however, can be much more complex, can have many more variables and typically a longer term time horizon as well and will be 'used' only when it matures. Questions such as: 'Where should I invest?' 'What in?' 'How much?' 'What proportions?' 'When?' 'How often?' 'For how long?' 'What is the risk versus reward profile?' 'How can I have access to it?' etc', can make it extremely difficult to understand and to compare with others. Additionally the investor also has the questions in his mind 'How do I know that this is the best value, or right for me?' and 'How do I know that you are competent?'

Intangibility

This is further compounded by the fact that financial services offerings are intangible – that is they cannot be physically delivered and neither can they be resold. This is the case with all services in as much as the opportunity to sell it has passed once it has gone. Eg a cinema seat that would have yielded £7 on Friday 20-11-02 but was not sold and therefore empty, can never be re-sold because that day has passed and the £7 is lost. The potential income cannot be recouped if it is occupied the next day because the next day's sale is part of another revenue stream.

Financial services are the same although there are tangible aspects to them, eg an ATM or a statement where the former is a physical manifestation of the infrastructure that allows you access to your money, but is really only a means of dispensing it, in the manner of a vending machine for chocolate or drinks, rather than the end product itself. This is known as 'physical evidence' of the service and is defined as:

Physical evidence[2]

Physical evidence of the service offer or of the company are the only tangible attributes that the service consumer may use to assess a service. This may include the physical state of repair, decoration and design of the building, company promotional information (brochures, letters, and business cards) and even the physical appearance of staff.

Similarly there is no delivery of an overdraft except a line on a statement (which says £1340.89 DR in red and is really like a delivery invoice). It is argued by some that this compounds the complexity – but few people worry about that aspect. It is therefore difficult to 'take an overdraft for a test drive' or to engage in 'tasting' or 'sampling' of loans or insurance policies and as a result people either rely on previous experience or on third-party recommendations – friends and family or advice from financial advisers (see purchasing decisions).

Finally financial services offerings pose some severe problems in marketing because they tend not to be one-off purchases such as a newspaper or a house but usually involve a long series of transactions such as the continual writing of cheques or drawing of cash, or monthly payments into pension funds, or loan drawdowns and repayments and therefore it is difficult to pinpoint the precise purchase and re-purchase times.

In financial services, and in particular since the greying of boundaries between the different sub-sectors, customers can often be on both sides of a value chain. They input to a bank by having money in their bank accounts, and they borrow from a bank – often at the same time. They also save with other financial products and this can complicate analysis of the chain and where customers sit.

3.3   Delivery channels

There have been some great changes to distribution of financial services. Products have metamorphosed through:

- ◆ Face-to-face personal channels
- ◆ Branch networks
- ◆ ATMs
- ◆ Telephone banking/insurance
- ◆ Internet
- ◆ And even virtual money (Mondex)

Figure 3.1: It is a more complex and diverse world than before

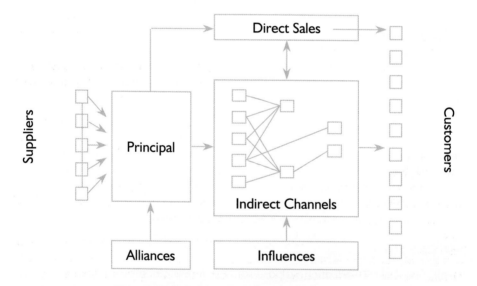

Customers have diverse needs ... many players are involved in serving them ... it is difficult to maintain a seamless, consistent promise to them ... and deliver it efficiently.

Financial services is a much more complex world than before (see Figure 3.1) and this has been driven by several factors:

- IT as an enabler of change has had the most profound effect and the scale and pace of change has been breathtaking by normal financial services standards. It has changed the way information is held and processed and enabled centralization of processing to out-of-town and even out-of-country/continent locations. It has enabled on-line access to records and customer accounts that has disintermediated the organizational staff to a very great degree.
- Major amendments to legislation altering regulation and cosy monopolistic positions out of recognition (from Competition and Credit Control (1971), through the Building Societies Act, various EU Banking, Securities, Insurance and other indirect directives, Big Bang and the Financial Services acts).
- As a result of the freedoms the rise of competition both from players within the market, from overseas, and from other external (non-fs) players.
- The changes in ownership (banks own insurance companies, securities trading organizations, factoring companies and many more; similarly insurance companies own banks and others). This reflects the rise of Bankassurance, or Allfinanz which despite all the brave words written about it is purely a mechanism for securing distribution channels.
- A greater acceptance by the public of changes (people now queue in the rain outside a bank branch to use an ATM while cashiers are unoccupied inside) – and an expectation of greater and increasing change.
- The rise of cash substitutes which has been geometric (debit, credit, charge and smart cards as well as electronic wallets) since the first tentative steps to introduce credit cards in the late 1970s.
- A shift in emphasis facilitated by the change from local in-branch processing to centralization, thus freeing staff to sell more products (if they can meet customers – who now only visit branches once or twice a year!).

Many also believed that these changes would lead to radically different living with virtual transactions and a cashless society – but this has only been partially achieved, although the trends are undoubtedly there – with 6 – 7 million UK banking customers using the Internet. This growth has slowed but there is an inevitability about it because it is still increasing, and given the changing demographics, younger, newer customers are much more likely to move straight to Internet or remote banking than the previous generation and it will continue to change.

Although cash is still used by most people every day – by far the greater value, if not number, of transactions take place via cards of some sort and cheques are virtually redundant now. This has caused serious cost implications for traditional branch-based organizations. If 10 per cent of your customer base shifts to using remote banking, for example, this does not equate into a 10 per cent reduction in branches – on the contrary it hardly allows branch closures at all – but still requires investment in newer channels as well! And the 90% of customers still demand 100% service from the network.

Figure 3.2: Channel economics

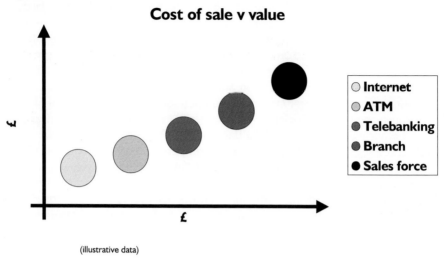

(illustrative data)

The array of channels available offers different opportunities for value creation due to their inherent modus operandi but also incur different costs.

Channel functions

Distribution channels have a set of functions that they perform:

◆ Promotion – spreading communication about product and service offerings
◆ Contact – finding and preparing potential customers for purchases
◆ Matching – bringing customers' needs together with producers' products by turning them into solutions
◆ Information – gathering, storing and disseminating information on customers, market forces and competition
◆ Risk-taking – sharing the costs and risks associated with the process of selling (eg commission-only sales forces get nothing until they have sold, thus sharing the financial risk with the producers).

Some distribution chains may be very complex – eg CD players, cars or lawnmowers involving many steps and third parties. Others, eg a corner shop selling fruit and vegetables or meat, may be very simple involving only a few steps.

Figure 3.3: Distribution chains – examples

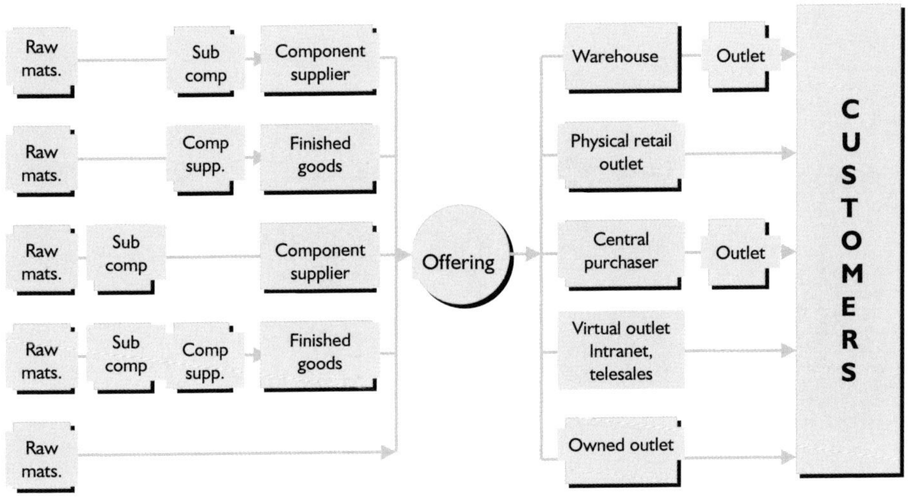

One of the characteristics of financial services, particularly since many sales tasks have been brought in-house, is that much of the distribution channel is internal to the bank (the HQ develops products, then disseminates it through regions and through branches to customers).

However there is a bewildering choice and many organizations use many at the same time – see Figure 3.3.

Figure 3.4: Financial services distribution

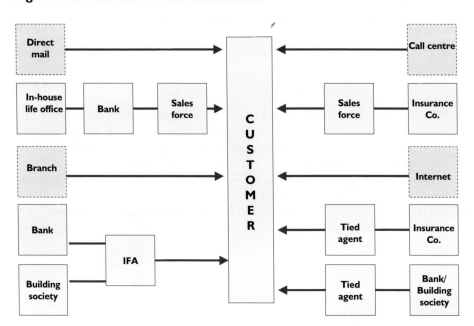

Figure 3.3 shows the array of channels that can be used and, in major financial conglomerates, often coexist at the same time. The boxes with dotted outlines represent direct contacts. This can give rise to several issues, notably channel conflict – as channels vie with each other for the same customers and this requires good management to reconcile. Also you are not allowed to differentially price between financial services channels and it is important that this does not happen.

Conclusion

Financial services is a very difficult market sector in which to operate because of the heavy and increasing legislation as well as the complexity of the product range and the inherent nature of many of them – intangibility, long term, risky and with customers throwing off inertia to change ever more frequently. It is, therefore, imperative that all steps are taken to be up to date with legislation but more importantly to understand your customer so as to maximize the opportunities from them.

Summary

Financial services is different from other sectors because:

1 Money has no intrinsic value and financial services offerings tend to be about money or advice.
2 Many products are complex and difficult for unsophisticated consumers to understand.
3 The offerings tend to be intangible and therefore compound the complexity.
4 Financial services is a highly regulated industry partly because of the previous points and therefore requires greater diligence in customer interactions to ensure that errors are not made that might fall foul of the law.
5 Many customers are on both sides of the value chain, having deposits, investments and loans at the same time.
6 Distribution can be very complex in financial services and must be part of a well thought through strategy, into which marketing has had considerable input.

Select bibliography

Financial services marketing – Tina Harrison (FT Prentice Hall) Chapter 1

FSA guide to regulated lending (FSA)

Notes

1 On 1 December 2001 the Financial Services Authority assumed its full powers and responsibilities under the Financial Services and Markets Act 2000. It is now the single statutory regulator responsible for regulating deposit-taking, insurance and investment business. It also took on certain new responsibilities – for example, tackling market abuse, promoting public understanding of the financial system and reducing financial crime.
2 *Marketing Management'* by Helen and Richard Meek, published 2001 by Financial World Publishing.

1

Marketing

Introduction to this section

This section covers the first stage of the three-point model shown below – that of **Marketing**. Marketing is about creating the environment at the macro level to try to motivate customers to want to buy your products and services. It is concerned with the theoretical aspects of buying and selling, demand etc and not how you actually sell at the sharp end. That will be covered in Chapters 10-15. The third point of the model – **Customer Service** – is about how you manage your customers once you have 'sold' them something and is concerned with relationship management and will be covered in Chapters 16-21.

Three-point marketing model

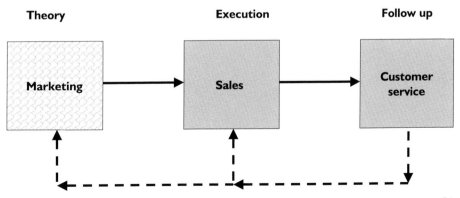

Four

Basic building blocks

Topics in this chapter

Value

CVP

4.1   Introduction to this chapter

The basic marketing cycle is shown in Figure 4.1. At the very heart of marketing lies the customer. The marketing cycle flows around it from analysis, into strategy, leading into plans, followed by implementation, which feeds back into analysis, and then further strategic refinement. Before moving into this cycle there are some basic issues on which marketing is founded.

Successful marketing, and indeed selling, is about getting the customer to purchase your offering in preference to everybody else's. You achieve this by developing a **value proposition** that is better than your competitors' and then you tell the customer about it. Marketing looks at how you develop that proposition, how you tell the customers about it and of course how you position your offering within a defined market, but unfortunately these markets are not always as simple as they might seem. This is because there are several factors that act to distort them.

Figure 4.1: Marketing cycle (1)

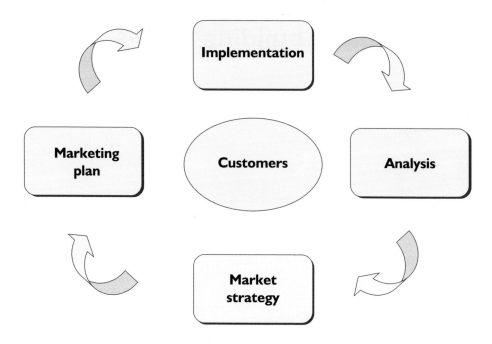

4.2   Market distortions

While in theory prices should be driven purely by supply and demand, unfortunately this is rarely the case and all too often the market is distorted by many factors. If there were no restrictions, in some markets prices would almost always be very much higher than they usually are. This tends to happen where monopolies/oligopolies exist or where there are cartels (there is usually legislation in place to stop this sort of distortion).

In the situation with an unregulated monopoly, the provider simply charges what it feels like, because the consumer has no other place to go for the goods. Where cartels exist, the main providers simply get together and decide on a price, thus performing like a de-facto oligopoly.

Imagine the situation where you live on a remote outpost (say a large farm in the wilds of Scotland) and although you have a car, there is only one store within a reasonable distance. It will tend to charge what it believes that it can get away with for its goods and services. Although globalization and the Internet have affected this type of circumstance to a degree they have not wholly eradicated it. Amazon would find it difficult to deliver cheaply, and frequently the needs of the residents in the Outer Hebrides.

There are many other things that also distort the markets and, accordingly, the prices that an organization can set. Some are internal and within the ability of management to influence or control and some are external and therefore largely outside the control of the enterprise. The major factors are:

External

Competition
Changing markets and customers' demands
Technology
Legislation

Internal

Costs
Profit targets
Growth

These are briefly considered in more detail.

External factors

These distortions are caused by another entity doing something that impacts on you as an enterprise. They are usually out of your direct control but may be subject to indirect influences – lobbying, press campaigns etc. They usually act to force prices down, but not always.

Figure 4.2: External factors distorting markets

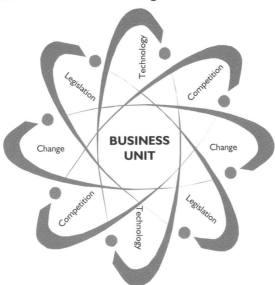

Competition represents the activities of other players in your markets. This can be direct competition where the product/service is an exact substitute for yours (eg betting shops where there are hundreds of variations on the same thing); or it can be indirect competition from something that is a direct competitor but is not the same eg the Football Pools and the National Lottery (which was introduced in the UK in 1994 and was subsequently used as an excuse by some executives for poor performance in betting organizations and others – including restaurants who see a marked decline in custom on roll-over days).

It can also be a totally different type of product that impacts on the price of your product.

Competitive markets are usually typified by major price wars in the mature phase of the market. Consumers have plenty of opportunity and time to shop around and so providers fight to attract them, as in the credit card and mortgage market.

Legislation is, by and large, passed to protect customers from being taken advantage of and tends to reduce the potential price that would be charged if firms thought they could get away with it (eg monopolies commissions or anti-trust bodies). It can also, however, push prices of the offering up where it requires changes to the way a product is produced or sold. Quite often government interference in markets (to restrict things, or try to define what markets must do) is driven by ideology. This usually operates to increase inefficiencies (eg in Communist countries governments try to plan demand and supply – it just does not work and one is always out of balance). This also happens in 'Western' style democracies when governments interfere – vide EU wine lakes, beef mountains, stakeholder pensions etc.

Health and Safety is a very good example where legislation requires that safe practices be introduced and that goods are safe to sell. In financial services very high regulatory requirements were introduced throughout the EU in response to the feeling that clients were being sold inappropriate products/services. The cost of complying with this is very high for organizations in this market.

Some governments try to control prices directly through price and income controls. This distorts the market very quickly and in the long term has very harmful effects on economies, usually resulting in an explosion of inflation when the lid comes off (or breaks) and high wage demands are put in, leading to higher prices etc.

Legislation can also put prices up by imposing tax on the offerings. Cars, spirits, tobacco and petrol are good examples of this. In most countries there is also some form of sales tax levied on goods and services. In the EU it is called Value-Added Tax [VAT] and is levied on each stage of the value chain, being reclaimable back, usually, from the next step and netted off. It is a very complex tax and unwieldy as well as being very unpopular – particularly with institutions who have a specific tax status where they are unable to set off VAT input against VAT output – eg financial services. (It also flies in the face of most of Adam Smith's canons about tax.) There is a healthy, if not altogether legal, arbitrage market between different customs duties. As a result many people go from the UK to the continent to buy tobacco and alcoholic goods where duty is cheap to exploit this disparity. It is legal for your own consumption but not for re-sales.

Customer demand affects prices in both directions. Where there is increasing demand for the offering then, unless the supply expands quickly to meet the demand, the cost will rise as the demand/supply relationship is rationed by price. Similarly where customers' perceptions change the demand may fall, thus causing prices to fall until demand and supply are back in equilibrium.

Customers can also exercise distortion by demanding more value from products/services, usually at no extra cost – particularly where there are lots of substitute offerings or their perception of what is a fair value changes. In the car market for example quality is now a given. No-one can sell shoddy cars – therefore more demands are placed on sellers by customers for different items and also if they feel that a particular product is below the new standard for quality it will not sell.

Changing markets will affect prices in several ways. A new product/service may render your own obsolete – eg the fundamental change to information availability in the 1990s destroyed *Encyclopaedia Britannica*'s value proposition. Similar information is now available easily and cheaply on CD-Rom and thereby forced the prices of their books down and also forced it to sell on CD; or it can result in the price rising as suddenly the offering becomes the flavour of the month – eg in the USA where consumers besieged shops to buy Cabbage Patch dolls, forcing the price up.

A good example of this effect is the Foreign Exchange (F/X) market where prices bounce all over the place in response to fears about US inflation, Bundesbank rates, UK or French unemployment figures, trouble in the Middle East, fears about the Japanese banking system etc. rendering long-term planning extremely difficult without hedging.

Technology has the ability to enable more efficient production but of course can push costs up in the short term because the capital operating costs are incurred usually prior to the benefits. In other cases technology distorts the market significantly by leading to the introduction of new working or operating practices. It is a fairly safe bet that many of the longer-term unemployed have been forced out of their jobs, not because the job was not required, but because a piece of machinery can do the task more quickly or cheaply.

Internal factors

These factors are those that are usually within your control and over which direct influence can be exercised. They usually act to force prices up, but not always.

Costs fall into two kinds:

◆ those incurred within your organization; and
◆ those that come in from outside as the product/service passes up the value chain.

Those within can be contained by management action whereas the external costs must be controlled in different ways such as supplier negotiation, shopping around and exercising purchasing power. The impact depends on the relative weighting of the cost type that is rising – in financial services historically staff costs have been one of the biggest (if not the biggest) proportion of costs and therefore a rise in this affects final prices much more than, say, the rise in the cost of paper.

> **'Part of our strategy is to become a much lower cost producer'** –
> John Windeler, Executive Chairman, Alliance & Leicester[3]

The following table shows some banks and major categories of costs (year 2000):

US$ millions	HSBC	Lloyds TSB	ABN AMRO	Deutsche Bank	Barclays	JPMorgan Chase	UniCredito Italiano
Staff	8,057	2,824	7,050	12,445	4,816	12,748	2,623
Dep'n and Amortization	1,591	577	889	1,852	458	2,545	332
Property, IT, Equipment	1,480	744	322	2,015	1,224	3,748 **	657
Commissions	1,266	717	*	1,478	479		1,690
Other	2,449	1,767	4,215	3,568	1,718	3,783	883
Total#	13,577	5,912	12,476	19,880	8,216	22,824	4,495

* Net commission only available from annual report
** Of which 1294m relates to occupancy, and 2454m relates to technology and communications.
# Total excludes commissions
Exchange rates taken at 2 January 2001

Source: Annual reports/Internet search

In financial services costs are difficult to shift – and usually result in what is euphemistically known as down- or right-sizing of staff – whereas income can fall rapidly. In 2002 many financial services companies were battered badly by equity falls in stock markets which hit reserves and liquidity; a downturn in the market which hit deals in M & A and investment banking and losses on loans which hit capital. In October German banks were held up as examples of a 'sick' banking sector because they reeled from the many problems facing Germany[4]. Similarly in state-owned (or quasi state-owned/controlled) European banks, due to restrictive labour laws, many are grossly overstaffed which impacts on costs and frequently forces them to 'beg' for capital injections from their governments to stay viable (maybe).

The following table shows some cost/income ratios:

US$ millions	HSBC	Lloyds TSB	ABN AMRO	Deutsche Bank	Barclays	JPMorgan Chase	UniCredito Italiano
Cost	13,577	5,912	12,476	19,880	8,216	22,824	4,495
Income	24,573	12,670	17,453	27,083	14,359	32,934	8,814
Ratio	55.3%	46.7%	71.5%	69.3%	57.2%	69.3%	51.0%

Source: Annual reports

> 'Cost/income is the most important statistic in the group'
> – Rainier Masera, MD SanPaolo IMI

In an effort to avoid this situation, however, in many sectors customer/supplier partnerships are becoming more of the norm, thus helping to control costs. In financial services huge cost reduction projects have been underway in many organizations for some time.

Profit targets/return will have the effect of forcing prices up as organizations strive to maximize the return on their capital investment. In many cases this behaviour is linked to the aspirations of shareholders, who generally like to see a reasonably quick return on their investment.

This tends to persuade companies to go all out for short-term profit, often at the expenses of achieving longer-term market share goals. This position is very different in other countries, particularly Japan, where investors are prepared to let companies strive for long-term market dominance, even at the expense of short-term goals.

Growth affects organizations because, in order to grow, higher expenditure is required in terms of assets and capital and cash to fund the business. This clearly pushes up the cost base until the benefits from this investment come on stream.

In the short term prices may be forced down in an effort to take market share (and thereby hope to achieve economies of scale). Extra orders may push up marginal costs as the current resources reach capacity, requiring further investment.

4.3   Value

'A cynic is someone who knows the price of everything but the value of nothing' –

Oscar Wilde

What Wilde meant was that there is a difference between the **price** at which something can be bought (which can be quantified) and the **real value** that people attach to it (which is an intangible, qualitative concept). Thus a painting by, say, Rembrandt or Da Vinci or a sculpture by Michaelangelo may be priced in millions of pounds and, whereas some people, or more commonly nowadays, corporations, would buy it because they see it as an investment, others would buy it because they **actually like** the picture. Still others would see it as just another picture or sculpture which could have been painted or sculpted by anyone and therefore regard it as overpriced. They thus perceive the **value** differently and accordingly will pay differing amounts for an item (or not buy it at all).

It is the **understanding** of this value perception that enables you to price differentially or target your prices to meet their expectations. This enables you to develop your Customer Value Proposition.

Customer Value Proposition (CVP)

This term was devised in the USA to describe the complex relation between price and benefits[5]. The basic premise underpinning the concept is that a customer will choose to deal with a firm that, in his perception of it, offers:

> the greatest **positive** combination of end-result benefits and price

ie the greatest value – over the offerings of its competitors.

Understanding what the customer values and therefore getting the CVP right is the difference between success and failure. It is a truism to say that the organization with a superior CVP will be the most successful in that field/market. In order to make them part with their money the firm must make customers believe that there is a good reason for buying its goods/services and not another's. That is the **value** that the customer places on your offering.

How is value defined?

In considering the CVP there is a precise definition as follows – always from the **customers' perspective**:

Benefits *Less* Price *Equals* Value

$$(B - P = V)$$

Where:

Price is the total costs to the customer. Note that this is as perceived by the customer **not** by you, your manager or your marketing department. It is usually in monetary terms but may include other, less tangible items, such as inconvenience or things foregone for this offering.

Benefits is the result to the customer of doing business with your organization (ie what the customers perceive that they gain).

Value is the outcome (or in a mathematical sense the product) or result of the **Benefits** minus **Price. NB** it must be *positive* for the customer to do business with you.

Note that it is not always easy to get this information from your customers – that is where deeper understanding of markets and your customer base is so important.

Other factors often play a major part in this. Eg many people shop locally for some of their goods despite the fact that it may not be wholly advantageous from a price perspective, but because it is more convenient; the service is perceived to be friendlier; the local shopkeeper knows you better; and it can be quicker. Many people will go to certain stores, eg John Lewis/Waitrose or M&S, because they believe that the quality of goods and services is better or the service is higher notwithstanding the price. In their minds they are making a price/benefit trade-off. Yet others will use the Internet for shopping because it is (usually) quicker and (sometimes) cheaper, and then have goods delivered – others prefer the physical 'shopping experience' and still trundle a trolley around stores. Some of course shop at the cheapest to tender to the market – often discount stores or poor-quality shops.

Benefits versus price – The 'trade-off'

When using this definition of what the customer perceives as value, it must be remembered that there is always a **benefits/price trade-off** that equalizes the two to arrive at the 'value', otherwise the only successful marketing ploy would be to offer your services at the cheapest price. Essentially customers will either:

◆ pay you **more than the competition** because they believe they are getting *better benefits* and therefore more value from you; or
◆ pay you **less than the competition** for an option which offers *less benefit*.

Therefore equalizing the **Benefit – Price = Value** equation in each case.

The key for an organization is to ensure that it can deliver that combination of benefits at that price which the customer is prepared to pay – **Profitably**.

A price can be defined as:

'an amount, usually in money, for which a thing is sold or offered'

or

'that which one foregoes for the sake of or in gaining something'.

The 'thing' referred to could be a product or a service and indeed in financial services can be money itself (an interest rate is the price you pay for use of money over a period). A price then is something paid for some product or service that, **in the perception of the buyer (consumer)**, is of value to them.

The perceived cost to the buyer (usually the price paid, often plus some other intangible items) is a measure of that value the customer places on the item. By understanding the value that consumers place on your offering you will know how to price it. One of the key issues, however, is that not all buyers place the same value on the same offering. That is why targetting of buyers for your offering is extremely important to ensure that the price reflects the value your targetted buyers place on the offering and therefore are willing to pay.

Case study – Pencil sharpeners

These are available in many shops, specialist stationers, art shops, retail stores such as Woolworths and W H Smith, sold in corner shops, department stores, even in 'grocery' stores such as Tesco, Asda and Sainsburys. The question that a customer will ask is – for what purpose do I wish to use this item (sharpening pencils obviously – but children's crayons, artists pencils or even eyebrow pencils?) and how much do I value the utility?

Where utility is low then a plastic pencil sharpener can be bought for as little as 20p – quality will be low and it will probably not last long.

Where utility is high – eg an artist wishing to obtain fine points on her pencils/crayons then she may decide to pay a lot more for a finely crafted metal sharpener.

Where it is a fun purchase – eg as part of a party bag for children – then cheap but 'fancy' sharpeners may be bought costing slightly more than the cheapest, because the customer is willing to pay a small premium for the 'fun' aspect.

4.4   Cost versus profit

There is a difference between these two concepts. You incur the former and you hope to gain the latter from what you do. If I buy a loaf of bread for £1.00 and sell it for £1.05 I have made a profit on the face of it of £0.05p. This may be classed as a profit, but it ignores any costs I had incurred in the transaction. If I had to get a bus or take the tube to buy it or sell it I would have incurred a further cost – say £0.50p – which when added to the cost of the bread itself means that in fact I made a loss of £0.45p. This also ignores my own personal time involved in the transaction, which would further compound the loss in this case. A profit can be defined as the income received from a transaction less the costs incurred in achieving that transaction. If income is greater than costs then the result is a 'profit'.

Discretion

Within organizations the discretion given to staff varies. Some prices are fixed, some are negotiable and still others are left to best judgement. In finance while many prices (fees, commissions and interest) are theoretically fixed there is often considerable discretion given to 'management' to reduce or waive them to the organization's and customer's advantage. Pricing is usually managed centrally to provide a framework and input to marketing, with the discretion delegated down to managers with profit targets to ensure that they do not give things away. Pricing is complicated and can be very difficult, especially when regulation is involved. (See chapter on pricing.)

Summary

In order to persuade a customer to take your offering you must persuade her that she will get the best combination of value (benefits less the price that she must pay). This value will differ between customers and it is important that you understand this difference when explaining your offerings to them.

1 Not all buyers place the same value on the same offering.
2 Differentiation is critical and you must develop a differential for those segments which you have chosen as your targets and offer it as solutions to customer issues – the Customer Value Proposition.
3 There is always a **benefits/price trade-off** that equalizes the two to arrive at the 'value', otherwise the only successful marketing ploy would be to offer your services at the cheapest price.
4 The key for an organization is to ensure that it can deliver that combination of benefits at that price which the customer is prepared to pay – **Profitably**.

Select bibliography

Loyalty Rules: F Reichheld
Principles of Marketing: Kotler
Value Based Marketing: Peter Doyle

Notes

3 John Windeler, Executive Chairman, Alliance & Leicester (annual report 2000)
4 *The Times*, Business section, Tuesday 29 October 2002
5 '*Building a Market Focused Organization* (BMFO) 1987-1995; Lanning, Phillips & Associates – white paper

Five

Marketing elements

Topics in this chapter

Supply versus demand

The four Ps

The four Ps redefined from the customer's perspective – the four Cs

The seven Ps

Introduction to this chapter

Marketing is about getting customers to buy from **you** rather than your competition. It is therefore about making your customers feel that by buying from you they are getting a better benefit than from anybody else. The higher the benefit they receive, however, the higher the cost to deliver it to them (usually) and so you must ensure that your prices have taken this factor into account and that your customers are prepared to pay for it.

Figure 5.1: High benefits usually imply high delivery costs

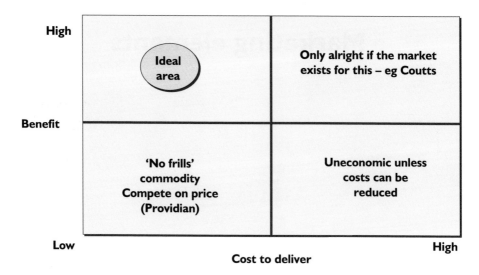

What does a customer want? What does it cost to
deliver? And how much will they pay?

The fundamental economic concepts of supply and demand play a critical part in marketing.

5.1   Supply versus demand

Prior to the introduction of money, trade (demand and supply) was by barter, which has inherent difficulties (deciding the equality of value between different items, portability (oxen are heavy) and lack of liquidity). Money provided an easy means of facilitating exchange between these two forces, acting as a means of buying and selling without barter. See Figure 5.2 where the demand and supply graphs meet at a price and quantity that equalizes the two.

Figure 5.2: Supply versus demand

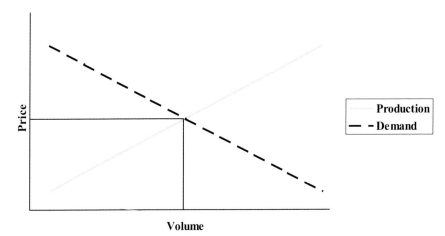

Because money is (relatively) stable it also regulates demand by acting as a rationing agent. As most of us have only a finite supply of money available (loans notwithstanding because they must be serviced) to satisfy wants and/or needs it must somehow be allocated across all the goods/services a person requires. The trick is then for a supplier to ensure that its offerings allow it to gain the most from transactions.

Prices must not be set too high or the offerings will not be taken up in the right quantity, and not set too low such that the supplier loses revenue. Experience teaches, however, that price is not the only determinant of demand. There are other factors that influence people's decisions and these must also be taken into account – otherwise all products would be the same and at the same price (see Introduction).

Marketing is about understanding these other factors and deciding which to give greater emphasis to in order to differentiate your product and therefore sell more of your offering.

Nowadays marketing is focused very much on the customer perspective. Marketing has not always taken this focus and has only relatively recently moved from 'selling' mode to true 'marketing' based on a real understanding of customer needs.

5.2 Historical antecedents – the four Ps

Marketing has its roots in production and then sales. Everything started with the perception that there was a need and that the 'entrepreneur' could produce something to fulfill that need. In the early days of 'mercantilism' this was not wholly incorrect; however, with the increasing sophistication of buyers and the growth of similar products and substitutes, this basic premise changed.

Traditionally, therefore, organizations were internally focused – ie they would say 'what do we make/offer, and how do we sell it?' Initial marketing theory and analysis was also based on this internal focus and this lead to the rise of product focused marketing and the four Ps:

Product   **Price**
Promotion   **Place**

For many years these four elements were the cornerstone of marketing for everyone and collectively are known as:

The marketing mix

It is the different blends of these four elements that enables organizations to differentiate their products from competitors (in theory at least) and provides the drivers for where the offerings are positioned in the consumers' minds.

Figure 5.3: Marketing mix

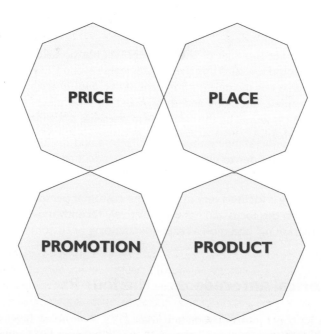

It is the different 'weights' of the four components that decide the marketing mix

These four aspects of what you offer must be aligned with your Customer Value Propositions – and will be different for each offering and each segment. Different offerings take different proportions of the four constituent parts of the mix.

Major retailers will always want to be in the best location – eg a high street or major shopping centre – because they rely on high footfall to sell lots of goods. Other retailers will have different views on this and will be prepared to take less prominent locations because they feel it will not materially affect their business – perhaps they sell by word-of-mouth or through other mechanisms (mail/Internet – where location is irrelevant). With increasing mobility of the population in the UK and increased usage of cars to shop once a week instead of daily many retailers are now responding to these demographic changes and moving to out-of-town locations. There is more space and they can not only offer a more extensive range of goods but also offer parking and additionally sell petrol, thus increasing turnover and profit considerably (extra sales, lower costs and greater economies of scale). These are often situated in retail parks where several different types of shopping can be undertaken at the same time – thereby re-creating the town centre in an out-of-town location. **(Place)**

Similarly while some organizations sell by offering the cheapest (pile it high and sell it cheap) others play on different subtleties and are very expensive. There are, however, perceived pricing 'bands' outside of which goods will not sell. If you go to any shop the price of a basic commodity such as cheddar cheese, although it will vary both within the shop by brand, and between that shop and others, will be within a pretty small range. This is because nobody pays a hundred pounds for a packet of cheese – no matter how good it is, because at that price it falls well outside of the 'band' with which almost everyone is familiar. For other goods such as wine, however, it is a completely different picture. You can buy a bottle of 'plonk' for less than £3.00 but you can also pay hundreds of pounds for a fine wine, and for others such as a Chateau D'Yquem even thousands of pounds. Many people are also unsure of the price bands for such goods and some sellers knowing this may 'jack up' the price and therefore customers might pay much more than they ought to. **(Price)**

These major components of the marketing mix are explored in more detail below.

Product

This is the substance of what you are offering. The concept also includes **services** if that is your market – eg consultancy, legal advice, painting and decorating and of course finance. It may be one thing such as a car loan or overdraft, or several things bundled together as a solution – eg for a corporate customer of a financial institution – Loan, Overdraft, F/X, Guarantees and Trade Finance limits all together as sub-components of an overall limit as a solution to working-capital needs. In the case of a personal customer an overdraft may be linked to a personal loan and a mortgage, often with life insurance thrown in. In many cases of course security of one sort or another may be involved which although it complicates the product does not change the underlying nature or essence.

Case study: The 'post-it' note

Nobody could have expressed exactly what it was that they wanted in product terms – but after it was 'discovered' by 3M in the USA it became globally ubiquitous. The 'post-it' note met a latent need and was a great success – and now it is found in every office, school, doctor's surgery, factory and home and is standard stationery. It comes as standard one-colour blocks, funny shapes such as hearts, faces, tools or fruits, in many colours, personalized with company logos and even with amusing phrases on the front and also as very useful small tabs for use in research!

The key factors in Product are:

- ◆ **Customer benefits** – special items;
- ◆ **Quality** – how good is it really – High net-worth 'premium' banking versus Providian or Delta cards;
- ◆ **Design** – basic 'vanilla' – comprehensive/complex derivatives;
- ◆ **Technical features** – bells and whistles [cashback, fees waivers, surveys included in mortgages or the option to invest in different proportions of securities in investment products];
- ◆ **Branding** (in-house, white label, 'cachet' – multi-brands within one organization – Lloyds/TSB/Cheltenham & Gloucester/Abbey Life);
- ◆ **Packaging** – how it looks or is presented;
- ◆ **Service** that accompanies it (follow-up, technical spec, instructions, customer helpline etc);
- ◆ **Training** – eg in software given to clients by banks to assist them in putting together cashflows.

Many organizations talk about the number of products they offer with little understanding of the fact that really they offer very few discrete products – and rather more product variants. A mortgage at 7% is exactly the same as a mortgage at 8.5% except for the **price**. It may have other features bolted on such as survey fees and so on but in essence it is the same.

If you buy a car – say a Land Rover Discovery – there will be a few different models and many different options – type of paint, type and number of seats, type of CD player and so on, but these would not be classed as different products. Financial services however tend to treat variations as new products, which causes confusion for consumers and difficulty in managing them. In part this is often driven by the need to account for variations separately on (often inadequate) systems for administration purposes which often require 'new products' to be established to cope, but equally often due to poor marketing thinking.

Basic banking in fact is built around only a few generic product types including:

♦ Acceptance of money
♦ Lending of money
♦ Advice on what to do with money
♦ Money transmission
♦ Exchange
♦ Insurance
♦ Advice

Most of the other services are just different variations on one of these core services so, for example, lending includes, *inter alia*:

♦ Overdraft
♦ Fixed-interest
♦ Floating-interest
♦ Libor-linked
♦ Base-rate linked
♦ Secured
♦ Unsecured
♦ Trade finance loans
♦ Working capital loans
♦ Etc

Figure 5.4 shows how many products can be built up in modular form – as the loan increases in complexity, so too do the steps involved.

Figure 5.4: Loan variations

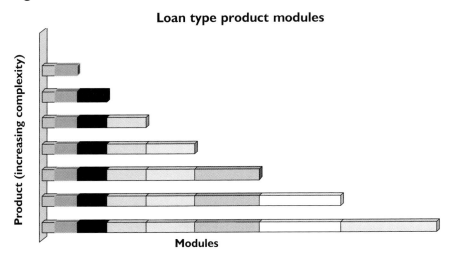

The different steps are all built on each other and are merely variations of the original product, but sharing an increasing number of features. At the basic level is an unsecured overdraft, followed by an unsecured loan. Then secured O/D, secured loans, mortgages, etc. Each type of product has a certain number of 'modules' incorporated such as security, type of rate (fixed/floating) and may include insurance, and so on.

Price

What you charge for your services. There are many ways of pricing including market-based and cost-based, but these are driven by internal considerations. You can also set prices by reference to competitors' pricing (eg base rates are very rarely out of line for good reasons as money soon flows into those organizations offering the highest deposit rates and out of those with lower rates who in turn are besieged by demands for cheap loans which would move the balance sheet returns into disequilibrium) or by what you think the market will bear – often useful if you enjoy a monopoly. Price is related to product and (usually) offering *less* value for more price is not regarded as a winning combination!

Price is very flexible and you can vary it more than the others because it is usually within your discretion (for some services this may not be the case – eg mortgage rate is often set centrally with no discretion in branches – however local staff can sometimes flex fees) and you can use it for long-term and also short-term advantage. Some possibilities include:

- ◆ **discounts** for special customers (ex-ante price reductions);
- ◆ **underselling** or matching competitors (eg John Lewis Partnership – 'Never Knowingly Undersold');
- ◆ **loyalty refunds** (eg Britannia Building Society 'Members Loyalty Bonus Scheme' or the Co-op 'Divi') (ex-post price reductions);
- ◆ **bundling** items together and offering overall prices – eg three services that separately might cost 1.0% pa (total 3%) each may cost only 2.5% as a bundle.

Although price is not (necessarily) a measure of inherent value received it is often used by customers as a benchmark, notwithstanding the other features or differences. (This can be irritating but it is the customer's perception that counts and the job of the client manager to clarify the misunderstanding and to change this misperception by making them understand the differentials).

It should also be remembered that price is the only one that brings in income.

All the rest involve cost!

Price is closely related to the perception of value (see CVP). Usually you cannot charge a very high price for a poor-quality product or service – at least not where there are others against which a customer can benchmark. Bowman refers to the 'strategic clock' of price versus quality.[1]

Figure 5.5: Bowman's competitive strategy options – the clock

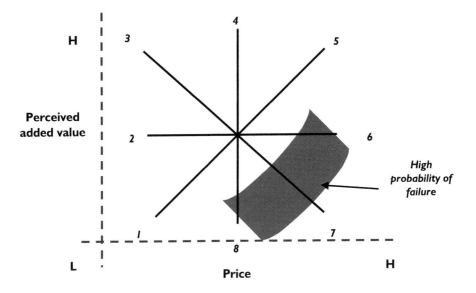

Bowman categorizes the possible marketing strategies into eight points on the clock as follows:

1. no frills
2. low price
3. hybrid
4. differentiation
5. focused differentiation
6. increased price/standard value
7. increased price low value
8. low value standard price

The following comments are relevant:

◆ options 1 and 2 are **price-based** strategies – with 1 being rock bottom value at rock bottom prices and 2 being price competition by matching value but at a low price – note you must have **price competitive advantage** for this. A good example would be the cheapest mortgage in a best-buy table where term and 'extras' are the same but the rate is lower;

◆ option 4 is to try to **differentiate** yourself from the competition with added value to achieve greater market share but offering your services at the same price or slightly higher. This requires a very good understanding of what the customer values in order to equalize the price benefit trade-off;

◆ option **3** is a **hybrid** between 1,2, and 4;

◆ option **5** seeks to offer **high value** and therefore charge a **high price** – equalizing the price benefit trade-off – eg Coutts & Co. which offers premium banking to wealthy and selected customers – at a price;

◆ those options in **6,7,** and **8** are destined to **fail** because they seek to offer lower value at the same price **(8),** higher prices for less value **(7)** or increased price at the same value **(6).**

Case study – credit cards

In the early 1970s in the UK there were few credit cards – there were only a few outlets that accepted them and there was generally no universal appetite for this new form of shopping and paying. Take-up was slow and most people still preferred cash or cheques. Barclays Bank took a new and interesting approach to this obstacle. The bank converted many of its cheque guarantee cards into dual cheque cards and credit cards – 'Barclaycards' – and thus introduced hundreds of thousands into the market – at little or no cost and with no need for a marketing campaign to get people to apply. It was very successful and Barclaycard – later co-branded with Visa – became a major contributor to profits (30%) and it still has a major share of this market. Later on legislation was passed to stop this happening – but by then it was too late because customers already had the cards and had become accustomed to using credit cards.

This market is now well and truly saturated with many people having several credit cards. The battle now is to encourage customers to switch from their current providers to you. This is usually by way of cheap introductory rates on transferred balances, lower fees or other combinations and is a very intensive marketplace.

Promotion

This is about how you inform the world about your offerings – to both existing and potential customers. It is all very well having something to sell to customers but you have got to tell them about the features and benefits (qv) in a cost-effective and (ideally) focused manner. Some of the more usual methods include:

◆ **Advertising** – on the radio, TV, in papers or magazines and increasingly on the Internet – indirectly on someone else's or on your own website, or via linking to a search engine;

◆ **Telephone selling** – effective but can quickly become an irritant if poorly executed – eg employment agencies calling up once or twice every day. One of the drawbacks with personal selling is that the best time to call people is when they are at home in the evening. Paradoxically this is also the time that they are least likely to respond positively because they often regard calls at home as an intrusion of their privacy;

◆ **Brochures** and catalogues;

◆ **Internet banners and pop-up web adverts** – increasingly common – although the effectiveness has yet to be proven conclusively;

◆ **Exhibitions** and third-party endorsement;

◆ **Home parties** (mainly focused on women and famously includes: Tupperware, Avon cosmetics, women's risqué clothing or 'marital' aids) where the selling is by peer pressure to buy something different, out of the ordinary, or 'sexy' in good company away from the hassle of shops or husbands etc;

◆ **Sales force** (eg man from the Pru);

◆ **Billboards** and other similar methods – fly posters;

◆ **Window posters** are very effective and a common feature in for example building societies;

◆ **Leaflets** – can be indiscriminate – (eg given out in the street or put on cars) or more targeted – despatched with statement – and/or linked to an event – (eg 'your policy reaches its tenth anniversary or matures – why not deposit the funds in our new account that pays you x%' etc). They can also be extremely cost-effective – they are cheap to produce and when targeted – eg a take-away curry house that leaflets dwellings within its delivery area – can yield substantial returns;

◆ **Face-to-face** – eg by cashiers or customer service staff when a customer enters the branch – 'have you had an account review recently?' – or when a customer is buying Dirhams – 'I notice that you are travelling to the Gulf – have you taken out life and travel insurance?' One of the issues for banks is that they have, by and large, lost control of their customer contacts. Few people now visit their branch with any great frequency – they can now bank either remotely via telephone or Internet or use the 'quick deposit facilities, and increasingly they live remotely (often hundreds of miles) from their original (domicile) bank branch. This means that banks have to use other methods to bring products to their customers' attention;

◆ **'Best-buy' tables** – where one of your products or services appears at the top of a value-for-money table which generates considerable publicity although is very hard to maintain consistently due to the fierce competition and shorter life cycles and therefore increased changes made to products.

See the following example from the *Times*.[2]

Savings best buys

Instant access	Account	Notice	Min deposit	% Gross	Int paid
Alliance & Leicester	Easysaver	instant	£1	3.5%	Yly
Tesco	Savings	Instant	£1	2.85%	Yly
Yorkshire BS	Access saver	instant	£100	3.05%	Yly
Bristol & West	Easylife	Instant	£100	3.00%	Yly
Bradford & Bingley	Pemier saver	Instant	£2,000	3.15%	Yly

Credit cards

Issuer	Monthly	Annual	Int free
Cahoot	0.565%	7.0%	46 days
Intelligent finance	0.713%	8.9%	56 days
Halifax h2x	0.793%	9.9%	59 days

◆ **Direct mail** – has become a permanent feature of our lives. Virtually every time you apply for something, belong to a society or order goods you are placed onto someone's mailing list. In theory this is a good idea, from a marketing point of view, because it should be a list of names that probably constitute a segment (qv) and to which you could market propositions strongly. Sadly what this means is that for most people not a day goes by without some unsolicited piece of junk mail arriving in the post touting wares or something similar. This causes considerable nuisance to customers but fortunately most are recognized and put straight into the bin unopened. Indeed one of the unexpected side-effects is that it has stimulated another market (complementary goods) and many people have bought hand-held shredders for their homes, expressly for dealing with junk mail. This sort of marketing is particularly bad because , by and large it is unfocused and not only wastes marketing resources and collateral but also misses real opportunities as things are lost in the clutter. This is a shame because it has devalued the asset of the mailing list and messages are simply not getting through.

It is vital that your message stands out from the clutter of everyday rubbish that assaults us continually.

For some of these techniques it is appropriate to tell the reader about the price of the product, in others it is not. For example an advertisement on the TV for food or beverages rarely tells you the price, but a car advert nearly always does. Interestingly they are almost always just under a sensitive threshold (known as a price point) where psychologically it would 'tip' over into another price range – eg they are £7,995 (£5 below £8,000). Similarly, many companies' adverts in the press are little more than glorified price lists (look at an example from a PC retailer, or the leaflets from local supermarkets). For mortgages – the price (interest rate) is almost always somewhere – but not always the fees – because they may vary depending on circumstances. With, say, insurance or investment there is no price – usually just (always favourable) comparisons with others.

There are no hard and fast rules on this topic, however. If products are somehow undifferentiated or available from a wide variety of sources the advertiser may perceive that the price is the key purchase determinant and choose to promote this aspect heavily. This is frequently the case with commodity-type purchases, for example fuel – no one type is distinguishable from any other and although much time is spent on advertising brands, what causes people to use a particular petrol station is that it is convenient to where they work or live or simply because their tank is almost empty and need to buy petrol at once. Loyalty cards do not work very well for petrol as few people really want or appreciate what goes with them – they just want to buy petrol.

Note: PR *is different, and is about name or organizational branding awareness, ie getting the name of an organization (eg Barclays, HSBC, Stroud & Swindon, Derbyshire, Prudential or CGNU) in the press or other media (in favourable circumstances).*

Place

Is about getting your product in front of your customers. It used to be called 'location, location, location' – however newer channels, which are generally remote, render this analysis largely redundant. It is really about distribution channels and, for financial services in particular, these are extremely complex now. You may sell directly, remotely, directly face-to-face, via third-party branches (agencies) through a sales force, via the Internet, through the telephone via 'warehouses' or third-party agencies – eg lead managers in syndications, co-joint lending etc, or you may be servicing other organizations' portfolios and trying to sell them your services as well.

Financial services companies often use all available distribution channels – but in many cases they are still wedded to their branch network. It is one of their durable assets and almost symbolizes what they are. The changing marketplace however militates against this and an increasing number of customers are conducting remote transactions and this now begs the question – what is the NPV (Net Present Value) of a network?

Many organizations have also understood this and progressively closed branches where they are no longer used sufficiently to justify their continuation.

This has in some cases provoked some fervent criticism from a minority who expect banks to provide social services instead of banking – but the changing trend is there and is not to be resisted. No bank will survive without Internet banking and indeed all major banks and most minor ones offer this facility. Currently that is where the best rates of interest are available and customers are voting in strength with their feet – or their mouse – your competition is now 'only a click away'!

Figure 5.6: New branches for old

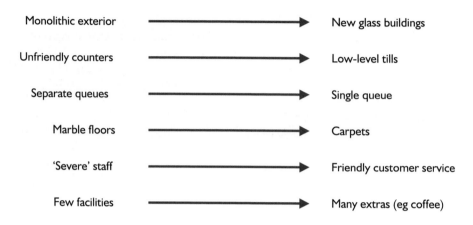

Monolithic exterior	New glass buildings
Unfriendly counters	Low-level tills
Separate queues	Single queue
Marble floors	Carpets
'Severe' staff	Friendly customer service
Few facilities	Many extras (eg coffee)

Over the last few years there has been a revolution in bank branches. The old 'Victorian Gothic' appearance of many branches has been replaced with a much more customer-friendly branch – very open and with huge expanses of glass. Figure 5.6 shows some of the major changes. Previously branches seem almost to have been built to overpower and daunt customers with their majesty and grandeur – 'we are a bank: you are only a customer'. Nowadays they are much more friendly places with comfortable chairs, newspapers, and often including coffee shops to make customers feel more at ease following the customer-centric approach, and include 'meeters and greeters' with cashiers now placed at the back of the site.

The lesson here is that branches can still be an integral part of the marketing mix – but need to reflect changes in demands by customers – and the changing needs of the organization to achieve different targets – eg product penetration and recapturing the customer contact. Where customers no longer use them then it is clear that branches should be closed and other ways found to service those customers in that area who are valued, eg by sharing with other banks or by offering remote banking. In many towns corner sites, so long monopolized by banks and in prime sites for footfall and therefore valuable assets when used by others, have been sold or leased out and are now occupied by other types of organizations – most frequently by wine bars or coffee shops, thus returning either capital or rental income to banks etc.

Other channels are also used – third-party distribution agreements between banks and insurance companies for products; the shifting of help desks and operations to low-cost areas – out of town and often in other countries continues – and in an increasingly global world will do so for some time to come.

Advertising

This is about informing customers of your goods in a non-personal manner and usually involves placing messages of some type in the media (newspapers, radio, TV, magazines, billboards and latterly the Internet.) It is used for many purposes – from selling fizzy or alcoholic drinks, food, shoes and PCs, to getting you to vote for candidates, to informing you of rate changes and to tell you about the congestion charge (local government) or about AIDS and smoking (public health). It is a massive industry with global sales worth hundreds of billions of pounds. It is not new – ancient civilizations used posters to advertise gladiatorial conflicts or other items and often used the ancient equivalent of 'sandwich men'. The first printed advertisement in English appeared in 1478! – just 28 years after Gutenberg invented the printing press.

Advertising is a study in its own right but briefly the key components are:

◆ **Setting the objectives** – whom do we wish to reach (target), why do we want to reach them (Sales objectives) and when do we want to reach them (campaign objectives)?
◆ **Setting the budget** – how much will it cost (depends on media mix), what will the benefit be (what will it earn us) and how much can we afford (corporate limits)?
◆ **Deciding on the messages** – type of message, focus on target, what is the theme and how does that translate into a message (eg we have thought about your busy life and want to help you by not adding to your burden – 'life's complicated enough').
◆ **Deciding on the media mix** – through which type(s) shall we disseminate the message – what reach do we want, when shall we place it and how often (frequency)? Typically there may be a TV and billboard/hoarding mix, supported by posters in the branch and maybe a mail shot as well. Many campaigns run adverts in short bursts over a short period of time – say a week at a time every three weeks to achieve persistency. Others may go for saturation to maximize take-up in a short time – eg during sales.
◆ **Post-campaign evaluation** – how well did we do; did we achieve our results? Very few do this well and as a result rarely find out what worked and what should be repeated. Targets should be agreed in advance so that real evaluation can take place, and the campaign should be output driven – eg increase deposits by x%, or £xxxm.

Different channels may require different (or seemingly different) products and services but beware of differential pricing rules and regulations.

Marketing mix strategies

In the example in Figure 5.7 two different offerings are being marketed. Each has different emphasis on the four aspects of the four Ps:

Figure 5.7: Marketing mix – different strategies

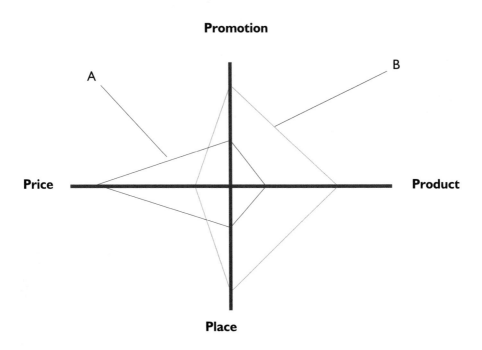

- ◆ offering A is heavily geared to price – ie 'pile it high and sell it cheap', conveniently – eg at a discount store.
- ◆ offering B is placing emphasis on product, then slightly less on place and promotion but not price – ie selling on the other attributes and therefore probably operating at the upper end of the market.

Each is aiming at different buyers whom they believe will respond to different stimuli.

Cahoot – the Internet bank that is part of Abbey National – ran a series of advertisements toward the end of 2002 placing emphasis on the low interest rate of its credit card and how easy it was to obtain it over the Internet – ie price and place. Its profile could look something like Figure 5.8.

Figure 5.8: Marketing mix – Cahoot credit card

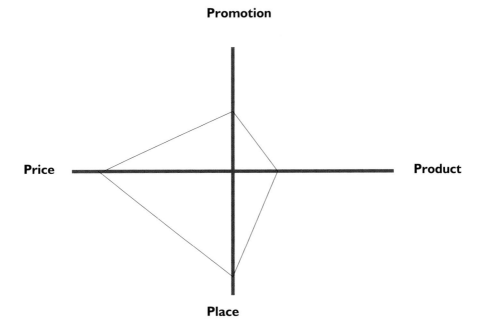

Case study[3]

Shell started to break into the fuel markets in the 19th century – largely by moving up the value chain from carrying oil or petrol on behalf of others and into supplying it directly themselves. Its greatest coup was to be the first shipping company to transport bulk fuel through the Suez Canal in tankers. This allowed it to ship vast quantities of fuel from the Caucasus to the Far East cheaply. The plan was to compete head on with the then major supplier – Standard Oil – whose product was locally branded 'Devoes'. This latter brand of fuel was transported in cans from the USA by ship and tended to arrive with the cans severely damaged (dented and rusty) after exposure to such a long sea voyage. Shell was very surprised, however, to find that it had great difficulty initially in persuading customers to buy its product – kerosene [in the UK known as paraffin] and branded as Shell Oil – even though it was cheaper.

Shell looked into the local market wants and needs and found, to its amazement, that the need for fuel was also bound up with the utility of the cans that the fuel came in. Shell supplied fuel direct in bulk to the local market – where customers could fill cans (Price and Place). The Devoes cans, however, despite being rusty and battered, were also used for a variety of other purposes after they had been emptied – including roofing for houses, bed-pans, lamps, cooking pots and so on and the alternative uses far outweighed the premium price charged over the Shell product.

Accordingly Shell changed its marketing mix from transporting and selling in bulk locally, to transporting in bulk to a local market and **then** putting it in cans for sale – made locally (and therefore increasing the economy there and buying local goodwill) from Welsh tinplate exported for that purpose – and painted them an easily identifiable red which further differentiated them. It thus moved to a more equal mix between *Price* (cheaper than Devoes), *Place* (available locally) and *Product* (nice new tins that matched the ancillary needs of the market). Even with the addition of the price of the tins they were still cheaper than Devoes rusty offerings and therefore they persuaded people to buy Shell fuel in nice new cans which could then be used for the ancillary purposes. The distinctive red colour also assisted the fourth aspect *Promotion* because huts changed colour as the tins were used and therefore the brand became associated with the ancillary uses of the cans.

A clear lesson – to outsell the competition the product must be:

– at least as good

– cheaper if possible

– provide added value to the customer

5.3   A new perspective

As further analysis has taken place, however, and greater understanding of buyers' behaviour has been realized, there has been a fundamental shift from the traditional product-focused, internal view to an externally-focused, customer-centric view. Marketing theory has, accordingly, changed to looking at, analysing and understanding things from the buyer's – ie customers' perspective. This is a totally different method of understanding and applying marketing techniques than the historical perspective and is now generally recognized as the better viewpoint.

You should note, however, that this change does not invalidate any of the four P analysis but shifts the emphasis away from the perspective of the supplier to the customers' viewpoint.

Figure 5.9: Inward versus outward perspectives

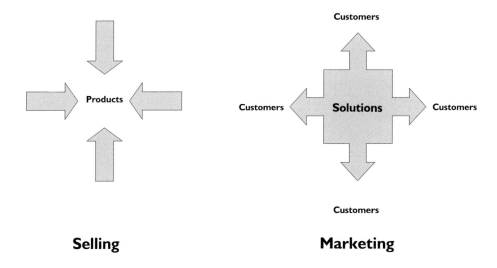

In Figure 5.9 the two types of thinking are contrasted – inward-looking **Selling** and outward-looking **Marketing**.

Selling:

- ◆ is introverted
- ◆ focuses on what we make
- ◆ is product driven
- ◆ asks how do we sell it?
- ◆ does not think of the customer's perspective
- ◆ is short-termist in outlook
- ◆ has very near time horizons – next week not next year – and short lifetimes

Marketing on the other hand is:

- ◆ outward-facing/extroverted
- ◆ focuses on what the customer needs/wants
- ◆ considers how we match those needs
- ◆ looks at things from the customer's perspective
- ◆ asks what does the customer think about us?
- ◆ takes a long-term horizon – next year; lifetime values

This has led to the emergence of a new understanding of buying behaviours – called the **four Cs**[4] – which looks at the buying cycle from the *Customer's* viewpoint and gives a different perspective which can be summarized as:

Cost   **Convenience**
Customer needs and wants   **Communication**

This view seeks to be the customer's who is **outside looking in** rather than, as before, the supplier who is **inside looking out**. What is it that the customer thinks about the offering and what makes him buy it – or if he is not buying it – why not?

Figure 5.10: Four Ps versus Four Cs

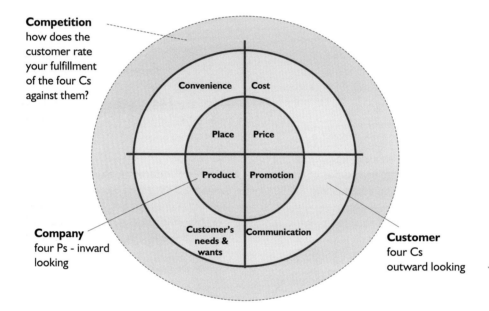

In this case competition has been added as the customers' perception of whether, and by how much, you meet needs and wants is measured against the competition. You need to keep this aspect in mind as well as your customer interactions because customer choice is a relative thing. For example John Lewis (UK Department Stores) send staff to check prices of its major competitors locally to ensure that they meet its stated aim of 'never knowingly undersold' because it cannot let its competition undersell it.

Cost

This represents the cost to the customer if he takes your product or service. He does not pay a *price* in his perception but incurs a *cost* (see Customer Value Proposition), ie not only what he has to pay, but also what he has to forego, or do (eg excessive form filling) in order to obtain your product. This could include intangible and non-physical issues such as time spent, foreign exchange support needed, comparisons of quality or value and other things done before even any money changes hands. Customers will put a cost on non-cash effort even if they cannot quantify it absolutely.

Convenience

This is more than just 'location' (ie where you as a supplier are or where your outlets are situated) but from the customer's viewpoint – what is the easiest way to get hold of the good or service required, or to deal with a query, or resolve an issue or problem. Customers are often prepared to trade off a lot for convenience. This might, for instance, include using different channels rather than bricks-and-mortar branch networks. You might spend a lot in informing your customer base that your service is the best but if the only cashpoint in the village belongs to a competitor he will use that one and not go to the nearest outlet of your organization because it is more inconvenient so to do – even where your competitor charges an extra cost (provided it is not too great).

What seems intuitive to you will not seem so to them (every day you see bank customers queuing outside in the rain at ATMs when cashiers have nothing to do inside the branch!). Similarly the changes demand different skills – no longer is customer handling a prerequisite, it is now fast, timely, error-free delivery. One of the downsides of this is that for many people getting to their own branch of a bank (or even to a branch of the bank that is not necessarily theirs) has become difficult.

Customer needs and wants

These two things are different and it is important to understand the difference. **Needs** are real – **Wants** are aspirational. For example I would *like* **(want)** a mansion in the country but I *require* somewhere to live that is within my budget **(need)**.

This will mean that *no matter what the customer may look at*, she will buy what she needs, at a price that she can afford.

It is possible, however, to sell something to someone by seemingly focusing on their wants; and often marketing is couched in this way. The closer that you can align your offering that meets the customers' **needs** to the customers' **wants**, then the more likely you are to succeed in persuading the customer to buy your particular offering. The more that you can supply something that meets (or partly meets) a **want,** but at a price that is closer to the **need,** then the greater your probability of success will be. This difference between **wants** and **needs** is known as a **'perception gap'** and is important in understanding your customers.

Figure 5.11: Price-value trade-off

When selling anything there is a price – value trade-off. Customers will pay highly for something that they believe adds value to their lives – even if it is not necessarily so (Dreams not perfume) whereas if they think it is a commodity they will differentiate only on price. (NB the Bowman clock referred to above takes this simple graph and expands it into the 8 marketing strategies.[5]) Often promotion of a product is linked to glamorous lifestyles to try to meet aspirations (see branding).

For example customers may come in and say 'I want service X', but this may be inappropriate for them (too expensive, does not deliver what they want – you might not have it). By understanding the underlying need, however, you can try to develop an offering that will satisfy them and by customizing it to meet as much of their aspirations as possible you may lock them in for longer than with a basic commodity purchase.

Case study: 'What colour is your card?'

American Express started off with the ordinary 'green card' and marketed it strongly, with many campaigns aimed at promoting it as the thing to have (**'don't leave home without it'**). Amex was pursuing the theory of increasing 'Market share'. Unfortunately this rapid and massive (and successful) expansion had its adverse reactions. As its success grew some people felt it was no longer a privilege to have one – because anyone could – and they started looking to other cards (eg Visa and Mastercard etc.) and its share of premium customers fell – even though Amex had increased its base enormously. It then introduced a 'Gold card' for premium customers to reflect their need to be different. This enabled Amex to recapture premium customers.

More recently Amex has introduced the 'Blue card' aimed at younger people who want to be associated with **'cool and trendy'** living and be visibly seen to be different from the other green or even gold holders. For those at the top end of the market it also has the 'Black card' – for those who have great wealth and high spending habits. Each card comes with different range of services and privileges. There are also corporate cards aimed at companies' staff. This is highly focused targeting of customers and meeting their needs and wants by differentiating the services offered. Other card companies have followed suit with their own variations on gold, platinum or silver cards.

Communication

This is about getting your message to the customer – and getting it to stand out from the clutter and background noise that surrounds it. A golden rule here is to focus your communication on your customers' (segmented) wants and needs. Instead of viewing it as promoting your product – think of it as an exercise in communicating a value proposition to your customers and prospective customers. Why should they listen/read it? Focus on their needs and wants and customize the contents to them. You would not usually advertise in the Russian language in France (unless you were targeting expatriates) – because hardly anybody would understand it and it would be wasted. Apply that analogy to any communication and you will soon see why the customer focus is key.

Successful selling then is, paradoxically, about increasing your internal emphasis from just *selling* to including *marketing* and using different strategies, tactics and approaches to increase your share of the customers spend.

Case study: Shell

Consider the earlier example from Shell. When it reviewed its tactics it changed its marketing mix to maintain:
- the reduced **Cost** over its competitors by bulk transport of fuel;
- the **Convenience** of a locally available product;

- and also it met the **Customers needs and wants** by selling the fuel in nice new cans which they used for ancillary purposes;
- the usage of its new red cans by customers, when they had used the fuel, to build accommodation also **Communicated** a strong message to potential customers.

In the classic Anshoff matrix[6], shown in Figure 5.12 this would be classed as quartile 1 – *market penetration* – ie selling more into your existing market (customers) by understanding their needs, linked with judicious forays into quartiles 2 and 3 – extending your product penetration and developing new customers.

Figure 5.12: Marketing/risk assessment matrix (Anschoff)

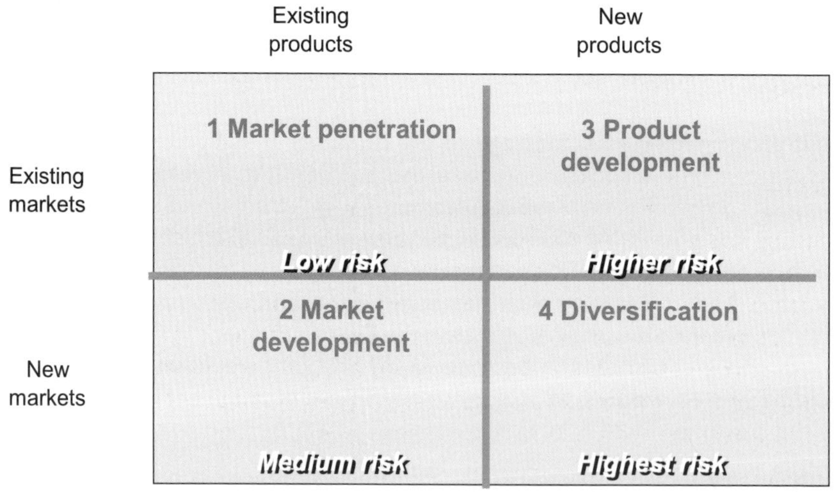

	Existing products	New products
Existing markets	1 Market penetration Low risk	3 Product development Higher risk
New markets	2 Market development Medium risk	4 Diversification Highest risk

Need to formulate your own strategy and understand your competitors' likely response and what the risk is therefrom

There are four types of marketing strategies as shown in Figure 5.12 with different risk profiles attached to each. The greater the degree of unknown (new markets, new products) the greater the risk of failure – but paradoxically if you get it right the greater potential for rewards, providing you have carried out your analysis correctly.

Market penetration: where the objectives are to increase market share; increase sales to existing customers/make sales to new customers by selective price reductions; selling alternative services; accepting smaller orders; improve selling methods; improve customer service or add extra value (Customer Value Proposition equation must be equalized).

Market development: where you must segment current market; focus different blends of services at different segments; price by segment; develop new markets.

Product/service development: change current services; develop new services; new capabilities and enhance current services; change service mix; unbundle services and premium price.

Diversification: acquire a supplier; acquire a distributor; enter a new area of expertise; brand extension; service extension or exit some markets and re-focus.

5.4   The seven 'P's – four 'P's augmented

For the financial services sector which is heavily people based, for which there is little or no evidence of products, and due to the increasing fragmentation of delivery, an extra three 'P's are worth considering in more detail. These are in addition to place, price, promotion and product, **Process**, **People** and **Physical evidence**.

Process

A process is a mechanism for making something happen and, for a process to exist, there must be a change in state of some sort. Delivery to clients is the end result of a process. Business processes are a fundamental component of any business and efficient business processes have a major impact on the success of an organization and shape the way in which people work. In today's knowledge economy people may well be the most important assets of a company but if they have to work within the constraints of inefficient processes they cannot work effectively.

There are three major issues with processes:

◆ efficiency and effectiveness;
◆ mechanisation rather than automation;
◆ fragmentation.

Efficiency and effectiveness

The twin goals of processing are efficiency and effectiveness:

◆ Where a process maximizes efficiency - it is doing what needs to be done as accurately and as fast as possible; and
◆ Where it maximizes effectiveness it means that what is done delivers value to the customer and the organization.

(It is no good carrying out a process efficiently if it is of no value, and similarly a process can be theoretically effective but if it contains inherent inefficiencies then it does not deliver when it should.)

Mechanization rather than automation

Similarly although new technology can deliver huge benefits to a company, both in terms of cost savings and efficiency, if it is not harnessed within well-designed processes it can never achieve its full potential. Typically technology support has only **mechanized** existing processes, rather than changed them to improve effectiveness and introduced real automation. This often results in extra steps in processes as people try to get round the system, to do what was done before - even where the system contains the opportunity for a step to be automated or renders it unnecessary – which usually makes things worse. Real attention is needed to yield real benefits.

Many processes are inherently inefficient because:

- ◆ Most processes have evolved – they were not designed;
- ◆ Improvements often focused within functions, whereas increasingly processes cross several functions and more often than not different legal entities and physical locations – even continents;
- ◆ Computerization has, until recently, tended to concentrate on mechanizing the existing activities;
- ◆ They often contain significant duplication and double checking;
- ◆ Often value added is countered by activities which add no value;
- ◆ They take poor cognisance of true customer needs.

A good example of a poor process in most organizations is the sales process where, typically, most of the effort is expended prior to the decision. Take a typical bank process for new customers:

- ◆ identify prospects;
- ◆ develop relationships;
- ◆ find loan opportunities;
- ◆ perform analysis;
- ◆ propose loan;
- ◆ credit decision;
- ◆ yes:
- ◆ underwrite deal;
- ◆ prepare documentation;
- ◆ close deal;
- ◆ no:
- ◆ turn down.

Such processes are usually insufficiently focussed, the tasks to achieve sales goals are not carried out well, and the emphasis is on new business 'hunting' rather than 'farming' existing client base. In addition cross-disciplinary efforts are usually poor and the organizations' talents under utilised.

By moving the focus of effort to the **decision** more effective usage of time can be made – eg by pre-approving decisions, or by delegating greater authority down to managers etc or by automating the process to be one-stop capture of data and auto-acceptance. Key steps to improve processes include:

- ◆ ascertaining the time value of activities;
- ◆ mapping the processes and then changing them to drive out the inefficiencies;
- ◆ ensure that MIS provides the right data at the right time;
- ◆ strip out non-value added activities;
- ◆ streamlining the processes to reduce wasted effort;
- ◆ move to self managing teams.

Benefits would, therefore, include:

- ◆ faster throughput;
- ◆ better quality (reduced errors);
- ◆ focussed marketing efforts;
- ◆ increased profit;
- ◆ improved customer satisfaction.

Fragmentation

This is increasingly becoming one of the most difficult issues for staff to manage. Given the globalisation of the world and the increasing separation of process execution from initiation, often transaction processing can take place within a radically different timescale (eg at night) and in far flung locations (E Europe, Asia etc). As a result the customer-facing member of staff is disenfranchised to a degree.

Figure 5.13 shows this.

Figure 5.13: Process hierarchy

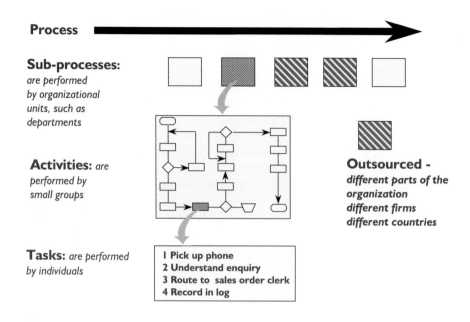

Process

Sub-processes:
*are performed
by organizational
units, such as
departments*

Activities: *are
performed by
small groups*

Outsourced -
different parts of the
organization
different firms
different countries

Tasks: *are performed
by individuals*

1 Pick up phone
2 Understand enquiry
3 Route to sales order clerk
4 Record in log

A process such as requesting a chequebook is very simple in essence, but may involve a very complicated process. A customer may go into a branch (not necessarily the account domicile) to request a chequebook. The order will be despatched to a central area of the bank, which will then process the request. This might then be passed onto another organization (eg printing firm where this piece of the process has been outsourced) and then sent to the customer. An organization has no direct control over the outsourced parts of the process and a member of staff in the account domicile branch hasn't even been involved. Where the customer information system is first class then this fact (the request) will have been noted and the branch can then monitor the transaction – where it is not first class however...

Figure 5.14: Process – fragmentation

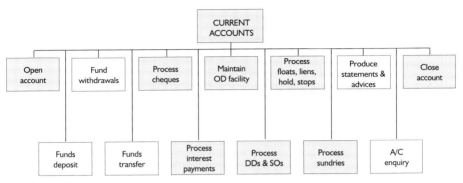

Figure 5.14 shows a typical range of tasks associated with the current account process. Many of these tasks (examples hashed on diagram) can, and often do, take place at locations remote from the branch (eg through ATMs, via telephone or Internet and of course in other branches and banks in some cases.) What this means is that the individual involved in the principal organization (eg account domicile branch), when interfacing with the customer, has to deal with issues which may have been caused by actions in other organizations, and of which the customer is unaware. The resolution of an issue may lie with this third party, over whom she has no direct leverage and on whom she must rely for rectification: the third party may not perform to her standards and may be in a completely different time zone.

People

Within most organizations staff usually have a functional specialism and sometimes a little knowledge of other areas. These are known as 'I' shaped (deep knowledge in one area) and 'T' shaped staff (deep knowledge in one area and a smattering of knowledge across the top). In order to offer enhanced service and to facilitate cross-selling and product penetration, staff, in particular relationship managers, need to acquire a broader, and at the same time deeper, set of skills and understanding of products and organizational capability. Figure 5.15 shows this.

Figure 5.15: Staff skills metamorphosis required

Typical organization –
largely functional specialist

New CRM focused organization
with many staff having broad
product knowledge

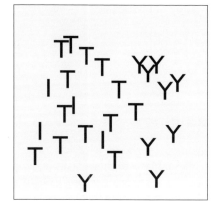

To ensure more sales and better service the organization needs
to migrate its staff competencies from largely 'I' with some 'T': to
largely 'T' with many 'Y'

For an organization this will necessitate:

◆ Ensuring the right staff fill the roles;
◆ That staff and relationship managers have the right training;
◆ That product knowledge is sufficient;
◆ That they understand the breadth of the organization's capabilities;
◆ If necessary recruiting (novation);
◆ That remuneration levels and form is right to drive and set the new behaviours.

Physical evidence

As the services offered in financial services are intangible – such as insurance, overdrafts or loans – there is no physical product that a customer can touch. It is important therefore that there is instead some other evidence of the service. This is called physical evidence. These types of things are often the only tangible attributes which the service consumer may use to assess a service or a company. This may include the physical state of repair, decoration and design of the building, company promotional information (brochures, letters, and business cards) and even the physical appearance of staff or a piece of paper that states that you are insured (certificate).

Similarly there is no delivery of an overdraft except a line on a statement (which says £1340.89 DR in red and is really like a delivery invoice). It is argued by some that this compounds the complexity – but few people worry about that aspect. It is therefore difficult to 'take an overdraft for a test drive' or to engage in 'tasting' or 'sampling' of loans or insurance policies' and as a result people either rely on previous experience or on third party recommendations – friends and family or advice from financial advisers. (See purchasing decisions.)

It would therefore be easy not to place adequate emphasis on such manifestations of service which are corollaries to the sale of goods (for example the sale of a television set – which sits in the corner of a room) but they are important.

Summary

The basic marketing mix is often referred to as the four Ps. This has now been revisited from a customer's perspective to yield the four Cs. Successful marketing is about communicating the right message about your offering to the customer – that meets his needs and wants conveniently and at a cost that he considers appropriate.

1 Marketing is about getting customers to buy from **you** rather than your competition. It is therefore about making your customers feel that by buying from you they are getting a better benefit than from anybody else.
2 The higher the benefit they receive, however, the higher the cost to deliver it to them (usually) and so you must ensure that your prices have taken this factor into account.
3 Marketing is often referred to as the four Ps: **Product, Price, Promotion and Place.** For many years these four elements were the cornerstone of marketing for everyone and collectively are known as the marketing mix.
4 More recently the focus has shifted from the internal view – the four Cs: **Cost, Convenience, Customer needs and wants, and Communication.**

Select bibliography

Loyalty rules: F Reichheld

Principles of Marketing: Kotler

Value Based Marketing: Peter Doyle

Notes

1 '*Exploring Corporate Strategy* by Johnson and Scholes (Prentice Hall), fifth edition, Exhibit 6.4

2 *The Times – Easy Money* – Wednesday, 13 November 2002

3 *A Century in Oil – The Shell Transport and Trading Company* 1887-1997; Stephen Howarth, Weidenfeld and Nicolson, 1997

4 **Robert Lauterborn**: '*New Marketing Litany*' (article in *Advertising Age* October 1990)

5 See above

6 **Igor Ansoff**: *Strategic Planning*, Penguin

Six

Segmentation

Topics in this chapter

Segmentation, profit:cost relationship

Introduction to this chapter

This chapter looks at segmentation. This is a very useful tool for marketing purposes because it facilitates better understanding of target consumers or organizations and allows you to focus resources and effort on the right customers.

A useful definition of a segment is that members will respond in a similar manner (more or less) to marketing stimuli. For example first-time buyers will respond in similar ways and wholly differently to 20-year mortgage holders due to the differences in their status, earning power, family needs, lack of equity etc. The value of a segment is not that you will necessarily produce a new offering for it (although you might) but that your offering will be tailored such that the benefits from your offering are *directly related to its specific needs and wants*.

What is segmentation?

It is analogous to an orange or a grapefruit, which is split into segments, or a cake which is typically sliced up before eating because they are not all eaten in one go but segment by segment, or slice by slice. When applied to, say, the UK, it recognizes that the cake (the population of 60 million) is not an homogeneous entity, but that it is composed of 60 million different and discrete individuals with different needs and wants. It is not possible to sell the same thing to all people all the time, neither is it possible to sell to each individual as an individual cost-effectively. If the EU is considered as the target market then it becomes even larger at 300+ million and the world globally is around 4 billion people, making selling the same thing in the same way generally difficult.

Why segment?

Acute observers, however, have noticed that people in a group often share the same needs and wants as the other members of that group and that it is possible to 'slice and dice' the general population by breaking them into groups or segments. It should be noted that many people belong to many groups and that they may belong to groups with different characteristics; but within these groups they will, typically, share the same needs and wants – although membership of one type of group does not imply membership of any other. Segmentation is an artificial analysis and offers a proxy for group wants and must be understood in that context. Few people would recognize themselves as a member of the group that comprises, say, church-going, fast-car driving, marathon-running, accountants with three children, although these characteristics may well be true for some people.

As an individual you may belong to several groups that have no shared characteristics, except that you belong to them. You might collect stamps, play golf and enjoy gardening at the weekend. Others who play golf will share needs and wants in relation to golf but far fewer will collect stamps and most will have no interest in it whatsoever. To target golf-playing stamp collectors would probably be very difficult (you bought our clubs – now buy a penny black!), however, targeting golf players with golf and golf-related products and services is very easy – either through direct advertising aimed at their needs and wants (golf equipment, golfing holidays) or through specialist magazines bought only by golfers. Similarly stamp collectors would be targeted via specialist magazines or perhaps at stamp fairs or similar events.

These groups can be considered as a series of Venn diagrams that overlap. Marketing focuses either on one circle on the diagram or large areas of overlap.

Figure 6.1: Different groups to which an individual might belong, with some members sharing interests and some not

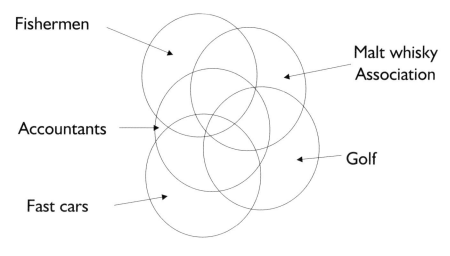

Fishermen

Malt whisky Association

Accountants

Golf

Fast cars

(illustrative data only)

Segments may consist of people, residential types, organizations, region(s), a country(ies), religion, language, or history (new world, third world). They can also be based on purchases by product, brand, usage, benefits received, needs, problems and even price.

Organizations need to segment to ensure that they firstly understand what the needs and wants of a segment are (it is of little use targeting bacon at orthodox Jews, or beef products at Hindus because not only will they not buy them but they will also probably be highly offended and may stop buying other products you may wish to sell them).

Benefits

The benefits of segmentation are:

◆ You can focus your efforts and therefore maximize results from that focus by looking at similarities within groups that are meaningful for your business. If you are a small regional building society it is of little value in segmenting the UK into regions – it makes much more sense to focus on the market within your 'boundaries' [however you define them] and to develop offerings that meet the specific needs of sections or segments within that area.

◆ You can develop an expertise in a particular segment – eg Ecclesiastical Insurance – which focuses on church and related insurances, or a 'special risk' broker at Lloyds.

◆ You can build a very strong brand based on your reputation and knowledge of a particular segment – eg Citibank has an unrivalled reputation in the field of payments and Chase is considered at the top with regards to safe custody.

◆ You can more easily 'weed out' those customers that you do not wish to service by setting criteria that you know form the boundaries of the segment (eg Coutts [free asset value] or Riggs bank [embassy banking] or the smaller regional building societies which tend to lend only within designated geographical areas), or some organizations have formed alliances with 'affinity' groups (eg NUS, Mini owners etc).

◆ Your marketing can support the segments you have chosen and reinforce your position within them.

◆ You can more easily cross-sell relevant offerings to the members because you will know that they are likely to give them higher consideration than those outside the segment and you know [or should know] more about their specific needs and wants.

'We know that there is a gap in the market – but is there a market in the gap?'

Profitability is key

There is no point in looking at a segment where you cannot make money. This has been the cause of many problems for organizations where they have not undertaken analysis adequately. Rather they have been adopting a 'me too' approach in following others into segments where they have neither the right product nor the understanding of the needs and wants that might have enabled them to tailor the product to meet them and therefore (assuming cost was right) to make money. You are in business to make money and while some people do not like to think in these terms it is a fact. The only reason for requiring customers to take your offerings is to make money. Unless you have a strategic and sustainable advantage within a segment, which allows you to make money, **there is no point on going into it whatsoever.**

6.1   Segmentation by profitability

Segmentation, as discussed, is a mechanism used to divide the whole universe of customers into manageable portions or slices. Historic marketing spoke of segmentation by all of some of the following:

◆ Gender
◆ Religion
◆ Race

- ◆ Nationality
- ◆ Age bands
- ◆ ACORN (A Classification Of Residential Neighbourhoods)
- ◆ Wealth/income
- ◆ Geography

Category killers

This has been a recent phenomenon where organizations have focused rigidly on one segment and attacked it very aggressively – usually with incredible success. Good examples of this include:

Budget airlines – where they have focused on only short trips and offer no frills and no extras (except at extra cost). The trail blazer for this was South West Airlines in the USA which focused on only 'hops' within Texas originally with no links to other airlines, no seat reservations and made lots of money; followed by Ryanair, Buzz, Easyjet and Go.

Toys R Us – which has attacked the toy market and by developing vast shops stocking hundreds of toys and therefore getting huge bulk discounts, has taken a large market share.

Furniture – such as IKEA, which followed similar strategy to that of Toys R Us with huge shops in out-of-town locations stocking hundreds of items in the 'home goods' category, selling them cheaply with essentially self-selection in flat packs for assembly later. These types of shops are attacking the traditional department store which offers a very broad range but with only a few items in each category.

Clothing – stores such as Tierack and Sockshop take a similar approach where they focus on a particular item and offer very broad ranges of a small selection of goods.

It is interesting to note that few of these as yet have emerged in financial services fields – due to the more complex nature of the offerings and the less relevance of discounted bulk purchases although it could be argued that the Internet banks offering high rates for deposits are some way down this road. The initial success of Direct Line was also similar because it 'cherry-picked' specific types of insurance (car) with a very cheap offering based on low overheads centralized in an out-of-town call centre.

However there are difficulties with segmentation – it not only tends to embrace large 'generalizations' but also each buyer has his own needs, wants, attitudes etc and could therefore represent a segment of one. Clearly this would pose severe problems for marketing because everything would be personalized or individually customized.

Customization, however, need not be producing a product or service explicitly for each person but may be a modular approach based around a combination of standard or easily available products/services already in existence. This can give the feeling to a customer that he is being looked after personally while at the same time using products in existence that require no development and therefore no extra cost. It might not always be possible to reach a 100% fit – but you can usually get very close.

Case study

A family of four are going on holiday and come into a travel agent to make enquiries and possibly book it. They discuss options with the agent and eventually decide what they want. The holiday is based around a set of core items:

♦ type of holiday
♦ destination
♦ flight times
♦ convenient airports
♦ type of hotel
♦ duration of holiday
♦ cost

…and some ancillary items such as:

♦ car hire
♦ trips
♦ extra services

Based on these factors a holiday is chosen. The holiday is in fact personalized to them – and it is unlikely that any other holidaymakers will have exactly the same holiday but nothing 'new' has been created or developed, merely a unique selection of modules/options already available. The agent will also possibly take the opportunity to sell extra services such as currency, travellers cheques or travel insurance.

Where you produce for only a few customers (eg if you are building luxury holiday cruise ships) it is relatively easy to customize for them – where you sell to larger markets it is clearly impossible. Segmentation helps to make sense of an amorphous mass of many individuals (or companies in the corporate sector). What are traditionally recognized as segments, however, contain pitfalls for the unwary or inexperienced.

Take residential areas – often used as proxy segments on the basis that they are relatively homogeneous; however this can be misleading. Within the same post code in London, for example, you might have houses that have large families, small families, childless couples, retired people, several flats in the same building or even council-owned houses or sheltered accommodation, tenants or even squatters and all of these would have widely differing needs and incomes and disposable levels. Any campaign targeted in this way would be a waste of time and may not generate any business at all.

Case study

Royal Bank of Scotland has several different segments at the macro level, including:

◆ Its branch network for the majority of the customers – branded as:
   Royal Bank of Scotland, and
   NatWest;
◆ Premium banking within the network of ordinary branches with special teams of premium bankers (relationship managers);
◆ Premium branches run on the same platform as the network, eg 'Drummonds';
◆ Coutts – a separate bank for HINWIS customers, with its frock-coated bankers.

Prices for services of course vary accordingly, but customers are prepared to pay extra for the differential service – or the cachet of banking at the 'Queens' Bank' (Coutts).

6.2   How to do it

If we use the definition referred to in the introduction where segments are 'sets of buyers who have similar needs and who respond to marketing stimuli in similar ways' we get closer to a true segment.

It is, therefore, far better to use a combination of factors – which implies very good information – and segment by **potential profitability** to the company. In fact this latter method of segmentation is the only way to make money. You must therefore take the following steps:

◆ decide on what bases you will segment;
◆ analyse the attractiveness of those segments for you;
◆ decide in which you will make money and prioritize them;
◆ choose the position of your offerings in those segments;

◆ develop your Customer Value Propositions for each.

This therefore implies that you must manage your customer base (segments) very carefully and get rid of those that do not make you money (or perhaps migrate them to a different service level where they can make you money). This is where the customer-service aspect of operations is useful because it provides feedback on the performance of those segments and allows you to analyse them and take the right business decisions accordingly.

Understand the 'hive' of customers

Consider the two key aspects of a customer:

◆ what level of product take-up do you have now?
◆ what do you consider it should/could be in the future?

This enables you to categorize them into the 'hive' of customers.

Figure 6.2: Hive of customers

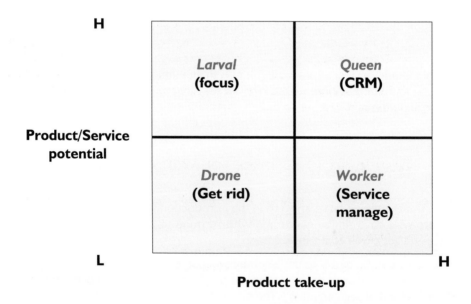

The best **(Queen)** customers are those with high take-up and likely to have high potential. They need careful management now and close management into the future and probably high levels of service and contact.

Next are those with high take-up but little potential in the future (**Workers**). They need good service management to ensure that you maintain their custom and that they receive the service required.

Those with high potential but low take-up (**Larval**) will probably need to be induced into taking products on the short term (eg free banking for students or accountancy/ solicitor trainees) to ensure that as their needs mature so does the relationship.

Finally those that have low take-up and low potential (**Drones**) offer no real value to you and are unlikely so to do and therefore they should be managed out as soon as practicable.

This may mean taking tough decisions – but it is the sign of good management that it is able to act on information and take the right actions. This enables you to ensure that you are focusing your effort in the right places – ie on those accounts or customers that will generate the best income and not on those that take too much time and yield little by way of returns.

Building societies are often faced with these dilemmas. Many of their accounts have small balances but still require the same amount of effort as those that contain higher deposits. In addition many customers use what are in fact savings or deposit accounts as quasi-current accounts, which costs the societies money and makes them little.

For them the difficulty is to maintain the balance between the perception of mutuality (cheap services to all and sundry) and profit-enhancing decisions – higher charges or closure. Good robust analysis of their accounts can assist them in understanding those customers who are unprofitable and then it can assist them in formulating a strategy and a plan to close, or manage out, the unwanted accounts and allow them to focus on the ones that make them money.

6.3 Decide on what bases you will segment

As mentioned above – profitability is key. Segments chosen should be those where you can make money. This implies that you must:

- ◆ understand the market better
- ◆ have a better offering than your competitors
- ◆ tailor it more specifically to wants and needs

or

- ◆ be able to deliver it at a lower cost

Segmentation, therefore, must be based on those factors where you have sustainable competitive advantage as outlined above. It is perfectly reasonable, feasible and can be extremely successful to define your own segments – that are different from your competitors and that enable you to play to your strengths – provided that they are real segments and not just inchoate groupings.

Different ways of segmentation might include:

◆ Demographics and socioeconomic factors (often used but not very focused)
◆ Lifestyles
◆ Product usage (eg if they use an Amex card for buying shrewd analysis might lead you to offer products that reflect their purchasing)
◆ Needs/wants
◆ Attitude to service
◆ Benefits sought

Figure 6.3: Analysing segments

| Idea | What is the real need (overt/latent)?
Are customers interested?
Do they see the value for them? |

| What is the opportunity | Who are the target customers?
What revenues can we get?
Are they sustainable?
What is the time horizon? |

| Implications for us | What assets do we need?
What additional competences do we need? |

| Who is in the market | Who are the competition - now and in the future?
How will we compete?
What risks are there - how do we contain/manage them? |

| Actions | How do we get into this market?
Acquire? - Ally? - Cooperate? Build? |

General segment strategy

The critical issues in deciding which segments to attack are: firstly, whether the segment is attractive to you (ie can you make money easily in that strategy – given what you do); and secondly the strength of your CVP within the segment by comparison to the competition.

For example Coutts would have little chance of making money in the low-income segments of society because what it offers is simply not relevant and its cost structure is wrong. Similarly banks geared up to mass account management with minimum levels of service would not take too many customers away from Coutts because their CVP does not compete.

Figure 6.4: General segment strategies

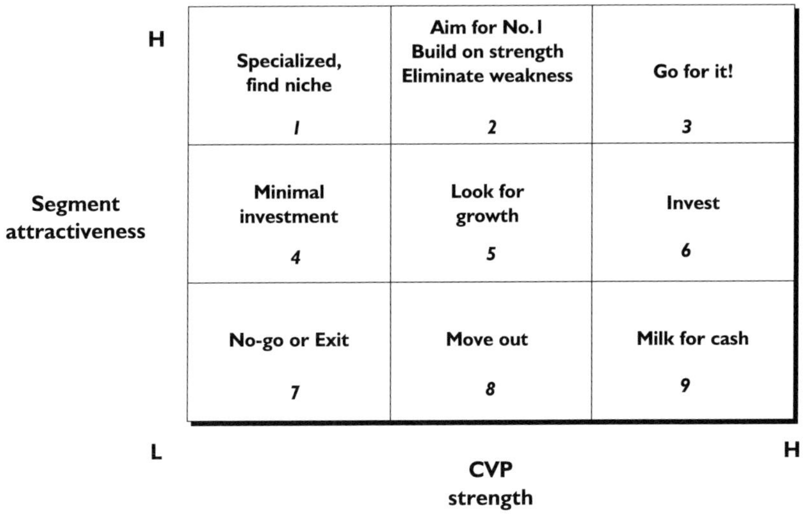

H	Specialized, find niche *1*	Aim for No.1 Build on strength Eliminate weakness *2*	Go for it! *3*
Segment attractiveness	Minimal investment *4*	Look for growth *5*	Invest *6*
	No-go or Exit *7*	Move out *8*	Milk for cash *9*

L   **CVP strength**   H

Based on the segment attractiveness and the strength of your CVP there are a number of generic competitive strategic initiatives that can be followed.

Figure 6.4 shows some generic strategies that can be adopted after you have completed your segmentational analysis and understood the strength of your Customer Value Proposition in that segment.

They are as follows:

No.
1 The segment is very attractive for you but your Customer Value Proposition is weak. You need to find a niche for your Customer Value Proposition and harvest market share.
2 Build on the strengths of the Customer Value Proposition to oust the leader – try to improve the Customer Value Proposition.
3 You should easily be the market leader – nothing to stop you, but you need constantly to review your customer feedback and check that your Customer Value Proposition still meets their needs so as not to lose the position.

4 Try to exploit the segment without spending too much, ie selling standard products without too much effort.

5 You must look to grow your market share – and customer share.

6 Invest to gather customers based on the strength of the Customer Value Proposition which should allow you to exploit this segment.

7 Get out – no hope – segment unattractive and Customer Value Proposition poor – place investment elsewhere.

8 Begin to move out – and put investment elsewhere.

9 No investment – merely sell your products based around the Customer Value Proposition to maximize return and generate cash.

The key issues for consideration here are what the competitive response might be to your actions (see competitive analysis) and how easy it is to divert investment across into those segments where Customer Value Proposition is high and they are attractive.

It is worth highlighting the difference between previous segmentation and new thinking in this context:

◆ Traditional Segmentation (ex ante) – the market is segmented based on age, income, geography, type of business, etc. It is often difficult to find a relationship between these segmentation parameters and the customers' purchase decision and usage.

◆ Needs-Based Segmentation (ex post) – Because the customer's purchase decision is closely linked to the individual's needs and preferences, customers with similar needs are grouped. When a group of customers with distinct needs and preferences is found (eg very little price sensitivity, and interested in new product features), common background for the group is analysed in order to operationalize this segmentation model.

This then allows you to:

◆ choose your segments – get rid of unprofitable segments
◆ agree your Customer Value Propositions (CVP)
◆ understand your customer-shared goals
◆ develop customer-focused activity processes to deliver to the shared goals
◆ develop the 'logical roles' to carry out these processes – with the right Attributes, Skills, Knowledge (ASK)

which will lead to better profit from more focused sales and marketing.

Summary

Segmentation is a very useful tool for marketing purposes because it facilitates better understanding of target consumers or organizations and allows you to focus resources and effort on the right customers. It must be used carefully and you should enter only those segments where you have a sustainable advantage that will allow you to make money. To achieve segmentation you must follow a robust process based on your general marketing strategy to ensure you hit those targets that will yield the desired results.

1 It is not possible to sell the same thing to all people all the time, neither is it possible to sell to each individual as an individual cost-effectively – but people often share the same needs and wants as the other members of a defined group and it is, therefore, possible to 'slice and dice' the general population by breaking them into groups or segments.
2 Segmentation facilitates focused marketing of targetted offers.
3 A segment is defined as: 'sets of buyers that have similar needs and who respond to marketing stimuli in similar ways'.
4 There is no point in looking at a segment where you cannot make money.
5 Segmentation is an artificial analysis and offers a proxy for group wants and must be understood in that context.
6 Key issues for consideration when choosing segments include possible competitive response and how easy it is to divert investment across into those segments.

Select bibliography

Principles of Marketing: Kotler

FT – *Mastering Marketing*: pp 55-58 'Slicing and dicing the market' – Green and Krieger

Seven

Competitor analysis

Topics in this chapter

Why analyse competitors

Types of competition

Information

Introduction to this chapter

It is not unfortunately just enough to understand your customers, because you do not operate in a world where you are the only game in town. It is necessary for you to scrutinize the competition to find out whom you are up against. In particular you need to know:

◆ Who are they now?
◆ Who were they in the past – and why are they no longer there?
◆ Who might they be in the future?
◆ What do they offer?
◆ How do our offerings compare?
◆ Which do customers prefer and why?
◆ What is the competitive response that they will take to action we initiate?

This is because your success is measured as a relative thing against your competition – other businesses in your marketplace. You can then split them into three types:

◆ Threats
◆ Opportunities
◆ Allies

'The key to investing is not assessing how much an industry is going to affect society, or how much it will grow, but rather in determining the competitive advantage of any given company and, above all, the durability of that advantage' (Warren Buffet)[1]

Threats

Those that are threats (or potential threats) need to be analysed to understand:

◆ Why they are or might be a threat;
◆ What they have that is different – or better;
◆ Where and how you can/might compete;
◆ What their response to this action might be.

And you can therefore formulate *defensive* marketing strategies. This needs to be done for each perceived different threat and might include such things as:

◆ **Changing your capability** – perhaps training new staff in, say, sales rather than deposit-taking, or developing new services to match competitors' offerings that also meet customers' needs;
◆ **Changing your technology** – eg building up an Internet facility, developing a call centre (note that this latter is not a few people in a room with some telephones) or developing a customer relationship management (CRM) database that allows you to understand your customers better and anticipate their needs;
◆ **Improving processes** – by re-engineering them to focus on those areas that provide maximum benefit to customers rather than those that meet internal historical procedures;
◆ **Recruiting different staff** – with different skills, or different attitudes to improve what you offer or that have experience of different methods of customer service.

Or if all else fails or the writing is on the wall:

◆ **Exit** – to a market where you have or can build/develop sustainable advantage.

Figure 7.1: Customer/competitor analysis

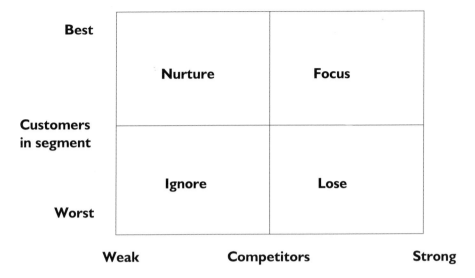

Figure 7.1 contrasts the relative strength of competition against the quality of your customers. Four strategies emerge from this:

◆ **Nurture** – Where you have your best customers and competitors are weak you must nurture them – you cannot be complacent because circumstances change and they could be cherry-picked at a later stage or by emergent competition.

◆ **Lose** – where your competition is strong and your customers are poor in quality (expressed as income earning for you) there is little point in worrying about them or developing a strategy – let the competition pick up the dross and bear the costs of servicing them for little return.

◆ **Weak** – where the competition is weak and customers are worst then ignore them – any that go are little loss and in general there is no imperative for them to leave.

◆ **Focus** – where your best customers are liable to a sustained attack from strong competition – you must develop defensive strategies against this and focus your efforts. NB not all competitors will fall in the same quartile with the same segments therefore your strategies must be cognisant of this and the analysis needs to be carried out on a competitor-by-competitor basis (unless they are very homogeneous and can be dealt with as a whole).

Opportunities

Those that represent opportunities need the same type of analysis but with a view to where you can attack their customers and how to win them across – ie you develop **offensive** strategies.

> Offensive marketing is defined by Hugh Davidson[2] as the mnemonic POISE where:
>
> **P Profitable** – means a proper balance between the firm's need for profit and customers' need for value
>
> **O Offensive** – must lead market, take risks and make competitors follow
>
> **I Integrated** -   marketing approach must permeate whole company
>
> **S Strategic** – probing analysis leading to a winning strategy
>
> **E Effective** –   strong and effective execution on a daily basis

This is really taking the fight to the customers and assessing where you can win and then driving into the competition's heartland and taking customers by dint of a superior offering. The objective of marketing is about making it so easy for a customer to choose your offering over that of a competitor that it becomes a 'no-brainer' because the argument is so compelling that they cannot resist. This is because you offer what they need at (in the customers' perception) a better combination of benefit and price. Similarly you must not give them any reason to go to a competitor.

Differentiation can be a useful tool here. Many organizations (bookshops, food shops and clothes shops for example) are turning their hitherto rather staid and moribund locations into part of what is called the 'customer experience'. Rather than just a collection of products sitting on shelves or a row of tills with queues in front of them and bored cashiers sitting processing they are adding many different items such as coffee shops, and even in some cases performances by artists, jugglers and so on.

While banks are still some way from the barbershop quartets seen in some shops there are some moves in this direction – Abbey National has entered into a joint agreement with Costa Coffee and in many branches the entrance is through the coffee shop – providing a different experience from many other banks and it is more common to see clowns giving out balloons to the children of financial services customers as part of branch promotions than before.

Allies

Where you perceive competitors as potential allies you will need to investigate where best to ally yourself and what is in it for both parties – eg sharing distribution outlets to reduce costs yet provide extended service to customers in outlying areas or sharing products between a bank and an insurance company.

7.1   What is a competitor?

At first glance the answer to this question might seem intuitive. You all know your competitors – you walk past many of them on the way to work; but the world is changing fast – driven by such things as:

- ◆ new means of **distribution** that are often location independent (web, mailshots, off-the-page adverts)
- ◆ changes to **barriers to entry** – caused by new regulation to 'level the playing field' or by technology (Internet, e-mail)
- ◆ increasing **globalizatio**n (foreign companies either talking over domestic players and altering the way they operate; new companies entering your market directly; new companies entering the market indirectly through alliances or remotely – at a distance through the web)
- ◆ **convergence** between markets and players as they seek to extend the brand into financial services (Virgin, M&S, Sainsburys etc) linked to
- ◆ increasing **commoditization** of products (eg many mortgages are now bought and investments made based on 'best-buy' tables – which focus largely on price – a sign of commoditization)
- ◆ easier access to greater and cheaper **capital** (interest rates are very low currently and there is a surplus of capital, also highly-rated firms can raise capital cheaply in their domestic market or elsewhere and use it in other markets)
- ◆ organizations moving up the **value chain** (to secure distribution, to reap the benefits of economies of scale by product penetration or to take advantage of greater margins in different parts of the chain).

As a result competition is not only getting more diverse but also much more intense. The natural result of this is that margins are squeezed and firms try to poach and cherry-pick the best customers.

There are really five types of competition:

- ◆ Pioneer (leading [and sometimes bleeding] edge)
- ◆ Early copiers
- ◆ Late copiers
- ◆ Resistors
- ◆ Differentiation from flow

Pioneer

Prime-mover advantage can be gained – eg the Ford Motor Co. in the USA where Henry Ford took the idea of task specialization from the meat trade and applied it to motor manufacture. He gained a virtual monopoly and only his intransigence in the face of customers' demands for extras allowed others to obtain market share. In financial services you could take Direct Line and First Direct, which brought telephone banking and insurance to a market based extensively on branch networks, with the attendant cost structures.

Early copiers

Alternatively there is a caucus of thought that suggests that the second mover makes more money than the prime mover because it can sell the service without having to develop the demand, eg Cahoot, Egg, IF etc.

Late copiers

Everybody else – can be left with rubbish. Often a 'me-tooism' where the market has moved and you have no alternative but to follow. Sometimes it can provide a benefit, because where the market moves very quickly you can enter with a later innovation and steal a march on early copiers.

Resistors

Those that will not go with the flow and try to resist – usually have too much tied up in old products etc. But if the market goes with the new flow, they will usually lose out heavily – or shrink to niche players – for example the few shops that still sell music on 'vinyl' – long since superseded by CDs elsewhere.

Differentiation to flow

Tries something radically different from everybody else – may in turn lead to their becoming a pioneer. A good example would be Direct Line insurance which successfully broke the mould of insurance with its out-of-town telephone-based sales via call centres.

Mondex, the electronic purse, was a good example of a company taking a completely different approach from anything that had gone before – but based in existing infrastructure.

7.2   Why analyse competition?

'We can learn even from our enemies' **Ovid**[3]

Sadly we do not live in a simple world where you have a unilateral relationship with the customer. Every day is a fight to keep those that you have in the face of onslaughts from the competition. They are also trying to sell their offerings to your customers – if not to try to take them away from you altogether. Similarly any attempts by you to win new customers will face defences (usually – unless you are really lucky) from the competition. Even though that great asset to banks – customer inertia – is no longer as prevalent as before, it is still in many cases difficult to win new business by wooing customers across to you from your competitors; therefore you need to understand them really well. It therefore becomes increasingly important to understand the competition because:

◆ You need to keep abreast of their offerings to ensure that they do not overtake yours and to enable you to highlight the positive differences between your services and theirs;

◆ You need to know not only who they are now, but also who they might be in the future – and the implications for you;

◆ There are lessons to be learned;

◆ Customers will often know about their products and expect you to as well – and to explain your Unique Selling Point (USP) – ie why they should take yours and not those of the competition;

◆ Knowing who the competition is enables you to identify segments of your customer base that might be at risk and to formulate a response;

◆ Knowing who they are and how they react enables you to calculate their own competitive response to moves you may make;

◆ By understanding who they are and what they do you can formulate propositions that will enable you to steal their best customers from them;

◆ In some cases you can cooperate with them where it gives positive mutual benefits (Britannia has come to an agreement with another Building Society to share branches/outlets);

◆ You can also focus your efforts on those that represent a real or a potential threat rather than on those who do not.

Michael Porter in his book[4] stated that it is the **competitive intensity** with a market that determines the overall level of profitability within that market. Many organizations have looked at markets and decided that the rate of return was too low for them to enter into it. This however misses a vital point that it is in fact the level of differentiation or **competitive advantage** that you enjoy *relative to those other competitors* that decides your own profitability, which for those with a good advantage will be greater than the rest and enable them to earn a rate of profitability greater than that of the market – ie someone else is earning below that overall rate because it is a zero sum game.

By understanding the competition you can change your services etc to ensure that you have the best competitive advantage and, therefore, profits.

Figure 7.2: Competition

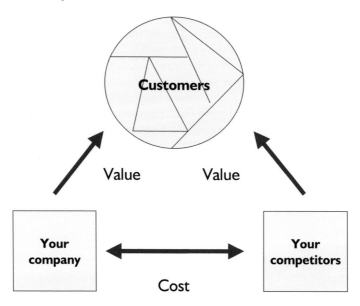

Customer/supplier continuum

Figure 7.2[5] indicates how you compete with the other suppliers in your market segments. Your customers will perceive the value that you and the competitors deliver differently but between you and your competitors there is a price differential driven by the different costs that you incur to deliver the same service to the market. (For example Direct Line pioneered low-cost insurance – competing on price but offering the same value thus delivering greater value to the client in his eyes relative to the competition.)

The sections of the customer circle represent different segments, to some of whom you may represent different value and where you may enjoy greater advantages than in others.

Figure 7.3: Relative competitor understanding

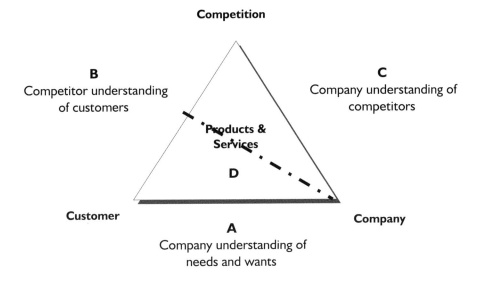

Figure 7.3 looks at the relationship between your company and the customer relative to the competition and from it emerge four analyses:

- ◆ A you sell to the customer based on your understanding of their needs and wants and how your services provide solutions to those
- ◆ B your competitors sell to the customer based on their understanding of needs and wants
- ◆ C the company analyses its competition to understand how it sells to its customers and what is different
- ◆ D you target your competitors' customers based on your understanding of your competition's analysis and offerings by tailoring your offerings or the way they are represented to provide extra value to the competition's customers over and above the competition.

7.3 Competitive comparisons

On a more local scale your customer is very likely to ask you about your products in relation to those of your immediate competition. An understanding of their offerings and the relative merits of yours over theirs is extremely helpful in discussing needs with customers. Not only does it show that you are aware of your competition but it gives an excellent opportunity to highlight the benefits of your offering over theirs.

The table below shows how you can develop this understanding by tabulating the relative merits and then preparing for questions about them. By listing the benefits that the offering gives and by weighting them with the customers' priorities you can then score your product against the competition.

Figure 7.4: Competitor service comparison

Criteria	Weighting	you		Competitors 1		2		3		n	
		Score	Adj	Score	Adj	Score	Adj	Score	Adj	Score	Adj
A	5	3	15	4	20	3	15	2	10	2	10
B	5	4	20	3	15	4	20	3	15	3	15
C	4	3	12	4	16	3	12	4	16	4	16
D	4	4	16	4	16	3	12	2	8	3	12
E	3	5	15	4	12	4	12	3	9	2	6
F	3	2	6	2	6	5	15	2	6	4	12
G	2	4	8	3	6	3	6	3	6	5	10
H	2	3	6	4	8	2	4	4	8	4	8
I	1	5	5	3	3	4	4	5	5	3	3
J	1	3	3	3	3	3	3	5	5	4	4
Totals		36	106	34	105	34	103	33	88	34	96
Difference					1		3		18		10

This enables you to see where you score highly and where the customer values the benefits. This enables you to emphasize the benefits of your offering while explaining that the competition's is less favourable. In the example shown the differences have been scored to show that in this case and for this customer your product leads slightly over the main rival, and increasingly over the others. Where the difference is slight the key is to emphasize other characteristics that are also important (branch location, opening hours, remote access etc) to further increase the probability of the customer choosing your products.

Summary

It is not enough to 'know your customers'; you must also 'know your competition' because it is they that will shape the market by what they offer against your own offerings.

1 Success is measured as a relative thing against your competition – other businesses in your marketplace. You need to understand who they are and who they might be in the future.

2 You should split competitors into three types – Threats, Opportunities. Allies – and decide strategies accordingly.

3 You need an understanding of the local competition's offerings and the relative merits of yours over theirs.

Select bibliography

Competitive advantage: M Porter – Free Press

Mastering Strategy – FT/Prentice Hall

Competitor Targeting (Winning the battle for market and customer share) : Ian Gordon: – Wiley

Notes

1 *'Mr Buffet on the Stock Market'* Fortune Magazine, 22 November 1999 p 220
2 *Even More Offensive Marketing (An exhilarating guide to winning in business)* – Hugh Davidson, – Chapter 1, 'Penguin 60' 1997
3 Publius Ovidius Naso (43BC-18 AD) , *Metamorphoses'*
4 M E Porter *Competitive Advantage* Free Press, New York
5 Kenichi Omhae – as used in *Strategic Management* Macmillan and Tampoe, Oxford 2000

Eight

Market research

Topics in this chapter

Desk research

Field research

Interpreting data

Data versus information

Introduction to this chapter

This chapter looks at market research defined as the systematic and focused collection of information on customers and markets for subsequent analysis and usage in formulating your marketing strategy. As shown in Figure 8.1 – *Marketing cycle II* – research fits into the overall marketing cycle by providing input to the analysis stage, and particularly as to the customers' needs and wants as shown below. This, when accompanied by internal analysis of strengths, weaknesses and offerings, and competitive analysis, provides the basis for deciding the marketing strategy.

Figure 8.1: Marketing cycle (II) (Research)

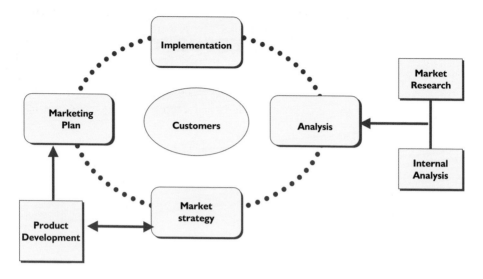

8.1   Why carry out research?

Collecting and analysing information that is relevant enables you to make informed and robust decisions as input into subsequent action. The objectives of research include:

- defining and evaluating your place in a market
- providing information regarding future trends in demand
- identifying customer needs and requirements
- discovering what they think of you and your offerings
- uncovering ways to delight your customers further
- providing an evaluation of advertising and promotional strategies and their content
- revealing opportunities for business development and improved competitiveness
- discovering opportunities for increasing profit/product penetration.

You may use research to address any or all of these issues.

There are two types of research:

- Desk research
- Field research

It is important to understand the difference between them. Desk research is usually easier and almost invariably much cheaper. It may not of course provide you with precisely what you need and you may have to resort to field research.

Desk research

Before commencing any external study and commissioning field research it is always worth asking – has it been analysed before? This is usually easier and quicker and the scale of information you can access has been altered radically by the explosion of information you can obtain over the Internet. This allows you to access all (published) information globally on a subject. The surprising thing about the Internet is that so much is available – and for free! (although an unfocused search over the Internet may take a long time and result in masses of data which will take forever to analyse).

Information can come from two sources – external and internal.

Typical examples of external desk research include:

◆ public library searches
◆ press cuttings
◆ sector and published surveys
◆ trade information
◆ Internet trawls
◆ books and other publications.

One of the major benefits of effective and up-to-date customer records is that it should facilitate the analysis of your own customer base. This will allow you to analyse:

◆ purchases made
◆ comparisons with peer customers
◆ patterns of consumption
◆ profit from products
◆ product penetration.

This will provide you with unique insights because no-one else will have this information. It might be necessary and desirable, however, to look externally as well – either for purposes of benchmarking, market trend analysis or competitor analysis.

Field research

This is where you have to go out and find information first hand by talking to current and potential customers. The major types of types of field research include:

◆ telephone research
◆ written questionnaires
◆ street interviewing
◆ face-to-face interviewing
◆ product tests

◆ consumer panels
◆ focus groups.

All these techniques have a role to play in collecting information but they result in different 'cuts' of information and some may not be appropriate. You must decide which are the best techniques and, having obtained the information, analyse the results.

One of the criticisms levelled against market research is that it is merely a 'front' for selling. This is called 'sugging' and it really upsets people, involving as it does lies – whether directly or by 'evasion' or 'omission'. It can also have far-reaching and damaging effects on your relationships because people complain and will also affect the value of the exercise, making it largely unproductive.

Whenever market research is undertaken, there are six crucial questions – to which you must have appropriate, detailed and supportable answers prior to commissioning the research:

The Sample	Who are you going to ask?
The Method	How are you going to ask them?
The Questions	What are you going to ask them?
The Results	What will you do with the information?
The Cost	How much do you want to pay for the answer?
The Timescale	By when do you need the information?

These are explored in detail below and in general apply equally to personal and corporate markets.

The sample

The number of people asked is an important consideration because if you asked just one person you would get a very accurate picture of her views on anything (probably) but this would not necessarily be representative of the world at large and may lead you down a completely blind alley. How many then should you ask and what sort of people? What is a good number – is it millions, hundreds of thousands, or what? Clearly there is a cost implication as the number increases both in terms of carrying out the research and also in analysing and interpreting the resulting data.

Fortunately a lot of research has been carried out into this area and some surprising conclusions have emerged. When you ask a number of respondents (known as the population) questions, after a certain number the percentage difference in the answer ceases to vary very much, or at least if it does then the degree of likely error can be calculated with a high degree of accuracy.

This number is known as a *'statistically significant number'* and although it needs to be calculated for each type of question, the numbers are surprisingly low. For consumer goods it is in the low hundreds and even for such emotive issues such as politics it is only in low thousands. Key points are that the sample must be homogeneous, ie sharing the important characteristics – eg four-wheel car drivers in the home counties, or British owners of Portuguese villas in the Algarve, in order that the data is comparable and that conclusions are meaningful and of course targeted. This classification is known as segmentation qv.

The method

There are several methods of obtaining the information as mentioned above and key characteristics of each are explored below.

Telephone research

Using the telephone to collect has one great advantage – it is cheap. One researcher can make many calls in a day without leaving an office. It is also both very focused because you are initiating the call and it is fast because interviews do not take long and the elapsed time to complete the exercise is also short.

There are some drawbacks however – often people do not like to receive unsolicited calls and it can be very difficult to use in a corporate – business-to-business – environment. It relies on a structured script and on obtaining answers in the same manner (eg interviewers tick boxes on a template in front of them).

Written questionnaires

This is probably the most common method of research and everyone will be familiar with it in one form or another. Unless used in the right circumstances it can be a passive method reliant on people to complete and return them, and in this case inertia rules and only those with a grievance or an axe to grind return them. By combining it with other activities however, such as checking out of an hotel, installing new software or making it part of the application process for loans or life insurance, and other services it can be turned into an effective method of research.

To be really effective it is best to use questionnaires that ask for boxes to be ticked or indications placed on scales. This has the advantage that it is easier and faster for the recipient to complete and also allows direct comparability of answers. It will not perhaps have the same depth as, say, a qualitative survey where respondents write comments but if it is drawn up well it is very useful and can cover more subjects than the qualitative type.

Types of questionnaire

There are several types of questionnaire and each is designed to explore different aspects or elicit different responses. Some of the more common include:

- ◆ Dichotomous
- ◆ Multiple choice
- ◆ Importance
- ◆ Bipolar
- ◆ Likert
- ◆ Rating scale 1 – 5
- ◆ Buying propensity

These can be used in any combination as long as the questionnaire is not too long and that it is focused.

In the fictitious examples below the data is merely illustrative.

Dichotomous

This is a fairly typical basic type of question, not too intrusive and merely asks you to answer yes or no. As such it cannot assess the degree of feelings in between the poles:

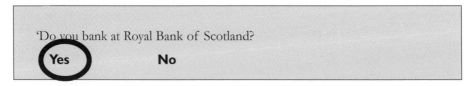

Multiple choice

This is a question offering three or more answers – and allows a greater breadth of response.

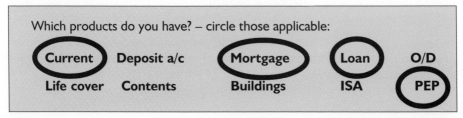

Importance

In this type of question the respondent is asked to rate the importance of an issue to them on a scale of 1 to 5.

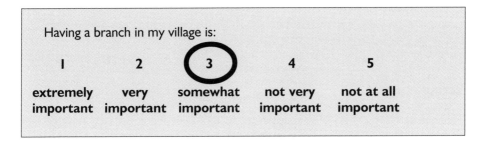

Bipolar

The question asks for a response to be marked between two opposite ends of the scale:

How would you describe the local branch of HBOS:

Convenient	—x— ——— ——— ——— ———	Inconvenient
Friendly	——— ——— —x— ——— ———	Unfriendly
Service oriented	——— —x— ——— ——— ———	Unhelpful
Efficient	—x— ——— ——— —x— ———	Inefficient

Likert

This question examines how strongly the respondent agrees with a statement and can help to assess the feelings of customers towards issues:

'Building societies generally give better service than banks'

strongly	agree	neither agree	disagree	strongly
agree		nor disagree		disagree
1	2	3	4	5

Rating scale

This question type rates the replies in terms of a scale from, eg, very poor to first class. As with all these types of questions it is sometimes necessary to have an even number of boxes (eg 4) to avoid the middle of the road response commonly taken by those trying to avoid making a stand.

How would you rate the service from your local Lloyds/TSB branch?

First	Good	Fair	Poor	Very
Class				Poor
1	2	3	4	5

Buying propensity

This type of question is trying to elicit a customer's future intentions by asking whether he might buy a product and can help assess the needs and likely take-up of a new product if developed. Care needs to be taken with these questions because they may reflect wants rather than needs!

If a Barclayloan for a car was offered I would?

Definitely	Probably	Be unsure	Probably	Definitely
take it	take it		not take it	not take it
1	2	3	4	5

All of the above are **quantitative**-type questions. What they ask is for a response within pre-defined parameters that allows input into spreadsheets and hard analysis.

Although this facilitates the input into data analysis sheets and subsequent number crunching – the respondent is not allowed to say what he thinks. He can answer the question only by marking the pre-designated boxes. This is of course of immense use – especially if the questionnaire has been well thought through and piloted. Sadly this is often not the case and many are rather poor!

As a result you do not get the qualifying comment that can often express his real feelings.

Qualitative questions can allow more freedom for answers but are much harder to analyse because each respondent will use her own words. Often the question will be couched along the lines of:

Describe in your own words your opinion of HSBC.

This has the advantage that the respondent can say what she likes, which can yield very interesting information that might not have been thought of at design phase; but she can also respond in an unlimited and often unconstructive manner, making analysis much harder.

Whichever question types are used they must always be designed with the express intention of:

- ◆ inconveniencing the customer as little as possible;
- ◆ being aimed at a homogeneous segment; and
- ◆ having been designed to elicit specific information that supports your marketing initiative.

Street interviewing

This an effective method of data collection although not always the most cost-effective because it involves people's time as researchers and may involve lots of non-value added interactions for every useful interview.

Usually the researcher is situated in a busy thoroughfare and asks a few questions to eliminate candidates and ensure homogeneity (known as screening questions) before either thanking them or passing on to the next set of core questions. This is to ensure that the quote sampled is statistically significant.

It is almost exclusively used in consumer research. Segments chosen must be wide enough to be meaningful but also focused to support the conclusions you require to achieve.

Face-to-face interviewing

This is basically a structured conversation. The interviewer should have a one- or two- sheet guide to the questions she wants to ask. These should be ordered so as not to give too much information to the interviewee to avoid prejudicing his views.

Eg asking 'Do you like XYZ bank?' before you ask 'Of which banks are you aware?' will prejudice the answers.

You must:

- Confirm the interview beforehand with a letter or fax
- Arrive on time, and make sure the interview does not overrun
- Guide the conversation gently, but firmly
- If the interviewee is not forthcoming then make your excuses and leave.

Product tests

These are widely used, especially in the consumer markets.

The manufacturer selects a group of potential buyers and offers a pre-production sample for people to use, on agreement that they report back their findings.

They are not very useful in financial services.

You should:

- Use experienced personnel (internal or external if they are not available)
- Choose an appropriate place to hold the tests (eg for food outside a supermarket; for audio equipment, in a hall)
- Make sure that everyone who participates is given a questionnaire to complete
- Circulate during the event to get off-the-cuff remarks, and record these for later analysis.

Consumer panels

Consumer panels, also called Omnibus surveys, are where pre-segmented panel members fill in a diary on a regular basis.

Panel members are usually recompensed by gifts or 'points'.

You must:

- Use a specialist firm.

Note – This is usually for Fast Moving Consumer Goods (FMCG) only, because of its nature – not many people take out loans every week or even month.

Focus groups

These are basically moderated group discussions but can be extraordinary useful in getting information out of people.

The format is as follows:

- ◆ an audience of between 6 and 12 people, with selected background is invited to the meeting. This takes place in a comfortable room (eg like a drawing room);
- ◆ a moderator or facilitator (often using visual aids) explains the purpose of the focus group and may give some background to the topic;
- ◆ the group is then invited to discuss the relevant issues. The discussions are usually recorded (or notes are taken by an assistant);
- ◆ the moderator guides the discussion to make sure that it stays on the subject.

You must:

- ◆ ensure that the audience represents the desired segment(s);
- ◆ make sure that the audience is relaxed and feels free to speak;
- ◆ ensure that the quieter members of the group are given a chance to speak as well.

The quality of the moderator is crucial. Specialist firms are usually employed to maximize value from the exercise.

The questions

In order to make informed decisions about anything you need the correct information. This must be based on analytical data and gives you the knowledge to make the decisions. One of the things that often emerges from research is that you actually know a lot less than you thought you did. (See Figure 8.2)

Figure 8.2: Knowledge is power

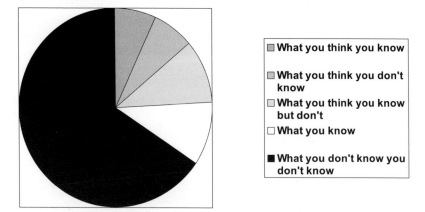

Legend:
- What you think you know
- What you think you don't know
- What you think you know but don't
- What you know
- What you don't know you don't know

What you know is a lot less than you think.
You must have the right level of information to make an informed decision

You must take especial care therefore in framing the questions to ensure that you receive the correct output. The type of research chosen will also affect the type of questions. There are two types of questions:

Quantitative – based on numbers or fixed answers – eg what percentage do you pay on your mortgage, or how much are your monthly life premiums?

Qualitative – based on words – how do you feel that your account has been handled in the last year?

Quantitative answers are generally much easier to analyse but qualitative answers can give you more valuable insights into what people really think.

The results

What will you do with the information?

It is critical that you think this through before starting any research. What you want to do with the information should shape the nature of the questions and possibly even the manner in which it is collected. It will certainly affect the analysis and conclusions drawn and presented.

The cost

How much do you want to pay for the answer? The cost of market research can vary widely, from a few hundred pounds to many millions spent by multinationals on major consumer brands. It is relatively easy to assess the cost of market research and the procedure to follow is:

◆ scope out the activities that you think will be needed (eg 100 telephone calls, 20 face-to-face interviews etc) and assess the amount of time input that this requires (see below for a guide);
◆ identify the daily cost of either your own staff or employing people of the right calibre to do the work;
◆ add in the preparation time for questionnaires and the time to analyse and write up the reports.

A brief guide to researchers' time:

◆ Telephone calls – around 8 to 10 completed calls per working day.
◆ Face-to-face interviews – typically only two face-to-face interviews can be accomplished a day, and if travel to other towns is required this may fall to one-and-a-half – this is to allow time for the interview to be completed and written up.
◆ Street interviewing – around 20 to 30 a day may be accomplished, depending on the questions.
◆ Group discussions – set aside at least a day for administration and half a day for the group. Do not forget that more than one person is required to run a group interview.
◆ Written questionnaire – typically a response of between 1% and 3% is considered normal.

The timescale

Work backwards from when the results are required to get start date.

Produce a bar chart (sometimes called a Gantt chart) showing the various steps and the interrelationship between each of them.

Typically the stages will be as follows:

◆ Scope the project
◆ Set-up phase (eg hiring contractors, preparing questionnaires, samples, purchasing mailing lists)
◆ Desk research – looking to see what already exists
◆ Test phase (sometimes called piloting). Test a small sample of people to check your approach
◆ Research – there may be a number of phases, one leading to another
◆ Analysis – leave plenty of time for this!
◆ Reporting – a written report should be prepared for the benefit of others in your firm, and to provide a reference document.

8.2   Exploiting data

The amount of information you need should reflect the magnitude of the decision that you are going to make. This does not mean that you need reams of paper for an important decision – but that you do need real and pertinent information that analyses the issues and gives useful conclusions.

There has been a true revolution in the last few decades – driven by the increasing power of IT processing capability – the progressive reduction in costs both from economies of scale and from vastly increased processing capabilities – as well as the unbelievable amount of data now available publicly from the Internet. This has of course led to an equal explosion in the amount of data processed and regurgitated within organizations. Unfortunately much of the data is unusable. This is because data does not equal information – and for all too many organizations – the old maxim holds true:

DRIP:

Data Rich : Information Poor.

As a result staff and managers are drowning in a sea of paper (the so-called 'paperless revolution' has in fact lead to an increase in paper because people still wish to read from the paper medium because they are more 'comfortable' with it. Sometimes this often goes as far as then printing out e-mails – writing their reply and giving them to a secretary to re-type!).

One of the key aspects of research is to deal only with that information that is truly critical and will yield the results that you want quickly. (NB This does not mean fiddling the results by sifting out unfavourable answers to prove your point but rather sifting the gold from the dross.)

Conjoint analysis

Customer perception is usually measured by using sophisticated market research and psychological techniques of which the best known is conjoint analysis. Potential buyers are asked to consider a series of features and then make a series of trade-offs among them. The analysis of the results enables manufacturers to understand the relative worth of each feature that customers value. Thus, when researching the price of a new car and trying to determine what to offer as extras, the manufacturer might ask a series of questions like the following:

- ◆ would you prefer a CD player or central locking?
- ◆ would you prefer a passenger air bag or sun roof?
- ◆ would you prefer a CD player or leather seats?
- ◆ would you prefer central locking or a sun roof?
- etc

The answers can be fed into a computer program to determine the relative perception of worth of each item. This is clearly not a trivial exercise and would be used only for major product analysis involving high expenditure on product re-design.

Summary

Market research can be a very valuable tool for assessing true needs and wants in a marketplace. To be effective, however, it must be structured, focused on segments and analysed in the context of the results desired.

1 There are two types of research – desk and field. The former involves making use of information already gathered. The latter in gathering and analysing information yourself.
2 The objectives of research include:
   - defining and evaluating your place in a market
   - providing information regarding future trends in demand
   - identifying customer needs and requirements
   - discovering what they think of you and your offerings
   - uncovering ways to delight your customers further
   - providing an evaluation of advertising and promotional strategies and their content
   - revealing opportunities for business development and improved competitiveness
   - discovering opportunities for increasing profit/product penetration.
3 The amount of information you need should reflect the magnitude of the decision that you are going to make. This does not mean that you need reams of paper for an important decision – but that you do need real and pertinent information that analyses the issues and gives useful conclusions.
4 There are six crucial questions you must answer before undertaking research:

The Sample	Who are you going to ask?
The Method	How are you going to ask them?
The Questions	What are you going to ask them?
The Results	What will you do with the information?
The Cost	How much do you want to pay for the answer?
The Timescale	By when do you need the information?

5 There are several types of questionnaire and each is designed to explore different aspects or elicit different responses. Some of the more common include: Dichotomous; Multiple choice; Importance; Bipolar; Likert; Rating scale 1-5; Buying propensity.

Select bibliography

Principles of Marketing : Kotler Chapter 4

Mastering Marketing: FT

Marketing Pocketbook: Russell-Jones & Fletcher

Mastering Strategy – 'Brave new horizontal world': FT – T Kinnear pp107-111

Nine

Strategy, planning goals and targets

Topics in this chapter

Corporate strategy

Planning

Marketing plans

Target setting

Introduction to this chapter

This chapter will consider what strategy is, not as an analysis of how to formulate strategy but to show where marketing and selling fit in with this. It is often said that plans are virtually useless but that planning is indispensable because it allows you to analyse things and develop understandings of the relative dynamics and therefore be prepared for changes.

> ' ….Strategy …has often come to be synonymous with the quantitative breakthrough, the analytic coup, market share numbers, learning curve theory, positioning business in a 4- or 9- or 24-box matrix…and putting it all on a computer.' Peters and Waterman[1]

9.1 What strategy is

Strategy means many things to many people. Many people mix up strategy with tactics, many people talk of strategies when they mean operations.

A dictionary definition is:

> *'generalship or the art of conducting a campaign or manoeuvering an army; artifice or finesse generally.'* (from Greek *strategos* [general] from *stratos* [army] and *agein* [to lead]. *Chambers Dictionary*

Leading gurus define it as:

> *' (business) strategy...concerns major decisions deliberately taken to establish what sets of customers a business aims to serve in the future and against what competition, in order to meet its financial objectives'* Mathur and Kenyon – *Creating Value*

> *' the essence of strategic thinking is about creating a sustainable competitive advantage'* Porter – article in *The Economist* (1987)

> *'strategy... is not enough to optimally position a company within existing markets; the challenge is to ... develop great foresight into the whereabouts of tomorrow's markets'* Hamel and Prahalad – *Competing for the Future* (1996)

It can be put quite simply as:

> *... the development of a set of unique and irreproducible competencies and customer value propositions that enable you to continue to generate value...*

You will note that virtually all definitions of strategy in this context talk about markets and value. That puts marketing right at the heart of a strategy and underlines the importance of ensuring that the marketing actions and campaigns fully support the strategic goals and objectives of the organization. The augmented diagram in Figure 9.1 – *Marketing cycle (III)* – shows that the strategic inputs are also vital for the development of a marketing strategy. Both the corporate and competitive strategy influence and in turn are influenced by the marketing strategy, product development and the marketing plan.

Figure 9.1: Marketing cycle (III) (Strategic inputs)

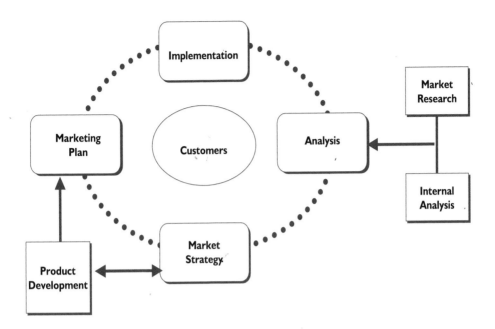

If your organizational competences are reproducible they will be copied by your competitors, and you will lose your competitive edge. If the CVP does not deliver what the market requires you will be unable to sell your offering at the right price to generate value.

Below is a quote from John Windelar of Alliance and Leicester. In it he mentions sustainable competitive advantage twice as well as, *inter alia*, brand, costs leadership and sales process (my emphasis). This underlines the fundamental relationship between marketing and strategy. The one (strategy) sets the overall vision and goals for the other (marketing) in order to realize the ultimate end – increased shareholder value by selling your services; but the strategy requires a great deal of input from marketing to be effective.

'Most bankers would agree that the overriding objective for any quoted company is to deliver long-term growth in shareholder value; however achieving this is dependent on *identifying and delivering a sustainable competitive advantage*. The key task of a board of directors is to ensure that your company performs well in the areas of: brand; logistics; costs leadership; research and development; sales process. *In particular you need to be clear about your chosen battlefield – the source of your sustainable competitive advantage*. Although this can prove tricky in the financial services industry, it's not impossible'.[2]

Organizations exist for different reasons and the reasons that cause them to come into existence will drive their ethos, culture etc. Organizations that have as their vision worthy ideals such as:

◆ 'to end world poverty'
◆ 'to eradicate leprosy'
◆ 'to succour world hunger'

will have vastly different approaches, stakeholders and measures than commercial organizations whose objectives are, *inter alia*, to generate returns on capital.

A mutual organization (eg building society, co-operative) will also differ from a commercial bank or major quoted retailer in that its principal duties (theoretically) lie to its members, who are also its owners.

Notwithstanding this each will (should) have a vision and therefore must have a strategy because that strategy is the means to achieve the vision. It is the emphasis placed on different aspects and the relationships with stakeholders that cause the differences.

9.2   What does a corporate strategy do?

It takes the **vision** and develops it into a framework and translates it into a **set of actions** – ie steps for achieving the vision (or at least in attempting that).

For a commercial organization this will revolve around creating and then sustaining/increasing value (equity). To this end it:

◆ sets long-term objectives
◆ drives actions
◆ gives resource allocation priorities
◆ defines the competency domain of the organization
◆ leads to core competency development through:
　◆ competitive strategies
　◆ functional policies
◆ is simple to grasp
◆ is flexible enough to respond to force majeure but changes must be defined, discussed, definitely agreed and not drifted into
◆ is viable

It is important, however, to understand the difference between **Corporate** strategy and **Competitive** strategy. This is why and where much of the confusion surrounding strategy occurs.

The existence of corporate planning departments can also be unhelpful because strategy is **not** about planning. This aspect is an ex-post activity once the strategy has been set. It is also impossible to plan for the *whole organization* but planning can be carried out for the *organization as a whole*.

It is further compounded by the use of the term **Functional** strategy to describe what, say, an IT department or an HR department or the marketing department does and which is more properly described as a **Functional policy** (in support of a strategy). Each considers different time horizons.

For a commercial organization the **fundamental objective** is to earn a return on capital that is *greater than the cost of that capital*. This is to ensure that it can continue to have the right to use that capital and, if necessary, to allow it the right to raise more to enable it to undertake further activities in order to meet its vision. All other objectives are **means objectives** in support of that fundamental objective.

Corporate strategy is, therefore, about managing the **Value** of an organization – often expressed in monetary or financial terms. Thus it is helpful to refer to this as **Financial value**.

Competitive strategy is about assembling the *Inputs* which, when put together with reference to a defined market as a **Customer Value Proposition (CVP)**, enable the *Outputs* to be delivered to the market for **Commercial value**.

Support strategies are in fact components of the competitive strategy (or strategies) and it is more helpful to refer to them as **Functional policies** because they usually refer to a particular organizational function such as HR, IT, Finance etc. Marketing and therefore the marketing policy is of fundamental importance in achieving the objectives.

There are some basic questions that a competitive strategy must answer:

- what does the market want?
- what are we going to offer?
- how are we going to offer it?
- at what do we need to excel to succeed?
- how will the competition respond?
- can we make money?
- what are the internal implications?
- what do we need to change?
- will we satisfy our stakeholders?
- what are the risks and how shall we manage them?.

9.3   Stakeholders

In essence a strategy is an articulation of the path to a vision – which is consciously accepted by stakeholders (or else they will not support it). Stakeholders can have one or more of the following roles:

Influencer

- community
- government

◆ pressure group
◆ union

Enabler

- ◆ staff
- ◆ equity providers
- ◆ distributors
- ◆ suppliers
- ◆ third-party suppliers (TPA)

Consumer

- ◆ customers
- ◆ distributors

Legislator

- ◆ government
- ◆ regulatory body

Shareholder value is determined by stakeholders' behaviour and they can be split into:

Primary:

- ◆ Customers
- ◆ Employees
- ◆ Investors

Others:

- ◆ Bondholders and Lenders
- ◆ Market Analysts
- ◆ Regulators and Government Bodies
- ◆ Competitors
- ◆ Suppliers

... and the combination of their actions/support for the organization will determine the value that it is able to generate. It is therefore necessary to determine what keeps stakeholders committed to working with an organization. It can be expressed as follows: stakeholders stay committed to an organization as long as they receive more back than they put in. This can be stated as:

Receiving more **Stakeholder Value Output (SV$_o$)**

(however they define it) from the relationship than the:

Stakeholder Value Input that they deliver **(SV$_i$)**

$$ie\ SV_o > Sv_i.$$

For some this will be financial, for others a combination of things (service, benefits, convenience etc).

Figure 9.2: Value added model

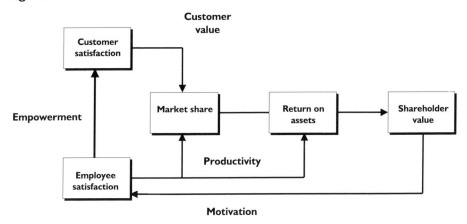

The model in Figure 9.2, as developed and used by Rank Xerox, demonstrates the linkages between key sets of stakeholders in generating value – employees, customers and shareholders. It exemplifies that it is important to consider all stakeholders (although not necessarily in the same proportion) when formulating strategies. Marketing strategies need to be cognisant of this and ensure that they support stakeholders' needs.

Michael Porter has arguably been one of the most influential strategic thinkers and writers of the 20th century. With the publication of his book *Competitive Strategy* in 1980 he became the definitive strategist with the book being required reading on all MBA courses and for business students generally. The book focuses on a series of techniques for analysing industries and competitors and is still regarded as the seminal work.

In the book he argues that there are five forces shaping strategy within industries: rivalry among firms; threat of substitutes; threat of new entrants; bargaining power of suppliers; and bargaining power of buyers. The relative strengths of these forces determine the profit of an industry which are of course different in each industry. The thrust of his book is that an organization needs to understand these forces in its industry and then position itself to defend its position against them and influence the factors in its favour.

Porter then goes on to state that there are only three strategic types of options that organizations can use:

Differentiation – ie make your offering such that it is perceived as being unique and different from the rest.

Cost leadership – basically selling on price but with such tight cost controls that you are profitable.

Focus – only to deal in a specific market or geographical location.

According to Porter failure to follow one of these three leaves you floundering 'somewhere in the middle'. His analysis is very powerful but more recently has been questioned as being too prescriptive and too simplistic. Some criticisms include that it tended to force organizations into Strategic Business Units and thence into portfolio approach to strategy, ignoring offerings that may be very different even though delivered through the same organization; he suggests that organizations should play off suppliers against each other and never be reliant on one. Recent success stories (South-West Airlines, Ryanair and others) have rebutted this assertion by striking very beneficial deals with single suppliers and overhauling long-standing and established competitors.

9.4   Where planning fits in

Figure 9.3 shows where functional plans support a competitive strategy. At the primary analysis level there is analysis of:

- ◆ the market
- ◆ yourself and
- ◆ your competition

in order to identify segments where you can make money. This is the playing field where you wish to get involved with your offerings.

Figure 9.3: Competitive strategy requires functional support

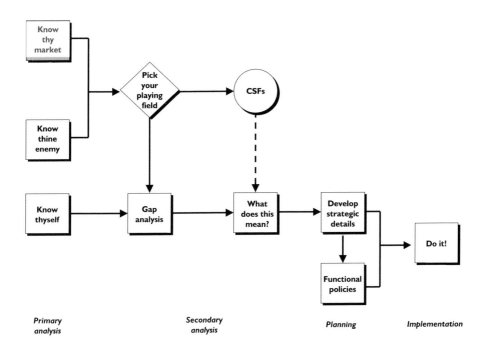

This then allows you to understand what gaps there are in your capabilities and what the critical success factors for success will be. You can then develop the strategic details to close those gaps and hit your CSFs.

This can then be translated into functional policies such as marketing and HR. These policies set out what they have to do to support the competitive strategy. Any such policies developed in isolation from this type of analysis will be worse than useless.

Figure 9.4: Competitive strategy and supporting, functional policies

The competitive strategy, while unique to each offering, is of course a blend of the offering and the supporting functional policies, including marketing.

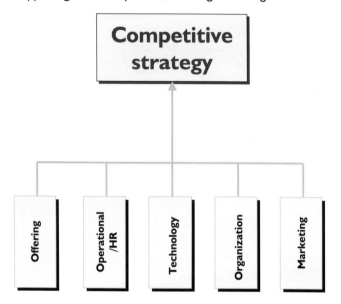

Each functional policy will require planning specific to its function.

Analysis

Any planning, whether strategic, functional, or even at the branch level requires some analytical data to support it. This needs to carried out by each line of business as well as at the organizational and functional levels.

One of the most frequently used types of analysis is called PEST. **PEST** stands for Political/legal, Economic, Sociocultural and Technological. It is essentially an analysis of the environment within which you must operate and which might influence your offerings. It enables a categorization of the key factors that you believe will have an influence in the future. (Note that analysis of past impacts is useful only as a means of predicting or understanding future impacts.) They can then be prioritized and the magnitude taken into account. PEST analysis is a vital input into such things as scenario analysis and will support the market analysis:

Political – anti-trust laws, green laws, tax, employment law, government behaviour;

Economic – economic cycles, GNP, inflation, interest rates, unemployment, energy prices;

Sociocultural – demography, income trends, education, life styles, fashions, mobility;

Technological – R&D spend, rate of change, communications, speed of transfer.

It is also sometimes seen as **PESTLE** with the addition of Legal and Environmental analysis.

Figure 9.5: Business impact assessment

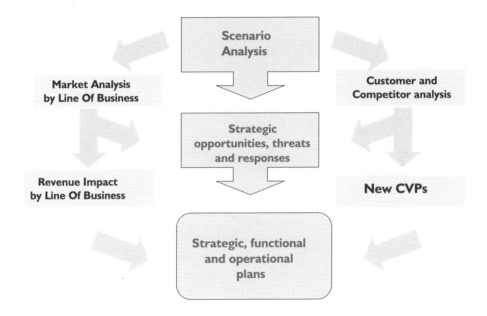

SWOT

Another type of analysis frequently seen is SWOT, which stands for:

◆ **Strengths** (where are we the leaders)
◆ **Weaknesses** (where our competition better than us)
◆ **Opportunities** (what are the opportunities that we can exploit given our internal strengths) and
◆ **Threats** (what could upset our plans and take market away from us).

Figure 9.6: Corporate time horizons

Figure 9.6: Corporate time horizons

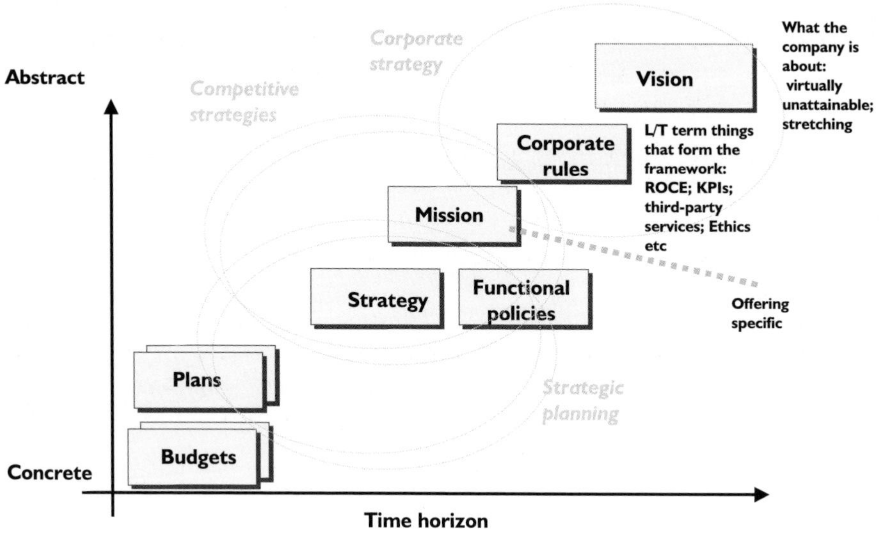

Difference between goals and targets

If the corporate strategy sets the overall goals and competitive strategy sets them in relation to offerings, it is important to know whether or not you are achieving them and therefore delivering value. To this end therefore some degree of measurement is needed. It is necessary to quantify all goals by setting the targets that must be measured. These quantified targets are known as the Key Performance Indicators and must be set for all aspects of the organization to enable you to measure success or not. They must measure all aspects of operations and should focus on these areas:

◆ measures for customer excellence that demonstrate how you are delivering your offerings for value;

◆ measures for stakeholders with the principal classes being management and staff and suppliers of capital; and

◆ internal measures for excellence which tell executives how well the organization is performing.

9.5 Marketing planning

The strategy of an organization sets out what it wants to do and where. The marketing plan covers to a large degree the how, but not the execution. It needs to examine each business product and brand, or rather the management of each business, product and brand needs to produce a plan for aggregation.

The plan will cover the business as a whole, but not the whole business. At that level plans should be delegated down to relevant local management (eg regional or branch managers). There are a few important points that shape a plan:

- Planning is data driven – that is you must have the right information to inform decisions.
- It is more likely to be used and to work if those involved in planning are closely concerned in carrying it out (central planning as used in the former command economies demonstrated the uselessness of remote thoughts).
- It must not be too rigid, and should have contingencies built in as well as flexibility to adapt to changing circumstances.
- Progress must be monitored against the plan.

What is a plan?

It is a:

- Statement of intent
- A set of instructions to a set of people to do a number of things, in a certain manner within a designated timescale
- It sets out action and precedes action but it is not action until it is carried out
- It helps quantify the future which is always uncertain and puts a framework around actions, by giving them structure and purpose (targets)
- It breaks up a large undertaking into a set of smaller and more easily manageable tasks and activities.

It:

- Has objectives that can be measured
- Answers questions that stakeholders and interested parties may pose
- Builds in options and contingencies as well as identifying and quantifying risks and issues that may arise.

It involves:

- Management time
- Commitment
- Cost
- Research
- Assumptions.

So it is important to get it right (or less wrong than the competition).

Why bother planning?

Some people might find structuring what they do second nature, for most however this is not the case. For organizations without plans they would get hopelessly lost on what they are doing with no structure. By producing a marketing plan therefore you go through a robust process that should result in useable and tangible outputs.

Planning, therefore, gives:

◆ Structure to actions
◆ Certainty
◆ Measures for success
◆ Confidence
◆ A 'route map'
◆ Evidence to readers, stakeholders and other interested parties of forethought and preparation.

When putting a marketing plan together you should ask:

◆ Does it say what you want to say?
◆ In the appropriate manner for the audience?
◆ With the right information at the right levels of detail (either in the main boidy or appendices)?
◆ Is it logical in content and flow?
◆ Does it support the organization's objectives?

Planning tips

◆ Ensure you have enough time
◆ Set realistic, stretching but achievable targets
◆ Do not underestimate resources or costs involved
◆ Think it through at high level first before engaging in detailed analysis and planning (proto-planning)
◆ Analysis must be robust and focused
◆ Make sure your numbers are right and that they cross cast etc
◆ Set out your assumptions and justify them
◆ Do not be afraid to change it if circumstances alter radically, but try to stick to it if possible
◆ Make sure it is produced in a timely manner – it is of little value halfway through the year that it deals with as there will be insufficient time to carry it out and too much will already have been done outside of the plan
◆ Obtain buy-in from all relevant parties
◆ Get help or assistance as appropriate

What a marketing plan contains

In general a plan should act as a guide to staff to help them work towards the organization's goals. A marketing plans usually contains:

◆ **executive summary** – an overview of the contents in precis form to enable management to review it rapidly
◆ **introduction** – sets out the contents and guides the reader through it
◆ **marketing objectives** – the sales and profit targets; the number and value of purchases; the penetration and value of usage; any enhancement or augmentation of the brand or company name
◆ **an analysis of the current market situation** – size, characteristics, expected development or growth (could be diminishing), segmentation and importance; will also look at the threats and opportunities and at the competition. Also an analysis of customers – current and potential
◆ **marketing strategy** – the broad thrust of the initiative that will be used to achieve the plan's objectives and including
◆ **product positioning** – the products/services you intend to offer, a brief statement of the benefits that they give the client, and their relative position vis-à-vis competition and segments. May also include analysis of sales history, product penetration, gaps and future developments
◆ **distribution analysis** – looks at the sales and channels to be used – including third parties; the expected product mix through them and profit etc
◆ **sales plan** – targets for areas, branches, regions etc analysis of the sales force; controls and accounting systems
◆ **marketing communication plan** – how much should be spent in each channel (direct mail, TV, radio, etc), by product, brand etc, how much on PR and so on, at whom should it be targeted, what follow-up for control and audits
◆ **action programmes and responsibilities** – what should be done, by when, in what way and who should take responsibility – link to targets, goals and probably remuneration
◆ **budgets, revenue forecasts** – how much will it cost, what resources do we need, what payback will we get
◆ **timings, milestones and controls** – the timetable, significant events, the controls on the programme

A plan will vary in detail depending on at what level it is produced within an organization.

Summary

Marketing is an integral part of achieving an organization's objectives and the marketing plan is a critical component of this. This section has looked at the marketing aspect. The next section will focus on **selling** – that is translating the theoretical ideas into positive tangible actions that achieve results.

1 Virtually all definitions of strategy talk about markets and value. That puts marketing right at the heart of a strategy and underlines the importance of ensuring that the marketing actions and campaigns fully support the strategic goals and objectives of the organization.

2 It is important to understand the difference between **Corporate** strategy and **Competitive** strategy and that Marketing supports the strategy by producing a **Functional policy.**

3 When putting a marketing plan together you should ask: Does it say what you want to say? In the appropriate manner for the audience? With the right information at the right levels of detail (either in the main body or appendices)? Is it logical in content and flow? Does it support the organization's objectives?

4 A marketing plans usually contains: executive summary, introduction, marketing objectives, an analysis of the current market situation, marketing strategy, product positioning, distribution analysis, sales plan, marketing communication plan, action programmes and responsibilities, budgets, revenue forecasts, timings, milestones and controls.

Select bibliography

Strategic Safari: Mintzberg

Competitive Advantage: Porter

Strategic Planning: Anschoff

FT – *Mastering Strategy*: FT

Notes

1 Peters and Waterman *In Search of Excellence*
2 John Windelar, Chairman of Alliance and Leicester. Quoted in *Financial World*, page 15 September 2002

II

Sales

Introduction to this section

This section of the book is concerned with selling – that is how you actually persuade customers, face to face to take your offering. In the financial services industry banking has undergone a major shift away from transaction processing (cashing cheques, taking deposits, changing currency etc) and into a more focused environment where selling products is critical.

This has lead to a change in the way banks are managed, the expectations placed on staff, how staff are trained and also in how the customer is handled. Many staff were and still are uncomfortable with the change – after all if they had wanted to sell then they would have gone to work in a shop not joined a bank. This is because selling still has the aura of something 'ungentlemanly' but also, and more to the point, because for most people it is inherently difficult.

A few years ago a customer wishing to open a current account would have left the bank having done just that – and just that. Nowadays the customer manager will have discussed a range of issues with him or her with the (c)overt intention of selling them several other services and products – this is known as cross-selling or customer management and sometimes customer maximization.

Three steps in the sales process

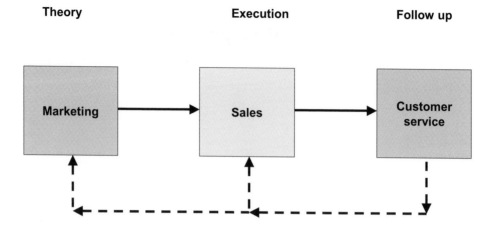

This aspect is the Execution part of the three-step diagram shown above and is about getting the customer to part from his money! The key components of sales are:

◆ Understanding the customers' needs
◆ Understanding how your organization can meet those needs
◆ Getting the benefits of your offerings across to the customer
◆ Pricing
◆ Setting targets and goals
◆ Incentivizing staff
◆ Presenting to customers

Ten

The sales process

Topics in this chapter

Hard versus soft

The process

Corporate decisions

Understanding the customer

Introduction to this chapter

Selling is about 'persuasive communication' – that is, giving a message to your customers (and potential customers) about your products that is perceived as adding value to you and your customer. It is therefore vital that you are clear as to what your organization offers.

Figure 10.1: Optimize your understanding

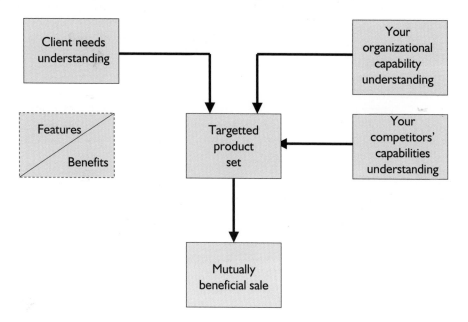

Therefore you must do your homework. You need to understand for each client:

◆ the client needs
◆ your capability in his context
◆ the competitors' capabilities in his context

and develop a targeted product set that meets his needs, better than the competition to close a mutually beneficial deal.

Why should the customer buy from you? ...rather than the competition? You must translate your products into benefits to the client – eg '....this means that...'

For example, a life policy could equate to 'peace of mind' and generate you better returns than the others from our investment performance; we have an easier claims service; we are flexible on premiums etc.

10.1   Hard selling *v* soft selling

Everyone, whatever his profession or trade, sells. Whether it is physical goods (in a shop or over the Internet), services (such as, insurance, legal advice or bank products) or ideas (teachers sell learning, vicars sell salvation). They are all bought in one form or another – whether with hard currency or through faith – the difference is how it is perceived.

The phrase 'hard sell' is often used to describe certain situations. For example anyone who has accepted an invitation to a lunch to discuss time-shares (bring your spouse) will understand all too well what a hard sell is. Similarly anyone who was visited by a life salesman (commission only) in the 1980s will also appreciate the concept.

This rather aggressive approach has tended to colour many people's attitude to selling. However, when you visit an optician for a check-up and he says you need glasses, but you might want to try our contact lenses – daily disposables payable by DD – and did you know that we also do prescription sunglasses or diving goggles? – that is a sale – it is just softer in approach – and probably in the longer term more effective. The differences between these generic approaches lies in the emphasis placed at the different stages of the sale.

The process can be decomposed into six steps[1] with different emphasis on the aspects depending on hard or soft approach:

	Hard	Soft
◆ Pre-approach planning	Low	High
◆ Introduction	High	Medium
◆ Needs analysis	Low	High
◆ Needs fulfilment	Low	High
◆ Close	High	Medium
◆ Follow-up	Low (or zero)	High

There is also a difference in the perception of features and benefits and relationship building:

◆ Features	High	Low
◆ Benefits	Low	High
◆ Relationship	Low	High

Hard selling concentrates very much on the close as the be-all and end-all – rather than the softer approach which emphasizes the needs analysis and needs fulfilment and follow-up, and this is reflected in the conduct of the meeting.

Hard selling

A hard seller, say, a car salesman, thinks that the need is for a car – he has a pre-conception of this before he even meets the potential customer. Very simple and usually wrong – it may be for a form of transport, a status symbol or a present. He will often start the meeting with the question – 'Are you just looking or buying?' A reply to the effect that you are looking loses his interest immediately as he does not want to waste time dealing with your queries unless it is related to a sale.

He does not need planning – he can sell anything. Product knowledge is sketchy and patchy and he will concentrate on features not benefits – it has a locking petrol cap! And silver paint! He introduces himself and then uses your first name as if you were long-lost friends, skims over the needs analysis and fulfilment and goes straight for the jugular. Follow-up is irrelevant because it prevents him from getting to the next customer.

Soft selling

Contrast the approach of the soft sell. Pre-planning is very important, involving product knowledge and how it satisfies needs (benefits). The introduction is important but the real meat is the needs analysis –'What is this person looking for?' – 'Why is he interested in this offering?' this leads into the needs fulfilment – 'How can I meet his needs with our offerings?' and 'Is this the right one or would something else be more relevant?' even can we meet the needs at all?. The close is incidental and unlike the hard sell where you have to close it the customer should close it herself by saying that she will have this one although you may need the assumptive close to confirm – but the follow-up critical. The art of soft selling is to focus on the customer and the needs and how you can match it – not on the sale itself as an end.

In financial services the repeat business and cross-sell is now critical, therefore it is long-term relationship building that is key. In other words although an increase in sales is still the **fundamental objective** this is supported by others known as **subsidiary objectives**. It is important to understand the difference between a fundamental objective and subsidiary objectives – often called means objectives – because these are the things you must achieve on the way to your fundamental objectives, and by focusing on them the fundamental objective is achieved virtually by default.

Transactional v relationship selling

It is important to understand the difference between these types of sales. Transactions are one-off sales with no guarantee of repeat business, although there may be regular transactions (eg weekly grocery shop) and little or no discernible pattern of consumption. Where you have a relationship however, there is a longer term set of interactions on which to build, invest in and make money from.

Nowadays, many low value high volume goods are nearly always sold as transactions. That is there is little or no relationship involved. The old cosy corner shop that was a place for a chat and to meet friends has disappeared in much of the UK. It has been replaced with large, impersonal, often out of town or special site outlets. Examples of this include:

◆ Petrol – tanks are filled when they are empty or it is convenient;
◆ Grocery shopping is carried out weekly at the nearest superstore. There is no feeling of a relationship. Goods are merely bought and paid for. Loyalty does not exist, or is very low and the slightest issue results in a change of sales outlet;
◆ Clothes are often purchased following a 'shop around' where many outlets are visited until the purchase is made.

The Internet has magnified this to a huge degree as you can now shop and source goods from virtually anywhere.

Clearly forecasting revenues from such fly-by-night or fickle customers is difficult, and whilst it might be possible in the general sense of a forecast of the many thousands of customers that might visit a Sainsbury, Tesco or Asda store, it is impossible at the individual level – and therefore customer profitability cannot be ascertained individually. Suppliers therefore try to convert transactional shoppers into relationship shoppers, to try and maintain their share of spend. Some of the ways of doing this include [qv] branding, loyalty schemes, long term discounts, added value services, differentiation.

The table below contrasts transactional and relationship sales:

	Transactional	**Relationship**
Type of good	Commodity	Service/high value
Level of service	Low	High
Nature	Discrete	Continuum
Interaction	Impersonal/self-serve	Personal
Specific Outlet	Neutral	Relevant
Customer Benefit	Price/convenience	Service/value-added
Revenure	Unpredictable	Consistent
Price	Low usually	Med to Premium

Financial services institutions, however, have both interactions with customers, from cashing cheques of other banks (or more likely non-customer account usage of ATMs) through to multi-service and often multi-generational relationships over many years. This is due to the nature of the majority of the products that almost demand continuous relationships. A life policy is paid monthly over many years, current accounts are used each day for many years and loan accounts have typically lives of between 3 and 25 years. This means that it is not only possible (and desirable) to measure the revenue individually, but also to put some effort into keeping customers. The complexity of so many financial products lends itself well to relationship selling.

Product complexity

One of the key components for good selling is product knowledge. Some products are very complex, some require a high degree of sales skills to obtain agreement and some require both. The art of good selling is to be able to make the customer feel that although some products are complex – you understand them and can explain them to him simply so he can have confidence in your handling of them – but that he needs you to help him. Figure 10.2 shows some examples.

Figure 10.2: Product complexity versus sales skills

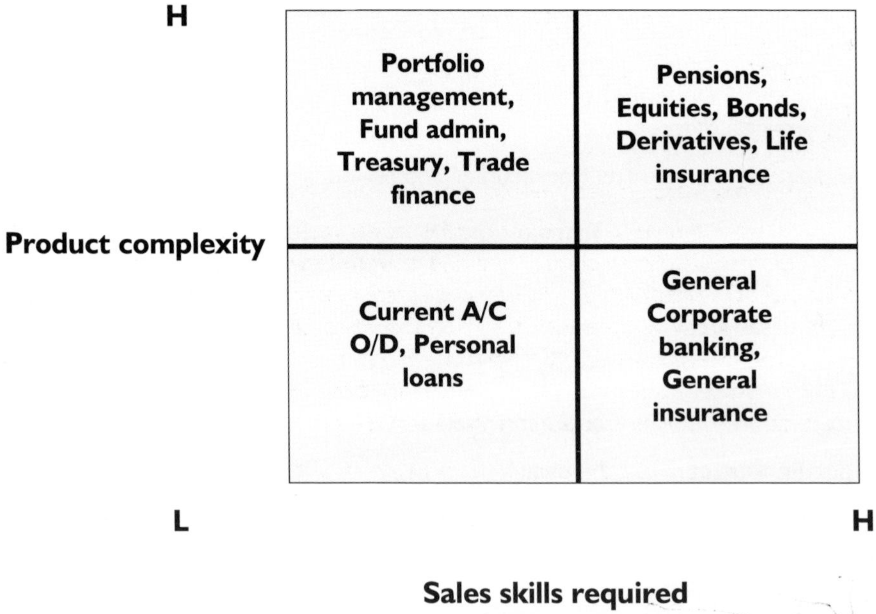

H	Portfolio management, Fund admin, Treasury, Trade finance	Pensions, Equities, Bonds, Derivatives, Life insurance
Product complexity	Current A/C O/D, Personal loans	General Corporate banking, General insurance
	L	**H**

Sales skills required

Do not try to sell very complex products without fully understanding how they work and how they affect customers – if in doubt get help. Customers usually have no issues with meeting domain experts – in fact it often flatters their ego and demonstrates that you have their best interests at heart.

Telesales

The telephone has moved from largely a device for making appointments or for sporadic queries into a new and major tool of sales – **the 'telechannel'**. Most customer contact currently is via this mechanism and for many organizations, without branch networks, wholly or jointly in addition to the Internet. It has spawned a radical re-appraisal of channel dynamics and offers a low cost business operating model – as pioneered by Direct Line and First Direct among others. The growth of call centres has been dramatic and has greatly altered the profit cost dynamics of many sectors of industry; and financial services, being based on intangible service offerings with no physical delivery required (except for documentation – see physical evidence), has lent itself greatly to this.

The key uses of telephones include:

◆ Customer service
◆ Customer support
◆ Distance transaction processing
◆ Outward bound sales campaigns
◆ Inward query resolution
◆ Lead generation for cross-channel selling
◆ Loyalty programmes
◆ Communication.

There are three major objectives for usage of telechannel:

◆ **Increased revenue** – from broader coverage of accounts and customers; lower cost customer acquisition; and targeted marketing/selling;
◆ **Reduced costs** – from lower cost lead generation; greater efficiency in processing low value transactions; and lower cost customer service support;
◆ **Enhanced customer satisfaction** – from more rapid customer responses; better issue resolution from centres of excellence; customer satisfaction surveys; and cheaper outbound contact for relationship management purposes.

An organization may use the channel for any or all of these purposes.

There are two main categories of usage – which can be termed telesales and teleservice.[2]

These contain the following:

Telesales

◆ **Teleselling** which is about inbound order taking and completion with little or no relationship with other channels – eg insurance. The emphasis here is on *product simplicity* not type of customer;
◆ **Telecoverage** – is about maintaining the relationship with major customers in support of other channels – eg sales force, account managers and is usually for

major, often corporate, accounts with complex and multi-varied needs and products. The emphasis here is on *customer* not product;

◆ **Teleprospecting** – is about generating new leads for closure by another channel – ie finding and qualifying leads for others to close using low cost methods.

Teleservice

◆ **Customer service** – dealing with customer requests – eg statements or telebanking;

◆ **Customer support** – dealing with technical issues and queries.

Teleselling is different in approach from ordinary selling and requires a different ethos and some would say a different type of person. It is about simple products, with good scripts and excellent product knowledge as well as a pre-prepared set of questions that a customer is likely to ask together with answers. A group of people in a room with a few telephones is not a call centre.

Verbal *v* non-verbal comunication

We communicate in a number of ways when interacting, and one of the key differences when using the telephone is that the **majority** of these signals – the non-verbal ones - are missing. As a result it is much harder compared to face-to-face situations where many other signals are received to confirm views, and it is important therefore to compensate. You cannot see a smile on the telephone – but you can hear warmth on the voice. Non-verbal communication includes head movements, facial expression, eyes, gestures, posture, touching, clothing and adornment, room layout/environment etc.

> 'Smile, dammit smile'
>
> *Body shop training sheet title*

Some differences between telephone selling and face to face:

Action	Face to Face	Telephone
Posture	Visible	*Invisible*
Speaking	Audible	*Audible*
Nodding	Visible	*Invisible*
Age	Observable	*Hidden*
Inflexion	Obscured	*Acutely audible*
Tone	Augmented	*Outstanding*
Environment	Shared	*Separate*
Gestures/touching	Usual/common	*Impossible*

Some key aspects of voice to consider and make sure that they are right include:

Loudness – many people speak much louder on the phone – conversely many mumble and there are no gestures to reinforce perceptions;

Pitch/Tone – make sure it is right;

Inflection – upward inflexions imply questions, downward inattentiveness;

Clarity – accurate pronunciation and measured speech;

Speed – many people speak too fast and as a result listeners do not grasp the whole sentence or message;

Accent – some are not acceptable for a variety of reasons and some, when strong, are incomprehensible.

It is also important to understand the basics of the telephone – you look ridiculous if you can't transfer a call or put it on hold – no matter how senior you are or how important you think you are – the customer is more important. Other issues to understand are how to leave messages on an answering machine; how to answer the telephone; and how to explain things to customers as well as how to close a conversation. Tragically these are often overlooked in day-to-day business (less so in call centres) and leave customers with the impression of, at best, a sloppy organization and, at worst, an organization that does not care about her or about basic training of staff – so why give it business or money?

Key tips are:

◆ Pay attention
◆ Listen
◆ Welcome the caller and introduce yourself
◆ Personalize the call
◆ Be polite but firm where necessary

- ◆ Do not give or accept abuse
- ◆ Listen
- ◆ Gather and give feedback
- ◆ Know what you are doing or seek appropriate help
- ◆ Inform the customer of what you are doing if there are any waits or delays for consultation
- ◆ Listen
- ◆ Close out properly and politely
- ◆ Diarize for action if appropriate
- ◆ Do what you say you will do (DWYSYWD)

Apart from these issues selling on the telephone follows the same basic sales logic as any other channel.

10.2   A sales model

There are three stages to any sale:
- ◆ Preparation
- ◆ Development
- ◆ Closing

and these are analysed below.

Preparation

This is about laying the groundwork such as product or service information that is relevant, any forms you will need, any referral names (for specialized information) initial needs analysis (based on any pre-existing relationship and depending on the nature of the sale) and scripting the meeting (laying out what you want to say, if relevant choosing a room etc).

Development

This is about the interaction with the customer (or customers) and includes meeting and greeting, introduction, objective agreement, questioning, needs identification/ confirmation, product or service matching, seeking confirmation of needs fulfilment and agreement.

Closing

This is where the deal is finalized and includes objection handling, next steps, and ultimately making the sale.

A good salesman will regard these three stages in the same way as an iceberg. Seven-tenths of an iceberg is below the water and cannot be seen. In selling that is your preparation. The development and closing stages represent only the tip of the iceberg that is visible above the water line.

The customer needs to make the decision to buy your product. Sales is about getting them to that point so it is useful to explore the decision cycle and how you can interact with it.

10.3   The decision cycle

The cycle for a sale is not simple and involves several steps. These steps may take place over quite some elapsed time and in the case of corporates are quite likely to involve several meetings.

Key steps

The key steps in selling are as follows – no matter what the situation is, whether it is a follow-on sale, a sale to an individual or to a corporate. It is just the emphasis that might change:

- ◆ Building a relationship and establishing rapport
- ◆ Making the opening statement
- ◆ Diagnosing the real issues
- ◆ Presenting solutions to the issues
- ◆ Handling objections to the solutions
- ◆ Closing the sale
- ◆ Follow-up

They need to be followed in order and the right level of effort put into them. Clearly this will differ depending on what you are selling and to whom, but the process does not vary.

Building a relationship and establishing rapport

Objectives here are break any tension barrier, relax the client, relax yourself and begin to analyse the characteristics of the buyer. For corporates this is often a group of people who have different vested interests in the outcome. Often you have to seek for the hidden questions underpinning their apparent questions. Some examples of hidden questions include:

- ◆ '..are you good enough for me to give you my business?'
- ◆ '..do you care about me or my business for me to buy from you?'
- ◆ '..will you give me the facts that will enable me to make the right decision?'

Making the opening statement

Objectives are to establish your credibility and fitness for what is under discussion (loan, insurance, investment etc), broaden and deepen the customer's understanding of what you can offer, to focus the meeting on the point at issue and to commence the understanding of the client. The customer will be looking for facts about you and your organization and what differentiates you from the competition.

Diagnosing the real issues

Objectives will vary depending on whether the customer is a corporate or individual, but include:

- ◆ to learn more about the client's business and issues (corporate);
- ◆ to understand where the individual(s) fit in with the structure and organization (corporate);
- ◆ what their goals are, to understand the real need and to start to look at their decision-making process – or that of the organization.

This is usually achieved by questioning the client, and narrowing the focus of the questions progressively, until you arrive at your end point. Examples include:

- ◆ general remarks to break tension and try to establish some common interest;
- ◆ questions on the organization and where it is going (corporate);
- ◆ questions on his personal situation, family etc (personal);
- ◆ the implications of this;
- ◆ the customer's needs;
- ◆ the organization's needs (corporate);
- ◆ what the opportunity is that arises by meeting these two areas of need;
- ◆ what is the value therefrom.

Presenting solutions to the issues

Objectives are to offer something that meets the customer's needs – eg an overdraft facility linked to working capital finance, trade assistance via letter of credit/trade advances etc; corporate insurance etc – to demonstrate how you will provide the solution eg as a single limit; as several limits greater than the whole within a smaller global solution; several facilities within an overall limit, or insurance for each office discounted down for multi-locations; and to gain agreement to the solution meeting the needs.

Many firms make the mistake of mixing up products with offerings – they are not the same – or not necessarily so. It is how what you offer meets the need or resolves the issue that is important – not the inherent contents. It is important to present the offering in terms of the **benefits** to him and the organization and not to talk of features or products.

There are some key criteria that will affect how a customer makes decisions:

◆ How your capability is viewed by the organization. This will be in comparison with what they are expecting and against others either currently competing or from past experiences.

◆ What your experience is of the service you are offering – and where else it has worked successfully.

◆ The service that supports your offering.

◆ Timing – when can it happen – duration and flexibility etc.

◆ What the competition is and how you and your offering compare.

◆ The cost/benefit trade-off (the Customer Value Proposition).

◆ Your relationship with the customer.

Above all you must be clear as to the real need and that you can offer a solution.

Handling objections to the solutions

In an ideal world you present the solution and the customer agrees at once and signs up on the spot. Unfortunately this is rarely the case and at the very least you will get questions of the '..what if..' category. It is important that these questions are heard, understood and reacted to otherwise you will not have agreement and the customer will not accept your offering. Therefore objectives are to refine the solution to meet objections or concerns or variations; to uncover opportunities that you may have missed – '..does it also cover x?; identify the real as opposed to the *prima facie* objection and deal with it; to establish the timescales and agree the next steps.

When people object it is not always straightforward to understand why. Sometimes they may say that does not meet my needs because of 'X' &'Y'. More often they will vacillate. There are several types of objections:

◆ **Procrastination** – They try to put the decision off until a later – and often unspecified – time (very common). You need to clarify the reason for putting the decision off – this usually means that there is another objection – eg they do not have the power to take the decision or that they have not yet obtained agreement to the budget. This needs to be explored, and sorted out.

◆ **Doubt** – They do not think that you can deliver either the service or part of it or in the time required. You need to clarify this, eg by asking a closed question, and then rebut the assumption (if you can of course). If there is something that you cannot deliver then come clean – do not lie – customers really get upset about that (quite rightly) and being honest usually pays great dividends as your relationship grows and deepens.

◆ **Misunderstanding** – real or imagined – about what you offer, the offering or the company. Clarify what it is that is misunderstood and then correct the situation by offering proof or further statements.

◆ **Indifference** – do not see the need – or do not see the solution. Clarify why they cannot see it and then re-iterate a solution to the issues.

◆ **Real objection** – eg price or you have not offered a service that they require, or there is something that they do not like. This can be a tricky one – especially if you cannot deal with it immediately. Try to place it in context with the other benefits and offerings and offer to sort it out later on.

Generally with objections it is important to prepare for the meeting by putting yourself in the customer's shoes and trying to raise objections and then derive solutions/answers. At all times try to clarify the situation and apologise for not making it clear if this is the case. Control your own emotions – even if you have covered the issue more than once. Ensure that the client agrees that the issue has been resolved satisfactorily.

Closing the sale

Where you try to close the sale and obtain the customer's agreement. There are two types of close:

◆ **Assumptive** – where you begin transferring ownership of the offering – '..so we've agreed that you require an overdraft for £x m – when will you draw down your first tranche?'
◆ **Presumptive** – where you ask them to agree.

And the closes can be:

◆ **Direct** – '…are you going to agree to this offering (OD, policy etc)?'
◆ **Choice based** – '…shall I put the facility in place today or next week?'
◆ **Logical restatement** – '…on balance then this is the logical choice for you…'

A good salesman however will of course have been using pre-closing – that is progressive or incremental closing where at each step they agree to the conclusion and at the end a slight nudge closes the sale – perhaps by way of a statement to the effect – '…here's what I think that you ought to do….' Or '…if I might suggest that we do 'x' and then 'y' and we can check up on 'z' later….' Or '… in the meantime you can do 'x' until 'y'….'

Closing the sale is a re-affirmation of the trust and builds on the relationship that you have established throughout the process. A common method is to say '…what **we** might do is 'x'…' because you are sharing the decision with the customer.

Follow-up

This is a vital part of the cycle and critical to customer service. Objectives here are to ensure that all is well; to fix any errors; and to seek new or further opportunities. There are two types of follow-up – where you have been successful and where you have failed.

Failure

◆ Try to agree when/if you should make a further visit/arrange a meeting
◆ Send a follow-up letter promptly
◆ Execute any interim commitments
◆ Try to monitor decision cycle and status and indicate readiness to open discussions again.

Success

◆ Obtain written commitment/signed agreement
◆ Send contract if necessary
◆ Agree timings and starting arrangements
◆ Put in hand necessary actions
◆ Ensure customer adherence to terms precedent and subsequent as necessary
◆ Monitor and problem solve
◆ Arrange reviews etc.

10.4   The corporate buying cycle

Dealing with corporate customers is very different from dealing with individuals. Selling a corporate your services presents a many-faceted problem for the following reasons:

◆ corporates are not people and so respond in different ways – they have cultures, their own ways of doing things and are composed of many people;
◆ they contain (often) many different departments and divisions with different goals;
◆ their staff are all different and will respond differently to the same stimuli;
◆ they often have different delegated levels of discretion which means that decisions are frequently taken by:
  o different people
  o at different levels within the organization
  o in different ways
◆ frequently there is a central control imposed in all or some aspects (eg many companies have a central treasury department that looks after much of its financial services needs) or more commonly central purchasing policies (eg we use this bank, this software, this travel company or this insurance company only);
◆ they are often in many locations within a country (eg major UK retailers such as Tesco, Marks and Spencer, Sainsburys) and in banking Abbey National Lloyds/ TSB, Halifax; frequently they operate internationally – across two or more countries (Walmart/ASDA, Carrefour, Barclays, BBVA, Banco do Brasil, CGNU, Willis Coroon) or globally (Shell, BP, McDonalds, Citibank);

◆ they may be subsidiaries of foreign companies and therefore subject to different rules and regulations and with an overseas head or regional office where many decisions are taken.

There are other reasons if you think about this, but suffice to say that dealing with corporates can often be much more difficult than individuals.

It is therefore of critical importance to understand the corporate buying process within an organization. This is part of understanding your customer but it is so important that if this aspect is overlooked it becomes virtually impossible to deal successfully with corporates. To this end you must find out and then cultivate the real decision makers within an organization. This is not as easy as it sounds. Most organizations have a defined decision chain which may be loose or very tight. The key question is 'Where to enter this chain?' and then of course 'How?'

Getting to maybe

It is very difficult to obtain appointments when calling cold and it is also becoming increasingly difficult to obtain them when they are referred or warm, because people are wary of anyone perceived as 'selling' them something and are busy. Part of the issue as well is that many people do not prepare for the attempt at getting a meeting and so either fail or only partly achieve their goals, thus assisting in reinforcing customers' perception of the pointless appointment for 'selling'.

It is not good enough just to ask for an appointment although many people still try this approach. In simple terms think of the Customer Value Proposition – what is in it for the customer? There must be some benefit to him far giving up his time and listening (the price) in order for him to say yes.

It is very important to let her know both what your objective is and what she will gain. A good technique is to put yourself in her place and ask – why would I say yes?

For example you might wish to say:

> 'I will be in your area next week and thought you might like to hear about a new product that we have developed especially for your sector (new customer).'

Or

> 'It is time for the semi-annual review of services (existing customer) and I would like to start the process.'

Or

> 'I would like to introduce a new colleague with some specialist skills that may be of assistance (eg Middle East energy if that is an area where the organization is interested).'

What you are striving to do is develop a 'business-to-business' relationship that transcends the more usual 'buyer-to-seller' relationship.

There are several factors that pull customers in different ways (real or perceived):

◆ Time pressure
◆ Resource constraints
◆ Internal pressures
◆ Sales targets which impose worries
◆ His own customers' relationships to manage.

Authority is ephemeral

Many staff within corporates are unwilling to admit how little authority they really have. Some of course are very happy to help you to find the right levels in the decision chain – but many do not wish to expose themselves and will not. As a result you can be stuck with your first contact who can be at the wrong level entirely and much time can be wasted in influencing the wrong person.

Typical sales theory focuses on the main types of customer contacts. Note that one person can be part of one group, all of one group, and also be in several groups depending on the type of decision the size of the organization and the importance of the decision:

◆ **Users** – the person with the need or the person delegated by the organization to fulfil the need. Eg the person to whom responses to an Invitation to Tender must be sent or the manager of the division that needs the facility. They can also be decision makers and budget holders but often sadly this is not the case, and it is also necessary to cultivate others.
◆ **Decision-maker** – the person or persons who actually makes the decision to go ahead with something – note that it may be formal or informal authority and ex-officio or de facto.
◆ **Buyers** – those that have the formal authority to agree to a decision to purchase – they are often the same person where the decision is routine or low level.
◆ **Budget holder** – the person who has the money to pay for your service. May not be the buyer – often is the decision-maker.
◆ **Coach** – a friend within the organization who, while not necessarily a party to the decision, gives useful information and advice.
◆ **Influencer** – someone to whom others in the buying process will listen and therefore whom you must have on your side. Note that in some circumstances surprising people can be influencers – eg with items such as photocopiers and faxes and often travel it is often people such as administrators who are key.
◆ **Gate-keeper** – someone who blocks access to others – may be your initial contact who is trying to keep the relationship at that level, an agent who wishes to keep control of the buyer, technical personnel, or often a secretary or someone working closely with someone who refuses to let you get to a customer.

Having established which players are in which category you can then go on to sell services and products.

Sales techniques

There are several techniques for remembering the vital ingredients in selling. Two examples are shown below. The technique is only a guide – it is what you do and how you carry it out that matters.

SPIN – stands for Situation, Problem, Implication and Need/pay-off[3]

Analyse the current position; identify the problem; understand the implications; meet the need, take the pay-off.

SPQR – stands for Situation, Problem, Question and Resolution[4]

Another way of looking at selling is to analyse the situation, diagnose the problem, answer the question in the mind of the other party (how do I solve this issue, will it make me look good, can I do this?) and then resolve the issue by your offering.

10.5   Tips in selling

- Never knock the competition. It is pointless and irrelevant – just emphasize how much better the benefits are from your offering for your customer.
- Translate features into benefits, directly to the customer's position or perspective.
- Sell solutions or results *not* products.
- Listen to what is said, but look for the unsaid (usually symptoms are described *not* the real problem).
- Be thoroughly conversant with your USP – and explain why it is of benefit to the customer.
- Ensure that the Customer Value Proposition is clear for this particular customer.
- It is always people who buy – it may be one or many depending on the circumstances – therefore understand the people with whom you are dealing and their agendas and needs.
- You do not have an automatic right to sell other products to a customer once you have sold the first product, although you would hope to build on the initial relationship and deepen it. You must earn the new right, or at least do nothing to deter them from coming back. A useful model for this purpose is the **customer corridor**, initially developed by Frederick F Reichheld from Bain & Co. Figure 10.3 is an example of the customer corridor depicted from a retail banking perspective.[5]

Figure 10.3: Customer-company interactions

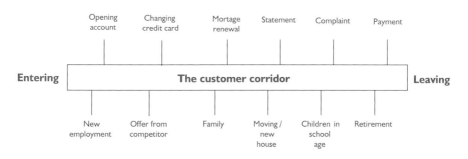

Events (out of control for the company)

This indicates the lifecycle of events of a customer with the opportunities for product selling along the way. At each stage or change there is an opportunity – but you have to be alert to them and work for them. You must also be sure that the relationship with regards to previous products is good to facilitate the next sales.

> 'The big growth areas are in savings and mortgages – less than 3% of Barclays' customers have a mortgage with us.'
>
> David Roberts, Head of Retail Banking Barclays.[6]

Summary

Selling can be hard or soft – but soft usually pays greater dividends in the long run. To maximize this you must really understand the customer's needs and develop solutions that match those.

1 Selling is about 'persuasive communication' – that is giving a message to your customers (and potential customers) about your products that is perceived as adding value to you and your customer.
2 Hard selling concentrates very much on the close as the be-all and end-all – rather than the softer approach which emphasizes the needs analysis and needs fulfilment and follow-up, and this is reflected in the conduct of the meeting.
3 There are three stages to any sale:
   ◆ Preparation
   ◆ Development
   ◆ Closing.

4 Often the customer will object to something and this must be handled by preparing for the meeting by putting yourself in the customer's shoes and trying to raise objections and then derive solutions/answers.

5 Dealing with corporate customers is very different from dealing with individuals because corporates often have strict rules for 'purchases' with several people involved. You have to work through this to be successful.

6 You do not have an automatic right to sell other products to a customer once you have sold the first product, although you would hope to build on the initial relationship and deepen it. You must earn the new right, or at least do nothing to deter them from coming back.

Select bibliography

Loyalty Rules : F Reichheld

Principles of Marketing: Kotler

Value Based Marketing: Peter Doyle

Notes

1 *Relationship Banking – Cross-selling the bank's products and services*: Dwight S Ritter – Probus Publications 1993, pages 11-15
2 Friedman and Furey – 'the channel advantage' Butterworth & Heineman
3 as developed by Huthwaite & Co.
4 SPQR (copyright Neil Russell-Jones 1997)
5 *Customer Relationship Development* : Ralf Blomqvist, Johan Dahl, Tomas Haeger IFS Publications
6 as quoted in Financial World, October 2002, p 15

Eleven

Features not benefits

Topics in this chapter

Features

Benefits

Introduction to this chapter

In this short chapter the difference between a product **feature** and a product **benefit** will be considered. This is an important distinction to make but unfortunately it is the most commonly forgotten or ignored. Organizations are always bringing out new products (even if they are old ones re-launched, tweaked or altered in some way) and this usually means that they have changed the features in some way (bigger, faster, cleaner, brighter, shinier etc). Most organizations and their salespeople focus on products or services and on what they **are,** rather than what they think the customers' needs are, and what their services can **do** for the customer.

This is the case not only in selling the service but also in selling the company. In many cases, especially in 'cold' situations, it is necessary to talk about your organization to inform the customer – but in the right context. Many people might say something like – 'My organization is ranked in the top 5 in the UK.' Very interesting but so what? The customer is more likely to think:

What does that mean for me? – Does it make your currency rate cheaper than your competition? – Does that make your loans cheaper? – Does it mean that you give better service? Or will it mean that you give worst service because I am unimportant to you? – Are you situated in more convenient locations?

Of course in the right situation it can be very important to talk about the size of an organization – it can show the strength, or the international coverage, or the service depth and breadth that it has – but only in the right context.

It is of critical importance then when talking to customers to understand the difference between a feature and a benefit. It is also important to note that some features can have more than one benefit and that different customers will find different benefits or different combinations of features/benefits attractive.

11.1   What is a feature?

A feature is a characteristic that your product or service displays. For example if you buy a new car the brochure will usually say what features this model has in total and what new standard features have been introduced with this particular model (locking petrol cap, CD player, tinted windows, heated front screen etc). Some of these may have been introduced because customers have asked for them, some because competitors are offering them or for internally-driven reasons such as standardization – and there will be other 'optional extras' (metallic paint, extra speakers and so on).

A feature on its own however means nothing and can often provoke the question – but why would I want it? With a mortgage there are too many variations to go into and the combinations are infinite – but typically they will have many features – such as cash back, fees included, fees paid for by the organization, fixed rates, floating rates, combinations, links to current accounts etc. These can often be bewildering for many borrowers and it is incumbent on the sales person to explain what they are – but more importantly why customers should have them. The **why**? Should be translated into a benefit.

11.2   Translating a feature into a benefit – 'so what?'

The most likely response from customers to a statement that 'this service does X' – is a 'so what?' In most cases they will not intuitively see the need for it and are quite likely to view it negatively – is this part of the cost – why do I need it – am I paying for something that I don't need/want? To counter this it is necessary to explain to the customer the benefit that this particular feature brings. In this context it is important to understand your customer and to translate the feature into a direct benefit for him. Remember customers have different needs and wants and one person's needs may be quite different from another. A customer does not want a loan – she wants a car, they want a holiday or the organization wants to import raw materials from China – the letter of credit (for example) is not required for itself, but because it will help to facilitate the trade that the organization wishes to engage in.

A statement such as 'we have a specialized department dealing with letters of credit' is not much help to a customer. It is only when you explain that the benefits of this include:

- ◆ We have expert knowledge of letters of credit and this helps us to assist you to design the right one for you;
- ◆ We have lots of experience in checking for discrepancies and this ensures that the documents etc are correct;
- ◆ Because of our knowledge we are familiar with the particular requirements in China and can help you round some of the difficulties there;
- ◆ We have excellent relationships with banks in China and can smooth the payments and documents etc.

To further underline the relevance of the benefits you must ask whether each benefit is of value to the customer. Where this is the case the benefits are adding to the benefit minus cost trade-off and this should help you in securing the business. Where it is not of value then it should be quietly dropped.

In many cases the client (particularly in a business context or an investment) may not understand the difference between the services that are available and will need help in choosing. The different features of the services can be translated into a different range of benefits and then contrasted to their needs and wants to help them to choose the right one.

Translating needs to benefits

In order for a customer to buy something there must be a need (see Needs and Wants) and to be effective in making a customer buy your particular offering over the competition you must translate your product features into the features that meet that need. Where a customer asks for something you must always be thinking at the level below. A request for a mortgage usually implies the need to buy a house – but the customer has translated that automatically into a product.

Often the expressed want may not be the real need. Eg 'I want to send money to Brazil – to be released on certain conditions' may actually represent an underlying need for some sort of secure trade finance – which may be better met by a different product such as a letter of credit. It is therefore important to think of the real need rather than the expressed want. This may require a few questions to uncover the lower level of need.

The model below may help you to think about this process:

Underlying Need	Translates into Product	Needs met by Benefits
Security in old age	Pension	Peace of mind
Cash access	ATM card	Fast cash anywhere, any time
Investment complexity	Financial advice	Reduction in complexity; solutions to other needs
Trade finance	Letter of credit	Security of delivery against payments; global access to banking

Bundling into solutions

In some cases the needs may be so complex or multi-varied that a single product will not meet the need. In this case a number of products should be bundled together to create a solution. In this case the bundle will have a number of features which when combined allow you to demonstrate the benefits of the solution that meet the needs.

The type of offering will be a combination of features and benefits and the price will accordingly be a function of that combination. It is very difficult to charge high rates for offerings that are low on functions and benefits, but it is much easier to charge more for those either rich in features or delivering high benefits. Those offering both, of course, will usually command premia over the rest. The grid shows the four types of purchase:

◆ Low Benefits and Low Features - commodity
◆ Low Benefits and High Features - product purchase
◆ High Benefits and High Features - unique purchase - probably customised
◆ High Benefits and Low Features - is purchased on the service offered

The greater the features offered then the greater the cost to deliver - so pricing must reflect this - unless it is a loss leader, or you are simply giving it away.

Figure 11.2: Benefits *v* features

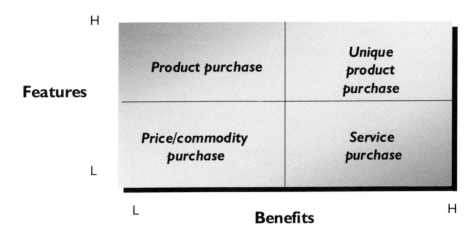

Any offering can be anywhere on this grid
- depending on where the offeror places its CVP

Your products versus the competition

When dealing with customers you must bear in mind that in many cases they will have spoken to others to obtain a broad range of ideas and prices. You should therefore be aware of the main competition's products and how they compare with yours. (See chapter on competitive analysis.)

The chart overleaf (Figure 11.2), from the *Times* 23-11-02, shows a route for probing the needs and then relate products/benefits to those needs.

Summary

It is vital that in dealing with a customer you adopt a customer-centric approach and understand what her real need is. You must then demonstrate how the features of your solution deliver benefits to her by meeting her needs. This will ensure that you equalize the Customer Value Proposition by offering her the best combination of benefits price trade-off.

1 Features of a product are meaningless to customers unless they are translated into the benefit that they bring to the customer.

Figure 11.2: Mortgage decision tree

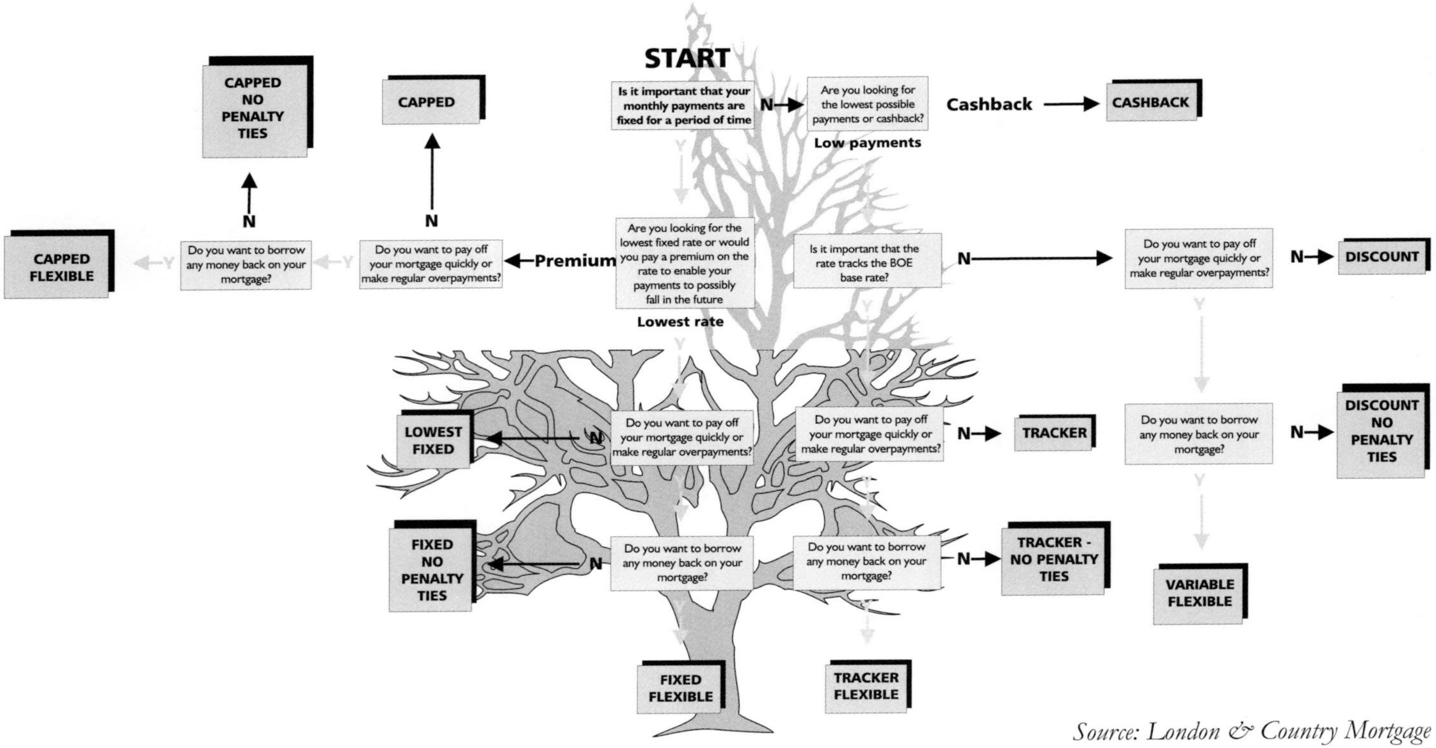

Source: London & Country Mortgage

2 You must be able to demonstrate the superiority of benefits that they receive from your product rather than that your competitor.
3 It is worth running through all products and translating every key feature into a benefit.

Select bibliography

Financial Services Marketing: Tina Harrison

Principles of Marketing: Kotler

Twelve

Branding and brand extension

Topics in this chapter

What a brand is

Types of brand

Brand features

The four Ds

Brand extension

Brand geography

Brand architecture

Introduction to this chapter

This chapter looks at branding and brand extension. It considers the question: what makes a brand and why is it important? It will consider the benefits from brands, the types of brand and the four Ds of branding.

12.1   What is a brand?

In a philosophical sense it is a light in the darkness – that is it assists customers to distinguish a particular make of one type of good or service from another. It represents familiarity in an unfamiliar, complex and difficult world. A brand also contains other things such as dreams, expectations, lifestyle etc and those core components that the competition does not have. It is therefore an extremely important part of the Unique Sales Proposition (USP) – that almost indefinable thing or set of things that sets you apart from your competition.

Knowing a brand helps us with decisions – we are very much creatures of habit – few of us are early adopters or innovators. Accordingly we tend to use and therefore to buy things that are familiar to us – they are within our comfort zone. It is because of this that brands acquire their value.

Case study

Rowntree Mackintosh was a familiar name to everyone on the UK – and everyone was familiar with its products- including **Kit-Kat** (a chocolate biscuit bar). Nestlé, a Swiss firm in the same market, could see vast potential from the product portfolio and accordingly launched a hostile bid for Rowntree Mackintosh. Nestlé won and one of the key determinants of its victory was the ability of the management to convince the market that the brands within the Rowntree Mackintosh portfolio were greatly undervalued and that it could improve their value.

Brands at one level help to reduce levels of stress in decision-making. For example, doing the shopping in a supermarket in a rush after work it is very unlikely that you will try or actively seek out new products. You will stick with those you know.

A familiar phrase to many corporate buyers is 'no-one ever got fired for buying Big Blue' (ie IBM). It is a well-known name with reliable products and the corporation plays on this in its marketing.

In a recent survey by Interbrand[1], the relative value of brands was calculated. The table below shows this. What emerges is that, in general, brand values are much lower in financial services compared with the rest of industry, where it is normally around 70%.

Interbrand survey of financial brands

Brand	Brand value 2002*	Market cap	Brand value as % market cap
Global			
Citibank	18,066	206,900	9%
American Express	16,287	47,800	34%
Merrill Lynch	11,230	33,500	34%
Morgan Stanley	11,205	46,143	24%
JP Morgan	9,693	65,682	15%
Goldman Sachs	7,194	34,500	21%
UK			
Barclays	5,994	41,000	15%
Royal Bank of Scotland	5,688	55,500	10%
Lloyds TSB	4,593	38,700	12%
NatWest	2,975	55,500	5%
Halifax	1,844	21,381	9%
Abbey National	1,716	20,000	9%
Bank of Scotland	1,107	21,381	12%

* calculated as NPV of earnings that the brand is expected to generate

This is usually attributed to the fact that customers do not really value their financial services supplier – regarding it in many instances as a necessary evil rather than as a great experience – but regard the difficulties faced in switching suppliers as too great to undertake. For banks the message here is that the brand value (NVP of expected earnings) is sustained by inertia rather than image and experience sharing, so they need to improve those considerably or they may lose customer share to other competitors who may be able to offer a different experience. One of the strengths of a valuable brand is that it can be translated into premium prices, but this is difficult for most financial services.

12.2   Brand factors

How we perceive a brand is a blend of four factors:

Personal experience

We may have used the brand before or have experienced it directly. In this case customers will probably have strong beliefs about it (we all prefer this type of wine, beer or cheese to other, possibly very similar, brands (eg there are many types of Chardonnay from different marques). This is demonstrated very well by the 'blind' test. People are asked to taste a number of products and rate them in order of preference. They are then asked to rate brands. The results are always different as our knowledge and experience of brands alters our perception and can raise them higher up the list (or if we have had a bad experience push them into oblivion!). Many organizations can copy many products and services easily – but it is not easy to dislodge the favoured brand in people's minds.

Personal recommendation

Friends, acquaintances, work colleagues or family have used the brand and mentioned it – or have been seen using it. We rate these recommendations highly. Many people will ask friends for reliable workmen or how their car/TV/DVD player has performed.

Direct approaches

Customers may have been approached directly by salesmen or received direct marketing from organizations (and may have read it!). This will contribute to a higher level of familiarity than if we have never heard of it.

Publicity

In a general sense – as part of the aural and visual wallpaper that adorns every aspect of our life. The service may have been advertised on TV, in a newspaper, on the radio even on the DVD you have bought or rented. Messages may also come over the Internet or by post or even just eye-catching displays in shops or malls or on the walls of the tube or stations/bus-stops. All these items help to familiarize people with the brand and makes it stand out from the rest.

12.3 Brand versus reputation

Many things contribute to an organization's success (measured as growth and/or profit). Figure 12.1 shows the key factors and also categorizes them into those that are lasting *(durable)* and those that are not permanent *(ephemeral)*.

Note that both reputation and brand are ephemeral. This is because whatever happens to a firm, at the end of the day they will still have their tangible assets whereas both of these can be destroyed – sometimes with remarkable rapidity. Although brand and reputation are different they are however linked and reinforce each other.

Figure 12.1: Drivers and contribution to growth/profit

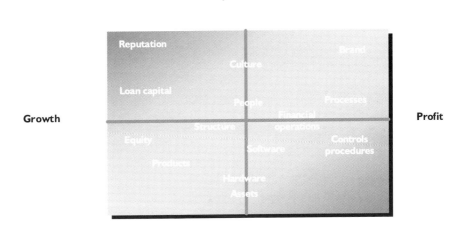

A brand can disappear almost overnight or your reputation can be damaged beyond redemption extremely quickly – sometimes by factors outside your control or by unrelated actions. (See below – Arthur Andersen & Co.) Building a global brand can often involve extinguishing other well-placed brands in order to focus efforts on one name (see below – UBS). They contribute however to different things:

◆ **Reputation** is a driver of *Growth* because your reputation allows you the right to engage with the customer;

◆ **Brand**, however, drives the price because it has an inherent expectation of where it fits on the cost continuum and therefore influences *Profit*. A premium brand allows you to premium price; but a cheap brand means that you will only rarely obtain premium pricing.

Case study – UBS

UBS, Switzerland's biggest bank, announced in 2002 that it was taking a Swiss franc charge of SFR 1 billion (£ 430m) as a result of its decision to drop its other brands. UBS – itself the result of a merger between Union Bank of Switzerland and Swiss Banking Corporation – will drop the names Warburg (a London investment bank acquired along the way) as well as that of Paine Webber – a broker.

The organization has also acquired other names in the past which have been dropped, including Philips & Drew, Dillon Read and Brinson O'Connor, in the name of creating a global brand. From the middle of 2003 all four divisions (wealth management; investment management; investment banking, and retail and corporate banking) will operate under the name UBS.

The Chairman Marcel Ospel said 'This is a further logical step in our efforts to define the future as one form. We need a flagship brand. Making this move is a signal of our unity, strength and momentum'. This is designed to place it on an equal footing in brand terms as HSBC and Citigroup – two of the strongest international brands in banking – and follows extensive consultation with customers globally who affirmed the strength of the UBS brand.[2]

12.4   Building a brand

There are three steps involved in building a brand:

◆ Develop the service or product
◆ Develop the basic brand
◆ Develop an augmented brand.

Develop the service or product

In order to develop a brand the underlying service must:

◆ be effective
◆ meet a need (may meet a want as well)
◆ be at least as good as competitive services
◆ have a name (NB it is only a label at this stage).

Selling at this level is purely in commodity terms – ie there is no real brand and no real added value – yet, and as result it is price-focused. A label distinguishes it from other services in the market (eg Bloggs Bank versus Groggles Bank) but does not signal anything else at this stage and carries nothing else with it. It is recognizable but carries no particular preferences. At this level it is impossible to build sustainable competitive advantage because it is easily replicable and, unless you have developed massive economies of scale, it is usually easily matched in price by competitors.

In most markets there is little difference in quality between competing services among peer-positioned services and indeed it is not possible to price the same as competitive services unless you meet this hygiene factor of quality levels. A service with lower quality will have to be priced against similar lower quality services or under the rest if it is out of line. In general offerings are bought to meet needs – ie they are solutions – so to focus on solutions, the brand must be built.

Case study

Arthur Andersen & Co., the auditing and professional services firm – which one day was one of the 'big 5' audit practices but, as the fall-out from accounting malpractices at some of its clients, notably Enron and World.com was uncovered, almost the next day it was obliterated. The name (brand) became damaged goods as the full scale of the enormity of the errors was revealed, it lost its reputation built up over many years, and it was stripped of the right to audit in the USA its main power base. It crumbled in days and many member firms walked out or joined other rivals.

Incidentally the former consulting arm of Andersen had split off some years before and changed its name to 'Accenture' – and therefore developed a new brand. As a result, therefore, it was largely untouched by the consequences of the audit practice and survived with its reputation largely intact.

Develop the basic brand

The characteristics of a basic brand are that it:

◆ Is different from the rest in some way (characteristics, or features or benefits) that can be easily recognized or described (washes whiter, has a different APR, better flexibility)
◆ The customers need to be aware of this difference so that they have a slightly different perception of the service and, more importantly, where the service sits against its competition. This is achieved by getting the message across by promotion, packaging etc.
◆ Emphasis is laid on the name, the quality or its features to build this perception.

This allows you to move into the next stage of building on the basic features to augment it.

Develop an augmented brand

The objective in this stage is to make your service the one that consumers want by differentiating through demonstrating, or creating a perception of added value. This means focusing their attention on:

- ◆ The extra services it offers
- ◆ The benefits to consumers from using this service rather than competitors'
- ◆ The product or service attributes that meet customers' wants
- ◆ Demonstrating a better value/price trade off.

This allows you to build brand loyalty, a reputation for consistency and quality, and requires a sustained campaign.

Unlike a service – where the characteristics are physical (a loan has a term, an agreed interest rate and agreed mechanisms for making repayments) – a brand is built on intangible items such as perception, emotion and wants. There are three parts to a brand:[3]

- ◆ **the core** – which is the essence of the brand (eg 'U be U');
- ◆ **the style** – how it is perceived; and
- ◆ **the theme** of the brand – how it looks.

Figure 12.2: Augmented brand – facets

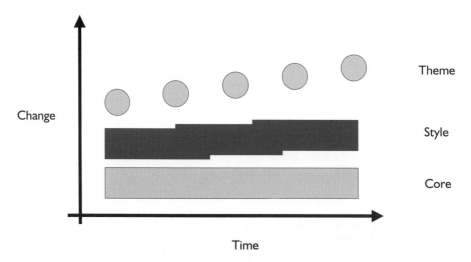

The latter two have three facets with the **style** of a brand consisting of:

- ◆ **culture** of the brand, ie the values that it personifies (eg Nike – 'just do it' or the Barclays set of adverts laying great emphasis on its large size or 'bigness' – similarly Swiss banks have been historically considered as stable and discreet);

- the **personality** – that is the character of the brand as it is perceived (for example Virgin is seen as rather iconoclastic whereas most high street banks are stuffy or more staid, or Abbey National – 'Life's complicated enough');
- the **self image** – how the customer sees herself in relation to the brand (someone using the Co-op may see them self as sharing its ethical stance or someone using an international bank may see himself as a globe-trotter or a mover or shaker).

Whereas the **theme** contains:

- the **physical** aspects of the brand and includes the name, colours, logo and packaging;
- **reflection** – the image of the targeted audience as reflected in its communications which may not reflect the total market (eg many advertisements are aimed at the youth market although the market is much wider, as many people want to appear young or younger than they are); on the other hand very few people under 50 would ever consider looking at a SAGA advert due to the implications of old age that go with it;
- **relationship** – how it seeks to interact or relate with the customer, ie is it experiential, attributional or aspirational (see below).

That is, how it looks to consumers, but obviously based around the core of the service.

The former – the **style** – changes only very gradually whereas the latter – the **theme** – can change over time and may vary with sub-brands.

The **core** does not change unless there is a fundamental need driven by market wants – it is difficult to see Virgin changing from its 'us against the rest of the financial services world' and is closely linked to its 'vision' – the long-term almost unattainable goal that drives it forward.

12.5 Types of brand

There are generally considered to be three types of brands:

- attribute
- aspirational
- experience

These are explored below.

- **Attribute** – this type of brand displays an image that gives confidence in the service's functional attributes. Customers will choose this type of brand where it is difficult to assess the relative qualities against competitive services (eg where most cars are equal in quality they might choose Swedish cars for safety or German cars for reliability, or in financial services a corporate contemplating a rights' issue might choose to use Cazenove due to its legendary placing power).

◆ **Aspirational** – these types of brands convey an image to which customers aspire, and to this end focus on lifestyles rather than products. Customers are lead to believe that they will acquire the image by buying these brands. The classic is Martini – depicted as drunk by sophisticated high-flyers and jet-setters. Archers adverts depict women leading fun-packed lifestyles and Rolex watches are shown as worn by the very rich and famous.

◆ **Experience** – this type of brand shares images and emotions with customers – almost shared philosophy – eg 'Fair deal' produce or Ben and Jerry's ice-cream, which claim to give more money to Third World producers than others. Remote banking is sometimes linked to busy professionals who do not have the time to go to their bank and can do their banking on the move. The recent NatWest adverts are aimed at those customers who want the branch banking experience and lay emphasis on the fact that they have stopped the branch closure programme. In many cases this is sharing values such as a bank branch's social function in a community. Bodyshop is a prime example of the shared worries about green issues which struck a very resonant chord with the public.

Different types of brands have more success in different markets. Very few brands aimed at the business-to-business market focus on aspirational selling – they are far more likely to focus on attributes (few buy mainframes to aspire to a better life). In consumer markets many companies try to move from attribute to experience to lock customers in by the sharing of principles. Attribute brands in a consumer market suffer from the increasing ease of replicability of features and benefits and greater information that reduces the uniqueness of the particular brand attribute as they read that others also share those attributes (eg safety is a main feature of most if not all cars).

The effectiveness of brands is often highlighted when blind tests are conducted. When customers are asked to name the best product or service the leading brand will usually come top. When blind tests are conducted the results are often very different. Eg recently in a blind champagne tasting the leading brands were eclipsed by one of the major supermarket's own brand!

12.6   The four Ds of branding

Successful brand management is about how you position the brand in the market. Where it is perceived as 'sitting' in the market by consumers drives the pricing and therefore profits. Positioning is about linking the brand with a category with which consumers can identify and – to sell the offerings with which they want to be associated – ie it must meet needs and, ideally, their wants.

Tyboult and Sternthal have developed an analysis that revolves around the **Four Ds** of branding[4]. They contend that there are four tasks that need to be carried out to be effective in positioning a brand:

Definition	Differentiation
Deepening	Disciplined defence

They then go on to make the point that failure can result in the emergence of a fifth **D** – **Decline** in market share and sales!!

Even good products need to be positioned carefully and this requires that you understand the effect and the implications of the four **Ds** – discussed below.

Definition

This is about defining what the brand is. It is usually achieved by highlighting what the brand stands for and in many cases the similarities with competitive offerings. These are called points of parity. Although you want your brand to be different, it is usually much easier to get a brand accepted, particularly if it is competing in an established market, if it shares attributes with the competing offerings, because this will put it in the customers 'comfort zone'. Clearly it should share the **good** points from the customer's perception – *not* the bad ones.

You are free of course to select in which category you wish your brand to sit. Re-defining it away from the typical category and into another can work wonders. For example Budweiser beer is perceived as a 'blue collar' working men's beer in the United States. In Europe, however, it has been positioned as a fun drink for young things about town and, therefore, it could seek to display parity and differentiation against a different set of competitors than in the USA. Similarly Guinness (a stout beer from Ireland) has been re-positioned over the years away from its old image as a drink for navvies and grannies into a universal drink that is sophisticated and fun.

Differentiation

Having established where the brand sits the next step is to build on these but to highlight the differences from the competition – which of course will (should) put your product in a much more favourable position than the rest: *'..not only does it do everything that brand X, Y, and Z do – but it also does this…'*

Digital radio is having a problem with acceptance in the UK. It is being marketed as a new way of receiving radio – but it is insufficiently different to make people go out and buy digital radios. Typically few people buy radios only – people now buy CD players combined with tape players and radio and few of these are digital, and they can see no reason to replace perfectly good CD players with a product that in their perception, at best, offers only a marginal benefit. Gradually of course, as audio products are altered to include digital radio reception, it will catch on – but this will take time.

Definition and Differentiation are part of the same continuum, as Figure 12.3 shows.

Figure 12.3: Brand definition versus differentiation

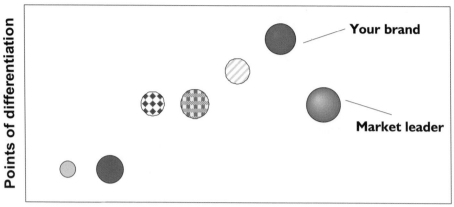

In this fictitious example your brand has been positioned against the market leader.

In terms of parity it shares many (but not all) points but has a few points of differentiation. A general idea of where to position your brand can also be gained from analysing the positions of the other competing offerings relative to the market leader (and of course your brand). In some cases the other products appear to have negative parity – this is because they share the bad features of the brand – and lack differentiation. Your brand has been positioned to share parity with all the others and be differentiated but also to be quite different from the market leader.

> Take the 'Virginone account'. It is a mortgage and current account combined. In this respect it shares all the general points of parity with both products – but by combining them it introduces a differentiation which is then used as a means of marketing it by majoring on the benefits (reduced interest payable on the mortgage by using the monies in a current account to set off against the mortgage). Of course the interest payable on a mortgage is generally greater than that received on current accounts – so the consumer is better off in the net interest payable position. For Virgin there is a trade-off between the float normally used by banks from current accounts foregone – and the opportunity to break into the mortgage market, linked to the funding issue.

The strongest points for differentiation are those that also coincide with the customer's goals – this is usually where the market leader has set its sights and why it enjoys that position.

Deepening

This is about making sure that your product meets those customer needs/wants by building on the competition-based positioning (points of parity) by using goal-based positioning. In this aspect the product features that are closely aligned with the customer's goals are emphasized. This process can be thought of a conceptual 'ladder' in which the concept is taken from:

- ◆ concrete points – 'this machine can photocopy 200 sheets a minute' – feature,
- ◆ through slightly more intangible issues such as – 'it will save you time' – benefit,
- ◆ to completely abstract ideas – 'you can therefore enjoy a better lifestyle as a result of buying our photocopier' – lifestyle or goal.

Figure 12.4: Positioning ladder

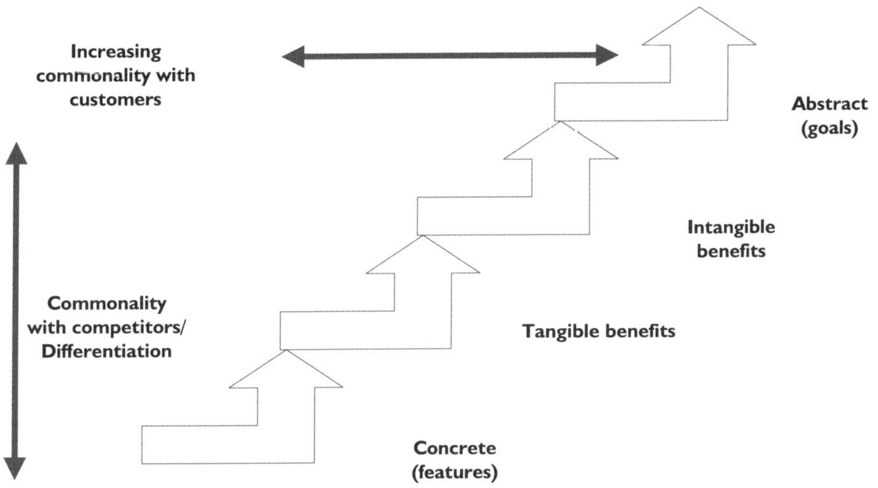

Eg the Coop bank states that ethics are important factors and its strap line is

'customer led, ethically guided'

It shares the other characteristics of banks, ie a safe place to put your money, with all the general products that a basic retail bank provides and that customers are important to it, but it is differentiating itself by aligning with those customers who feel that ethics are an important part of banking (eg not lending to arms producers nor investing in some types of research) and they want to be sure that their bank is ethical (however they define that). This is quite a focused differentiation and few other banks take this line – because it appeals only to that minority of customers who hold strong beliefs on the subject. It even says that if customers do not agree with its ethical stance it will show them the door!

One of the features of this is that products are lifted up the ladder from product features and benefits to customer goals. By looking at what customers want it is possible to start with those goals and then lead them down the ladder into your products because you have already established common ground and they are more likely to be well-disposed towards the products that have demonstrably fulfilled a goal of theirs.

It is important however to ensure that the goals are also those of the people that actually **buy** the product. Eg with children's foods – there are two aspects of selling children's goods. The adults – who pay and shop – often have views that are diametrically opposed to those of the ultimate end-consumers – children. Children tend to go for taste, not health, and in trying to meet adults' concerns about eg sugar or fat, you may alienate children and vice-versa. It is necessary then to try to hit both aspects in some way to ensure that each feels that the attributes of your product matches their goals (not too easy!). With some office technology for example – such as photocopiers or faxes – often secretaries use them but have little to do with the buying cycle; except to give feedback to management who might have bought on, say, price and features but the actually users require different functionality and benefits (low breakdown rate, fast throughput etc). Thus sales staff may focus on the wrong type of person and misunderstand the real goals.

Disciplined defence

Finally once you have achieved the position you need, strive to maintain it and if possible reinforce and augment it. Brands are ephemeral and positions can change rapidly if poor competitive and customer research is carried out. Both customers' tastes and thinking change, as can the competition, and they can both change rapidly. In some cases your product may be attacked by a revamped competitor product or in some cases eclipsed by a paradigm shift in the market. History is littered with products and brands that have disappeared – Betamax versus VHS – where the (perceived) better product disappeared – LPs and to a large extent cassettes eclipsed by CDs, and of course Ford – which had a dominant position in cars in the USA but by its refusal to allow extras that customers demanded (any colour as long as it's black) allowed others to break into the market and take market share.

One other thing that affects positioning is that, over time, differentiation points tend to become hygiene factors. For example in cars quality of performance (reliability) is now a given – it is very difficult to sell just on that aspect – except in some small segments (Rolls-Royce which is the eponymous term for quality) and other aspects need to be emphasized – although in many cases price is key. Mercedes used to sell on the cachet of quality – but now it is selling on the fact that it is good value and current radio adverts describe the surprise of customers in finding C-class Mercedes for less than £20,000 (in fact £19,995 – which is old-fashioned psychological pricing at a price point just under what is considered an important price threshold).

This does not mean changing a very good product too much in an attempt to respond to the wrong stimuli. As customers' perception changes it can be wrong to assume too much from press and media coverage. Although many people may be diet conscious and look for a drink that assists them, to change a product from its normal positioning where it has developed and built up considerable 'equity' can be a disaster. It can confuse consumers who do not understand the change and alienate those who do not want the change.

Coke

Coke – a company recognized for its marketing excellence and global success. It introduced a new formula coke to replace its previous flavour. It was a disaster and customers stopped buying it and switched to other brands. Sales plummeted and it was forced to bring the old coke product back. How much better it might have been to introduce a new coke in parallel – as it subsequently did with diet coke; caffeine-free coke, and diet caffeine-free coke. Thus consumers are not confused and those conscious of calories can buy the diet product if they wish. Those concerned by caffeine can buy the caffeine-free variety and usual product sales can be maintained. A further new product variant has recently been introduced – coke with lemon – again in parallel.

12.7 Brand extensions

This is where a brand has been developed to such an extent that the key features can be extended across one or more products or services that may in some cases be very different. EasyJet was started as a low-cost airline by Stelios Haji-Annou following in the footsteps of others such as South West Airlines in the USA and Ryanair in Ireland and the UK. Whereas Ryanair still just runs cheap flights, the 'Easy' concept has been extended across 'Easycomputers', 'Easycars' and more recently 'Easy everything'. The key concept is **value for money**, which is an easily transferable concept.

Why extend?

The major reason is that your marketing costs are reduced. You do not have to establish a new brand to sell a new product or service. You can piggyback on the existing goodwill of the market and provided it shares the same basic value will be accepted. Virgin has also extended its brand across from records to airlines, cola, weddings, trains, aeroplanes, cosmetics and spirits. Although they are not all owned by the same organizations they still use the basic idea of an irreverent, value-for-money, off-the-wall supplier. Many car manufacturers at the premium end of the market have extended the name to include consumables such as clothes, watches and so on.

The Co-operative movement long ago put this into place and covers shops, banking, funeral parlours, farms and many other areas based on the shared experience of all for the common good. Some concepts are much harder to extend – for example it would be very difficult to see Barclays extending its brand to chocolate or an oil company extending its brand into retail food – but not wholly impossible. Many garages now sell food and ancillary items on their premises. How long before we see the use of 'white label goods' branded as the oil company's own?

12.8   Brand geography

Branding can also be established at different geographical regions. Companies often have different names in different areas – often from historical associations, usually through acquisition.

The major geographical areas are:

- ◆ **Local** – where there can be differences in local culture or language – eg Belgium which is split, *inter alia*, into Wallonia and Flanders, the former French-speaking and the latter Flemish-speaking with different histories and cultures. Or the UK with four countries (England, Wales, Scotland, Northern Ireland). Some brands might be targeted at say Welsh or Scots whereas others are more pan-UK in approach).
- ◆ **Regional** – where there are shared characteristics, eg the USA which is a large market often split into several large regions with broadly similar characteristics – depending on the product.
- ◆ **National** – covers one whole country. Until fairly recently the chocolate bar called 'Snickers' was known in the UK as Marathon. The name was changed to bring it in line with the rest of the world. Aviva trades under different brands in many countries (NU, CU, NZI – see Aviva case study).
- ◆ **International** – this is where the brand is sold in different markets but with a local marketing mix – sort of federated national brands.
- ◆ **Transnational** (or multi-national) – where the brand has been developed but is tweaked for local consumption.

◆ **Global** – where the brand is truly global and is the same everywhere – eg McDonalds, Citigroup, Microsoft, Coke, BMW, Philips.

As a brand becomes increasingly global it is easier to conduct campaigns that have the same characteristics and therefore to achieve economies of scale in planning and execution.

12.9   Brand architecture

There are several levels at which brands can be set. These really vary the degree to which the brands share in the umbrella of the overarching name or brand. They range from:

◆ Product
◆ Line
◆ Range
◆ Parasol
◆ Co-brands
◆ Umbrella

Product – is where the product brand is highly unique and the corporate name plays no part. Eg 'Marmite' – the savoury spread which is a stand-alone product despite being owned by Unilever, Rolls-Royce recently acquired by BMW, or in financial services in Ireland Aviva trades as Hibernian Life and that is the local brand or C&G which is part of Lloyds TSB.

Line – where several products share the same brand but it is limited to minor variations, eg 'Fairy' which covers washing up liquid and washing powder etc, Coke with regular coke, diet coke, caffeine-free and caffeine-free diet coke or BMW with its 3, 5 and 7 series. It reinforces the brand's selling power.

Range – where there is a broader range of products in the line but within a similar area – eg Aviva plc uses Norwich Union (NU) in the UK covering common types of insurance.

Parasol brand (also known as endorsing brand) – where the service is loosely connected with the brand. The product is the dominant name and the brand is also attached, eg Kit-Kat is a strong brand but it also carries Nestlé on the wrapper (see Aviva case study below). Until recently the Midland Bank name was linked with HSBC, then it was dropped in favour of the global brand HSBC – c/f RBS/NatWest where the latter was acquired by the former a few years ago and shares identity. This is often a step between product brand and umbrella branding.

Until 2002 the Nottingham branch of the John Lewis Partnership traded under the name of 'Jessop and Son' (despite having been within the group since the 1960s) but associated with John Lewis through the brand name and the logo JLP. Then it changed its name to John Lewis, as did the Southampton branch (from Tyrell and Green) and others in accordance with its 'global ' branding policy.

Co-branding – is where the product is co-branded equally with the brand. Eg Cadbury's Dairy Milk or Nestlé's Milky Bar, Ford Escort and Ford Focus (but *not* Jaguar which is also owned by Ford). The product name focuses on a particular segment or market, the corporate brand supports the product and brings its attributes to the product.

Umbrella brands – where everything is sold under the one brand name – eg Phillips which sells shavers, TVs, DVD sets, CD players, and lamps all under the name Phillips. Also John Lewis and Marks and Spencer where all their own products are sold under their brand names of Jonelle and St Michael, respectively. Barclays also tends to use the global brand Barclaycard, Barclayloan etc.

Case study – Introduction to the Aviva brand[5]

Aviva plc is the new name for the former CGNU plc. The change represents part of the group's planned journey towards being recognized as a world-class financial services provider. From 1 July 2002, the Aviva brand brings together some 50 different trading names around the world and creates further opportunities for the group to harness the benefits of its size and international capabilities. Group chief executive Richard Harvey said: 'We are creating a new and powerful international financial services brand. The CGNU name was a pragmatic solution that was right for its time, but it was never part of our longer-term plans. The benefits of this change will be significant. We will be able to make more of our corporate brand, to the benefit of our trading businesses. We shall also be able to make more effective use of our marketing spend, particularly in advertising and sponsorship. The Aviva name tested positively in consumer research around the world, bringing with it associations of life, vitality and living well. This matches the aspirations we have for our customers.'

Other group brands

Most of the groups businesses will be re-branded Aviva in due course, from July 2002 onwards, however the group's strongest existing mass-market brands will remain, including:

Norwich Union in the UK; Delta Lloyd in the Netherlands; Hibernian in Ireland; Commercial Union in Poland; NZUI in New Zealand.

Such operations will benefit from their association with the group by carrying the endorsement 'an Aviva company' wherever appropriate. A number of specialist business names will also be kept, including: Morley fund management; Navigator in Australia; Pilot in Canada; Eurofil in France.

Essentially with the different types of branding there are trade-offs between service or product differentiation and shared identity and therefore economies of marketing scale, as shown in the table below:

Degree of focus on	PRODUCT	BRAND
By marketing as		
PRODUCT	H	L
LINE	H	M
RANGE	M	M
PARASOL	L	M
COBRANDING	M	H
UMBRELLA	L	H

And these can be graphed as well:

Figure 12.5: Product versus brand differentiation

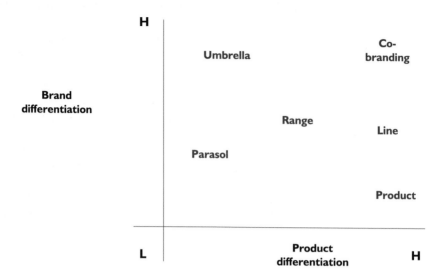

Different organizations use different brand architectures, depending on their strategy. As mentioned Aviva has changed its strategy to use the Aviva brand wherever possible but for the meantime has retained strong local brands. For this to be successful brands must have some added value over and above the service.

Thus adding the name 'Ford' to a make of car immediately lets people know that it is not just any car called 'focus' or 'escort' but is a Ford and therefore brings all the attributes of the brand name – reliability, service, smooth gearboxes etc., but because Jaguar is in a different class from run-of-the-mill cars – and is linked with sporty, high performance cars – Ford decided to leave it as a product brand. You can also use products to launch new offerings that may have risks attached to them that could damage the overall brand, and by keeping it separate you preserve that brand.

Summary

Brands are a very important factor in inducing customers to choose you over your competitor. They are intangible and must be 'nurtured' in order that they retain their value. They are built around a core, the style and the theme. In many organizations they are undervalued and poor attention is paid to them. Successful brands can be extended across very wide ranges of products and brands can be at product level, corporate level or a number of levels in between, including co-branding.

1 Reputation and brand are linked, but drive different things – profit and growth – they are also ephemeral and can disappear like frost on the morning sun if not nurtured and protected.

2 There are three parts to a brand – **the core** – which is the essence of the service; **the style** – how it is perceived; **the theme** of the brand – how it looks.

3 There are three steps involved in building a brand: **develop the service or product, develop the basic brand, develop an augmented brand**

4 There are generally considered to be three types of brands: **attribute, aspirational, experience.**

5 To be effective in positioning a brand you need to concentrate on the four Ds – **Definition, Differentiation, Deepening, Disciplined defence** – failure can result in **Decline.**

6 Products and services can be linked with corporate brands to give different types of brand architecture: **product, line, range, parasol, cobranded, umbrella**.

Select bibliography

Mastering Marketing: FT Section 4 – brand strategy

Principles of Marketing: Kotler

Value Based Marketing: Peter Doyle

Building Strong Brands: David Aaker – Free Press, N York (1996)

Notes

1 as quoted in Financial World, October 2002, p 51
2 *The Times*, Wednesday 13 November 2002 – Business section
3 after Jean-Noel Kapferer *Strategic Brand Management* (Kogan Page 1997)
4 Alice M Tybout and Brian Sterthal 'Connecting with consumers: the Four Ds of effective positioning' *Mastering Marketing*, FT/Prentice Hall 1999
5 from Aviva website

Thirteen

Buying decisions

Topics in this chapter

Wants and needs

Buying characteristics

Inertia versus conscious choice

Introduction to this chapter

This chapter looks at buying decisions. It explores what drives a decision (buying or other), what is involved in that decision and the factors that influence what people buy and how they buy.

13.1   Why understand the buying process?

This is important because each buying process is different depending on whom is involved. Individuals are driven to buy items by different reasons. Within corporates there will be defined processes, but nevertheless there will be variations depending on the precise needs and who is involved. It is therefore critical to understand the process involved as well as the individuals so as to:

- ◆ Ensure that you comply with the process
- ◆ Think through the needs of the buyer and what solutions are really required
- ◆ Understand the personality/ies involved

◆ Understand the consequences of their decision and how it will affect them and indeed you
◆ Focus your solution on the real needs.

There are two critical factors involved in any purchasing decision:

◆ the **involvement** of the individual and
◆ the degree of **assessment** required in the decision.

The interaction between these two affects the way that the decision is made and can be contrasted as shown in Figure 13.1 to give four archetypal decision types.

Involvement is the amount of time and effort required to take the decision, and also possibly the number of people involved. It is often high when:

◆ Money involved is high
◆ Risk is high
◆ Experience is low
◆ Issues are complex or difficult to quantify.

For example in a credit decision over lending for an oil refinery in the Caucasus, the amount is large, risk is high, this is new to the bank and there are complex political, environmental and economic issues. By contrast the decision to lend £10,000 to buy a car to a senior executive who has been a customer for years is simple.

Assessment is whether the decision is founded in *logic* or *emotion* (head or heart). Selection of a school for your children may be a mix of logic (is it a good school with the right academic record, is it convenient?) and emotion (one of the parents also went there and wishes to continue the tradition, you do not like the head teacher).

The four types of decision are:

Impulse	**Routine**
Emotional	**Rational**

Figure 13.1: Purchase types

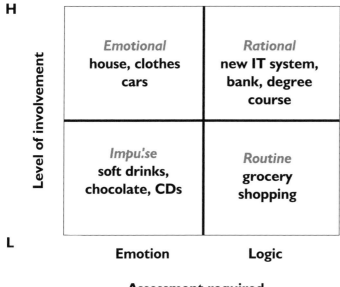

Impulse

An impulse decision is based in emotion and low on involvement – eg stop at a garage for petrol and buy chocolate and soft drinks – can also be what is called a stress purchase, one you undertake due to immediate circumstances – eg driving in the car with no music you stop and buy a CD – possibly one you might not normally have bought but you needed some music and it was the best available.

Routine

This type of purchase represents general purchases made regularly, almost on overdrive – eg weekly shop for groceries, stationery replacements, mundane insurance renewals, currency exchange before or after a holiday – with low involvement using logic.

Rational

This is where the involvement in the decision is high but it is logical rather than emotional (or should be!). Usually business decisions fall into this category – but being human beings, emotion often clouds judgement. Some domestic purchases such as houses probably fall into this category, because high logic is required, tinged with emotion

Emotional

In an emotional decision the degree of emotion is high but degree of assessment is low. Buying clothes or a car is emotional but does not require too much assessment. This is often closely linked to 'wants' rather than needs. I need clothes (to keep warm) but I want to look cool! – see below.

13.2   Wants and needs

This is really just an expression to help to define what the customer is looking for. Wants and needs are different, so for example, someone considering the purchase of a car might say:

'*I want a Jaguar*' (say as driven by James Bond in *Die Another Day*)

but will be thinking '*I need a car*'

The expressed **want** is aspirational – the driver dreams of a high-performance, classy car – in this case a Jaguar. However, because his real **need** is for transport and given that his wallet his probably limited he might have to settle for something more realistic (or use the tube or bus if that meets his need).

In the financial services arena a customer might say she **wants** a country mansion with 4 acres of paddock, but she **needs** a house (or somewhere to live). Similar constraints apply (to most of us anyway) and therefore she might settle for a small house in Wimbledon, a flat in Liverpool or a maisonette in Baseford, Nottinghamshire, within her mortgage-servicing capabilities near where she works.

Most personal and business requirements can be expressed in this way. People tend to think in terms of **wants**, but buy in terms of **needs**. The key to extremely successful selling, therefore, is to try to design your product or service to meet the need but to be aligned as close to the want as you can – and closer than the competition.

This difference between wants and needs is often called a perception gap, and aspects of it are familiar to everyone, both in business and personally.

Buying goods for subsequent despatch is a good example of this. Naturally enough you want it to arrive as soon as possible, maybe the next day. However most delivery services are normally priced relative to the expected delivery time, and so a next-day delivery might cost £30 whereas a three-day delivery will cost £15 (this is because the delivery company finds it cheaper to do it more slowly, because they have flexibility to take up slack time and can better maximize resources).

When you order the item your thinking will be influenced by how you are going to use the contents and the urgency or time horizon. If it is a spare part for a critical machine that is not working and that you need straight away then you will probably pay the high cost for next-day delivery. Your perception of the value of the delivery relative to price is high, and thus the extra cost is of no concern.

If, on the other hand, the contents are some books for a birthday present to be given next month, you will choose only to pay the lower delivery charge – perhaps even by the mail – which is considerably cheaper, if slower. Your perception of the value of the contents is now time-dependent. Thus although next day delivery of the books might be a thing that you might want, you do not actually need them for some time so they are not time-critical and you have a longer time horizon. You will, therefore, decide, and ultimately *pay*, according to your needs, not your wants!

13.3   The hierarchy of needs

Customers buy because they have (or believe that they have) a need for something. These needs lie at several levels and known as Maslow's 'Hierarchy of Needs' (hygiene, safety, social, esteem and self-actualization[1]). The need that drives them to buy something may be at a low level such as a 'hygiene' factor (food, shelter, heat etc) or something more esoteric – I need a holiday (esteem), or I want to buy a new DVD player (social/self-actualization). Recognition of this need drives them to action to meet the need.

Often wants are mixed up with needs:

◆ eg I **want** a Rolls Royce or a Ferrari or an Aston Martin
◆ but I really **need** a car
◆ or do I **need** some form of transport
◆ or do I really just **want** a status symbol for other people to see
◆ or am I so rich and bored that I don't know what I **need or want**?

They then enter into a process to meet this need. They will not of course follow this course of action consciously but more likely post-rationalize a decision or merely act on instinct (food) or even habit – there is no real need to eat at set times of the day – breakfast or lunch time – it is just a generally accepted thing.

The path is as follows (generic):

E   **existence** of a need (eg food) not recognized
R   **realization** that the need exists (he feels hungry)
A   understanding that something must be done about it **(action)**
S   information **search** (where can I buy/get food?)

E **evaluation** of the information (how far, how much, how expensive, type)
S **selection** of some food (and consumption) and thereby
ERASES the need.

Needs can be:

◆ immediate (eat now)
◆ repetitive (eat everyday)
◆ deferrable (change house)
◆ long term (buy house)
◆ cyclical (change car).

Sometimes things occur to change this perception of need:

◆ A woman gets married and takes out life insurance and mortgage protection
◆ A man gets divorced and cancels joint accounts
◆ A baby is born and the parents open a savings account
◆ A woman inherits a house and sells her own and liquidates the mortgage and the protection policy.

There are also several different types of purchase – notwithstanding the needs:

Brand new – no experience of the product or service, the customer will need a lot of data and you are trying to sell the product and establish a relationship at the same time. Eg an undergraduate opening an account for the first time or a young person thinking about taking out life cover (a very hard sell – known in the trade as 'immortals').

Replacement – routine, taking the same as before, eg re-booking your skiing chalet at the end of your skiing week, or rolling over an overdraft, or annual house/car insurance. (When engaging a decorator or builder it is common to obtain at least three quotes. Thereafter if service was good it is common to use the same one next time.)

Customer Service (next section) has a key role to play in ensuring that the rollover is as smooth as possible and this opportunity is not lost due a silly error, and to fight off potential competition. This stage or decision should also be exploited to facilitate product penetration by offering complementary or relevant products and services at the rollover.

Referral – where the customer has been recommended to you by an existing customer. You do not have a relationship but you must build on the existing relationship with the referee and take that into account – can be tricky sometimes, for example if the new customer does not fulfil criteria.

Substitution – where the customer is replacing the previous purchase but with a different offering. This is therefore a combination of brand new and replacement. You are trying to establish the relationship, but they have the experience of previous purchases (and if it is a similar replacement – presumably a bad service) or perhaps a change of circumstance (up-grade from a Fiesta to, say, a Mercedes E class).

Figure 13.2: Who really thinks about it?

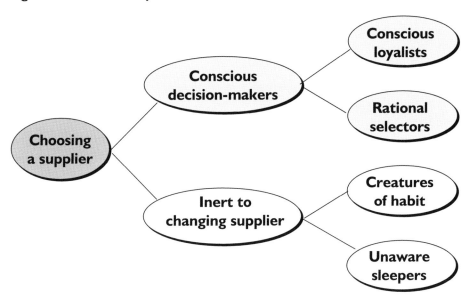

Decisions of course are not always taken in the right way or in the right frame of mind. Many are not thought about at all. Figure 13.2 considers someone thinking about changing a supplier. There are two basic premises – that they are consciously thinking about it or are not thinking about it at all. This leads to there being four states:

1 **Unaware sleepers** – who have no conscious input at all.
2 **Creatures of habit** – who think about it but prefer the known to the unknown. Much advertising is aimed at making people switch brands or suppliers because it is a well known fact that inertia is a powerful factor in your favour as a supplier. People do not change unless there is a stimulus for it, but once having changed they adopt the new supplier or way of doing things as a habit – especially where they cannot go back.
3 **Conscious loyalists** – those who think about decisions but consciously and deliberately decide to stay with the 'devil that they know'.
4 **Rational selectors** – people who will always take a rational view of what they are doing and will always open the field up to others – good for those struggling to gain a foothold in a company; less good for those established suppliers.

Clearly the best customer base consists of conscious loyalists and creatures of habit.

13.4   Buying behaviour

Customers typically take into account a wide variety of buying factors, including:

◆ specific product features and benefits
◆ support services provided, such as technical advice
◆ product/service availability
◆ company image
◆ delivery arrangements / packaging
◆ price per unit, total cost and 'value'…

….and different customer groups may have different needs and priorities. You must therefore understand the key factors for target segments and then optimize the Customer Value Proposition to maximize market share.

Figure 13.3: Customers buy for different reasons

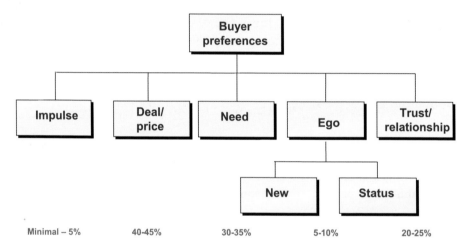

Typical Percentage in Each Category

The key question is 'What drives their preference?'

Customers buy for different reasons based on the drivers behind the decision. A purchase may be based on a combination of several drivers but analysis has shown that typically they fall into five broad categories:

◆ **Impulse** – where they are taken by the moment and suddenly buy something. Sometimes known as stress purchases. For example, you are travelling a long way in a car and you stop to buy food or a CD to play because you have forgotten your own. You will buy something that is there – even if it is not your best preference – you will choose the one that you consider you will have least cause to 'regret'.

◆ **Deal/price** – usually a commodity purchase where no extra value is perceived or where the purchaser likes the thrill of 'doing a deal' and demonstrating the bargain he drove based on his competence.
◆ **Need** – a major driver – see needs and wants.
◆ **Ego** – where the purchase will in his view give him credibility in his peer group or the world at large. Could be
  o **New products or services** – early adopters like to be seen with the latest gizmo or service to impress;
  o **Status** – by buying something they believe that they will receive referent charisma from owning the service or product.
◆ **Trust/relationship** – where they buy based on the trust that they have in the vendor.

Each purchase will be made up of a combination of these five areas but the emphasis will be different for each person and may exclude one or more areas (preference 0%). Understanding these drivers is crucial to selling to customers. A good understanding of your customer base provides the understanding of these drivers and enables you to sell the right products to customers by meeting these drivers and demonstrating the benefits in your customers' terms of perception.

13.5 Customer input to the purchase

This varies from decision to decision. Some purchasing decisions are very easy (buy a sandwich) and, although they involve choice, represent a very low 'risk' and will yield insignificant 'regret' if the decision goes wrong. Most purchases are of commodities (by volume not necessarily by value) such as bread, milk, petrol, etc. Little heed is paid to the brand in most circumstances and it is the price/convenience trade-off that is the primary factor. Look at the success of 'white branded goods' in supermarkets.

As a result therefore customers put little, or no, effort into these purchases; and have little or no compunction in changing should circumstances demand or facilitate it and it suits them. For example most people fill up with petrol when their petrol tanks are nearly empty and accordingly use the nearest petrol outlet – or when it is convenient – say at a visit to a supermarket or a motorway restaurant – and could not probably tell you which brand of petrol they purchased even if you asked them immediately afterwards. Brand therefore plays little or no part in the purchasing decision.

Where their need is a major one (car or house purchase) or is perceived to be important – clothes and goods that reflect style – the customer is more likely to devote a great deal of effort into the purchase. This is particularly so where goods have a high degree of 'visibility' (cars, clothes, music, furniture and may include other items such as credit cards or cheque accounts).

This reflects the **risk/regret** trade-off. What is the **risk** to me of doing this – in terms of price, people's views of me; and what will my level of **regret** be if I do not make the purchase – if I do not buy a house I have to pay rent which I might regard as dead money; whereas if I buy a house I have to service the mortgage and everything else that comes with it and represents a higher risk to me, but I obtain (*ceteris paribus*) capital appreciation and I might regret the lack of that benefit if I rented. Equally if I fail to insure my home against risks (fire, subsidence, flood, theft etc) and something happens I will be hit badly potentially and therefore will regret it very much.

These types of purchases have a high degree of effort and input/involvement from customers and are therefore important in the context of sales. By exercising good management when there is high input from the customers you can considerably influence decisions and also increase customer loyalty because you are seen to be helping them with a difficult or risky decision and they will appreciate it, and will have confidence in future subsequent transactions within the relationship. Conversely poor management here will conceivably turn them off you for life.

Factors influencing buying

In general there are four main categories of items that affect how people buy. They are:

- ◆ Their role
- ◆ Their background
- ◆ Their experience
- ◆ The information available to them.

Role

This depends on whether they are buying something personally in which case they will usually take on many of the roles, or whether they are part of a corporate buying process in which case they may be one or more of:

- ◆ influencer
- ◆ decision-maker
- ◆ economic buyer
- ◆ user.

It is necessary to understand which role they are 'playing' and tailor your sales pitch accordingly. Depending on the circumstances one person may play all parts, or many others can be involved (committees, sign-offs etc).

- An **influencer** is a person who has no direct involvement in the decision but may be able to influence the decision due to their position within the company or because of their experience.
- The **decision-maker** is the person who actually makes the decision to buy, but may not have the economic power and requires a sign-off.
- The **economic buyer** is the person who signs off on the payment for the purchase. She may not be involved in the decision at all but may merely exercise an 'audit' of the amount or supplier to ensure good value and/or proper procedural context. Typically they are a higher authority with the budget or more commonly a finance person.
- The **user** is the actual person who will be using the purchase. This person may have nothing whatsoever to do with the decision, or can be an influencer.

Background

They will be affected by their:

- Age
- Demography
- Culture
- Education
- And in a corporate – their position (or perceived position) within the hierarchy.

You must understand these in order to play to your strengths and make sure that your arguments do not offend either their sensibility or intelligence.

Experience

Is their experience of this purchase (and for a corporate the experience may be different from that of the individual):

- New and therefore risky
- Re-purchase
- Routine.

Depending on this they will have a higher degree of assessment to go through and may take longer or be less likely to buy.

Information

The degree of information will influence a decision to buy. Is their experience from:

- Having bought this service or a similar one before and therefore know about it;
- Have they obtained information from the market in which case has it been 'filtered';

◆ Have they received it from a third-party source which may be biased (for or against).

Summary

People and corporations buy for different reasons. Some are impulse buys, and some represent huge decisions by customers. Your response to these must be measured and accordingly the real reasons driving the needs must be understood.

1 Customers buy because they have (or believe that they have) a need for something. Recognition of this need drives them to action to meet the need.
2 The path to meeting this need is as follows (generic):
   E existence of a need (eg food) not recognized
   R realization that the need exists (he feels hungry)
   A understanding that something must be done about it **(action)**
   S information **search** (where can I buy/get food?)
   E evaluation of the information (how far, how much, how expensive, type)
   S selection of some food (and consumption) and thereby
   ERASES the need.
3 The key to extremely successful selling, therefore, is to try to design your product or service to meet the need but to be aligned as close to the want as you can – and closer than the competition.
4 There are two critical factors involved in any purchasing decision – the **involvement** of the individual and the degree of **assessment** required in the decision.

Select bibliography

Loyalty Rules: F Reichheld

Principles of Marketing: Kotler

Value Based Marketing: Peter Doyle

Notes

1 **Abraham Maslow**: *Motivation and Personality* (Harper & Row 1970)

Fourteen

Pricing and campaign management

Topics in this chapter

Types of pricing, discounts

Campaign management

Introduction to this chapter

A business is about exchanging your products or services for money – ie charging a price – and you need to sell them at a price that not only covers all your costs but also allows you to make a profit for distribution to shareholders. The price you set reflects this directly. In a simple example if you buy an apple for £1.00 and sell it for £1.05 to a friend you have made a 'profit' of £0.05p (not much). Of course this transaction ignores any monies you might have spent in getting the apple (eg bus fare to the shops) and in selling it (tube fare to your friend's house) and for a large organization this is much more complex, especially when you add in other items such as the cost of capital etc.

Profit therefore is your revenue (what you receive) less your total costs. The price you charge affects this enormously. If the apple had been sold for £1.00 it would have yielded no profit at all and if there was a glut of apples (say in September) then you might have been forced to reduce your price to £0.95 and then you would have incurred a loss of £0.05p.

Price in general has a major effect on the volume of what you sell. Not many tins of baked beans sell for £5.00 and even if they were very scarce they would not bear such a price because there are many substitutes, but at the price of around £0.15 they sell millions. A burger costs around £1.99 in the UK with fries and a coke, and few might think that you could charge much more than that even in a restaurant but the price expectations can be shifted depending on the circumstances. (See case study – When is a burger not a burger?)

Case study – When is a burger not a burger – and how much would you pay for it?[1]

New York bitten by king-priced burger

It comes sizzling from the grill, a 20oz oval of finely ground beef slightly larger than a CD, perched on half a soft wheat bun, topped with slices of grilled mushrooms. This burger of prime kobe beef requires no chewing. The barely cooked meat melts in the mouth as the palate savours the exquisite flavours. This is the burger that all Manhattan is talking about. At US$41 – about £26 – it is the most expensive burger in the city, quite possibly in the world, but since the Old Homestead restaurant in Chelsea first put it on the menu last Friday (10-01-03) it has been unable to keep up with demand. 'We ran out of ingredients the last three nights' Edward Gozdz, the executive chef who invented the ultimate gourmet burger said. 'I expected to sell 10 to 15 a night; we've been selling 60 to 70.' The morning that the burger went on sale a securities firm ordered 200 to be delivered. Yesterday two men arrived at 11.30 am, even though the restaurant does not open until noon. 'We don't need a menu' Gary Ciline, a car parts salesman from Long island told the waiter 'we want two of those kobe burgers.' Until Friday Mr Gozdz had kept burgers off the menu because 'this is an up-market restaurant' but this particular burger was different. The ingredients are a secret. 'It has a very high fat content' Mr Gozdz explained. 'The Japanese take a bovine cow, feed it beer to make it hungry and then stuff it with the best grain. Then it is massaged. Eventually it reaches about 1,600 lb, about 2½ times the weight of a regular cow. The secret is the marbling of the fat caused by the ancient art of kobe.' The US$ 41 price tag, excluding New York tax of 8.25% and the 20% service charge, is no deterrent, even though chains such as McDonald's sell burgers for 99 cents, complete with chips and a soft drink. 'We're talking about the best burgers in the city,' Mr Ciline, a customer said. 'You pay US$72 for a baseball ticket that five years ago cost US$27, so for 20oz of beef US$41 is good value.' McDonald's burgers do not come with miniature salad greens, garlic shoestring French fries and three small pots of relish: chipolte tomato ketchup, spiced with coriander and scallions, creamy horseradish aioli, and stonegrain mustard.

Price is very visible and can give a powerful sign of quality and value. As such it can affect and, if used positively, reinforce your image. Paradoxically in financial services customers for borrowing and similar facilities who are at the lower end of the scale pay more because of the higher credit risk which demands a premium, whereas those at the very top of the credit spectrum attract the finest interest rates.

There are different perceptions of price:

◆ To the seller it represents the revenue that can be generated from its sale – whereas to the purchaser it represents the value that the offering represents to them.

◆ For the seller it represents a reflection of the input required to generate the offering – to the purchaser it is the cost of that offering.

◆ Price represents the positioning in the market – to the purchaser it reflects the quality of the offering – a quality for which he is prepared to pay, thus equalizing the customer value price/benefit trade-off.

For the seller the price should cover the 'manufacture', distribution and marketing costs associated with the offering. It is not possible in the long run to continue to deliver the offering to the market at below this cost, unless it is always going to be subsidised by other products. While of course this is very much easier in manufacturing, it is often much harder in services and in particular financial services due to items such as shared facilities, multi-distribution channels, and shared costs with an inaccurate knowledge of how they should be attributed to products and where real revenue-generation takes place.

It is often said that price is flexible and can be 'flexed' for competition purposes etc – with financial services in many cases this is not, or less so – eg in the UK the Bank of England sets general interest rates and a wide deviation from those general levels soon causes economic disequilibrium in the balance sheets of banks. For example on 16 January 2003 every bank base lending rate, as quoted in the FT, was 4% – there were no variations whatsoever.

14.1   Factors affecting pricing

There are five main factors that affect how you price (see earlier chapter for factors affecting the market):

◆ The **price range** for the offering – ie many offerings sit within a price band and if the price is outside of that there will be no take-up. Currently mortgages are around 5% – and there would be no take up at levels of 12% – although this was not an uncommon price a few years ago – but the price band has shifted downwards as interest rates have fallen.

◆ **Segmental differences** – premium customers are not charged the same for services as ordinary customers (even if there is little discernible difference between the two).

Figure 14.1: Pricing layers – four Ps

Prestige/snob	**Highest level – feelings of exclusivity are paramount – Aston Martin, Rolls-Royce, Coutts, Black Amex, First class airfares**
Premium	**High level – based on strong brand – inelasticity of demand – Mercedes, Drummonds, Gold Amex, Club class fares**
Parity	**Ordinary level – no significant advantage – most banks, most credit cards, most cars, Economy class fares**
Pare away/discount	**Sub-optimal – weak players, 'give-aways' to break into markets, bottom level – eg Providian, loss leaders, poor image in market (Skoda)**

- ◆ The **strength and position of your offering** in the market – a premium will be paid by customers if it is in line with their expectations of price versus quality, eg ordinary, business and first class on an aeroplane or train, or different seats in a theatre, and if your offering reflects this extra quality then you should be able to charge a premium.
- ◆ The **costs to deliver** – you must cover and exceed your costs to make money (this includes direct and indirect costs as well as in financial services, items such as credit and other types of risk that demand a premium to reflect possible losses).
- ◆ The need for **flexibility on pricing** – is your market one where discounts may be a common feature, or where fees are commonly flexed by competitors (eg paying surveyor's or valuation fees in the mortgage market).

The mix of these factors will greatly influence how you price your offerings and of course you need to keep up with local market changes to which you might need to respond.

14.2 Pricing approaches

There are two basic approaches to pricing:

- ◆ Market-based pricing
- ◆ Cost-plus pricing

Their specific use, however, depends to a large extent on the market and products you are selling as well as the extent of information you have on your own business and your competition. It also depends very much on the characteristics of your customers, their wants and needs and their history, and finally, of course, your marketing strategy. Within these two main categories there are many variations of pricing techniques.

Types of market-based pricing

There are many tactics and techniques used in pricing, including:

Basic techniques:	going rate, perception, lump-sum and piece-rate pricing psychological, contingent, line, geographic
Specific objective:	loss leader, slot/gap, impact assessment, skimming, penetration, premium
Other:	Trade pricing, intermediary, dual or multiple, tendering, sealed bid, auctions

Some of these are explored in further detail below.

◆ **Going-rate pricing** – This name is given to the technique whereby an organization simply looks at competitors' prices and prices its own products slightly under or above the other prices to achieve a specific market objective (eg share, distortion of supply channels etc.). This technique is often adopted by smaller firms, those that have difficulty in measuring cost inputs or those in commodity or mature markets and could be argued that it is also used by banks in setting base rates etc. It assumes a kind of perfect competition (ie that there are no distortions, for example caused by loss-leader pricing) in each area and it further assumes that competitors know what they are doing. In essence, all the organization does is to look at the price everyone else charges and then simply adds or subtracts a very small amount. This differential against the reference price is then maintained.

◆ **Perception pricing** – this term describes a particular form of market-based pricing. This one is based entirely on the consumer's value of the goods on offer rather than on specific market conditions. The determination of a customer's perception is a difficult area to explore but is the foundation of premium pricing. Perception pricing tends to involve three main areas:

◆ where the customer is offered 'more for more'

◆ where the customer is offered 'more for less'

◆ where the customer is offered 'less for less'.

The customer perception is measured by using sophisticated market research and psychological techniques (for example a process known as conjoint analysis qv is often used).

◆ **Psychological pricing** – This could be described as a trick rather than a technique. It works by pricing products just slightly below a round number (eg one pence or five pence less than £20, being £19.99 or £19.95 instead of £20).

Extensive research has been done in recent years on consumers' perceptions of price points. Price points are the technical name given to the point where a product goes from being perceived as cheap to very cheap, or expensive to too dear to buy (ie outside their range of acceptable prices). Of course individuals vary in their perceptions, but understanding the price points in your market can pay huge dividends.

◆ **Contingent pricing** – This technique relates the price of the goods or services to the eventual outcome of the use to which they are being put. Readers might be familiar with its use in the football world. For example Arsenal might sell its centre forward to FC Milan. Milan might pay 1 million euro up front, and then pay a further 100,000 euro for each game the centre forward plays that season, and maybe 100,000 euro for each goal he scores. The overall price paid is thus contingent on the performance of the centre forward. These types of contract can be constructed in virtually any way, and can even be 'negatively contingent', ie the buyer will receive a refund from the seller in the event of non-performance.

Road repair in the UK has operated on a mixed type of contract for some time (called lane rental). In this the repairer quotes a price to repair (say) a mile of motorway. The repairer also agrees to 'rent' the motorway from the Transport Department for a fixed fee, per day. If the repairs are finished early, the repairer does not have to pay all of the rent and so receives a windfall bonus. If the repairer is slow or inefficient it ends up paying extra rent it had not bargained for. When a company is looking to buy another company it often employs the services of a firm of accountants or consultants as advisers. Because the takeover may or may not succeed it may wish to pay the adviser only a small percentage of the normal daily rates of its staff, but link this with a large success fee if the deal goes ahead. This is sometimes called contingent pricing, because the final payment is contingent on the deal going ahead.

For this to work the adviser has to have an idea how likely the deal is to go through. If the deal does not go ahead the adviser may well receive its costs back but make no profit, but if it does go ahead a very large payment is paid. Taken to its logical extreme the contingent fee can amount to 100% of the fee. Thus if there is no deal then no money is paid. If the deal does go through a very large fee may be paid. Intermediaries who act in this way are often called brokers.

◆ **Premium pricing** – This describes where the price of a product is set either slightly (or in some cases massively) above the 'real' or competitive price of the product or service. Typically premium pricing is used in conjunction with heavy advertising or branding where this promotes the ideas of quality, restricted appeal, 'snob' value, shortage of supply or the perception that the product is delivering more than it actually does. Premium pricing is very common in both the professional service sector (particularly financial markets) and in the so-called branded or quality goods markets. Premium pricing, if used carefully, can give a customer a very good feeling about the exclusiveness and value for money of a product or service and should be used where it can be justified.

14.3 Overt versus covert pricing

For many goods the price you pay is the price quoted, that is an overt cost – for example a gallon of petrol will cost you £x.yy. Equally, however, for many this is not the case because there may be hidden costs as well – eg so-called 'free banking' on current accounts – where of course there is no such thing as a free lunch. The customer pays for it through a variety of mechanisms such as minimum balances or very low interest rates, and there is an expectation that it will be cross-subsidized through the customers' take-up of other offerings – and indeed that is the main point of sales staff – to ensure that product penetration is as high as possible. This can be contrasted with the 'loss-leaders' that supermarkets often display to lure customers in to buy a cheap product and then purchase others as well.

One of the issues with the cross-subsidising concept is that it works only in a 'self-contained' world. You may have a customer that has free banking and a credit card as well as a loan. The loan and credit card will accordingly be priced above the market to recoup the losses on current accounts. Given the propensity for customers to 'shop around' and the increasing ease with which they can do this, it is now likely that they will take the loan or credit card from another supplier – where it is perhaps the loss leader and therefore the cross-subsidization relationship breaks down. Equally they may just point to the price differential and expect you to provide the product at a comparable price, thus having the same effect.

This type of covert pricing is also interest-rate sensitive. The value received and foregone (depending on which side of the equation you sit) changes as interest rates fluctuate. As interest rates fall the float benefit to the bank decreases, but the operating costs of the account remain the same, increasing the losses. Conversely as interest rates rise, so the interest foregone by the customer increases, operating costs remain constant and therefore the revenue accruing to the bank increases.

In some cases the free banking involves a flat-rate fee – which is charged regardless of the operating of the account. This is an attempt to recoup part of the costs. Customers are being given a fixed cost so that there are no surprises for them and because it contributes to the bank's operating costs it is a win:win. The key issue for the bank is estimating the potential use of the account. Therein lies the key.

14.4 Types of pricing used in financial services

- ◆ tiered pricing – mortgages/deposit accounts
- ◆ two-part pricing – credit cards (fixed fee plus interest or transfer balance and subsequent spending)
- ◆ bundled pricing – of products (saving and protection)
- ◆ captive pricing – eg must take in-house insurance product with other offering (where allowed by regulation)

- pricing of options – eg withdrawals penalty, minimum balances, notice periods
- product range pricing – eg mortgages of different sorts
- tailored pricing – related to value of business
- time pricing – to reflect balance sheet maturity needs – longer time horizons usually attract better rates
- transaction pricing – by the number of times a given activity takes place.

Internal information

To price confidently and accurately the key requirement is information. The less accurate your information, the less likely you will be to maximize your pricing return.

A summary of the main information requirements is set out below:

- **Cost Information** – Managers must know, for each item, the fixed and variable element of cost that each item picks up. In financial services this is usually the cost of money plus attributable overheads – and may include a charge for capital.
- **Demand/Price Relationships** – These are very difficult to determine in practice, but at the very least, the introduction of any new item or product to the range must be supported by a business case that shows projected volumes and target pricing to ensure that the economics of introduction are agreed and understood. These business cases should always be reviewed for accuracy at a later date.
- **Financial Modelling** – The business should be capable of being modelled to the extent that the components are shown at a level whereby business decisions can be taken. Thus models that show overall revenue etc. are not useful for day-to-day management because the detail cannot be seen. All data used in modelling should be capable of being viewed from either a customer or product view, or both. The pricing manager should have, at the very least, a spreadsheet model that shows the projected relationship between price and sales, and the likely return. This should always be checked and modified in the light of actual events.
- **Management Information** – Managers should be able to request (and regularly receive) information on any product, customer or combination that shows revenues, margins and costs at an individual level.
- **Strategic (rather than Tactical) View** – It is necessary to provide tailored information so that senior managers are able to take a strategic view of the situation and the use of price to alter outcomes. This includes an ability to override the internal systems in extreme cases and the authority to arbitrate between business units where there appears to be a conflict. For managers who are busy with operational issues, strategy development can be a problem because it involves a taking a long-term view that can conflict with shorter-term business demands (eg the sales force might be wanting to sell a large amount of product before the year end).

Case study

In 1994, Virgin launched a new type of PEP (Personal Equity Plan). This was sold direct to the public (and managed on Virgin's behalf by another company). The product was sold as being free of the large management charges that often accrue with traditional PEPs and became very popular in a short time, even to the extent that more traditional operators followed the same pricing strategy. The PEP was in fact a simple instrument that basically follows the market, and thus was free of management charges, because the management requirement was small.

It was clearly a mixture of strong branding (the Virgin name) and innovative pricing that allowed the success of this new venture. The moral here is that just because something has always been done one way, do not assume that it cannot be done differently. Innovative pricing can be a key to huge success, and remember also that innovative does not necessarily mean cheaper: it means different!

14.5 Price competition

Price cutting or price competition is very easy to employ as a marketing weapon, but for precisely that reason it is also the easiest to respond to. In general you should not enter into a price cutting 'war' unless you can sustain the long campaign, have a sustainable advantage or are prepared to take the hits for a different purpose – eg gain market share, dispose of stock, or because you need the cash urgently. The most likely outcome of price competition generally is a downward vicious spiral in price and therefore profit.

Case study

Marlboro is a major cigarette producer in the USA and had traditionally always sold on the cachet of better quality and therefore the cigarettes were higher priced. On the back of this they sold a lot of associated merchandise (clothing etc) and it had a very good stock price reflecting the premium cashflows thereby generated. A competitor aggressively attacked the market, offering cheap cigarettes and started to hurt Marlboro's share. The response by Marlboro was to reduce prices – a staggering response for a premium product and something that the board had always stated they would never do. As a result the perception changed into 'just another cigarette' and without the cachet price became a driving factor – customers accordingly switched to other brands. The result – on what has become known as Marlboro Monday – was a dramatic fall in the stock price and an alteration in perception of the brand overnight. It took a long and difficult campaign to re-establish itself as a premium brand.

This response by Marlboro was taken with inadequate regard for the consequences of damaging customers' perception of the brand by cutting prices in response to a very real threat that was viewed only in short-term price terms and, therefore, with a serious misunderstanding of the terms on which the Customer Value Proposition had been formulated. In this case it was predicated on the **Product/ Customers needs and wants**, ie a quality prestige product rather than the **Price/ Cost** and, accordingly, the poor judgement had dire results as customers and the market reacted adversely to the price cut.

Contrast that approach to the response to a similar threat to competition by Heublein:

Case study

Smirnoff was the leading brand of vodka in the USA. A competitor of Heublein, which makes Smirnoff, attacked this position by selling a vodka at a lower price while claiming it was the same quality. This started to hurt Heublein's share and the management had to respond to this threat.

The response was very considered and contained several elements that demonstrated a good understanding of branding and buying perceptions. It would have been easy to match the reduced price but that would have resulted in reduced profits and probably a price war, as well as destroying the perception of Smirnoff as a premium brand (*vide* Marlboro). Instead the company *increased* the price of Smirnoff and introduced another brand – Relska – to compete with the competitor's new brand.

They further compounded the defensive response by introducing a *third* brand – Popov – priced lower than Relska to sweep up those that bought on price. The result confirmed Smirnoff as the premium brand and the competitor came to be regarded as just another vodka. Profits increased handsomely. All three brands are of course virtually indistinguishable in taste and also in manufacturing costs – but customer perception when purchasing is all.

It is fair to say that in the last few years there has been an increasing trend to commoditization of financial services and, when coupled with greater price transparency, as a result a greater focus on price competition. This has placed a premium on cost control and contributed to the move to remote banking and insurance. Customers are now encouraged to move their transactions to these types of operations because costs are very much lower and therefore prices can be matched or in many cases reduced. This still leaves the question of what to do with the costs of the old infrastructure – but progressively these will become redundant and continue to be sold, altered or used for other purposes.

14.6   Campaign management

Introduction

This section looks at campaign management - that is how to manage a campaign or part of one, depending on your circumstances. It is unlikely that anyone outside a marketing department will be heavily involved in planning a major national campaign. It is more feasible for staff to be involved in the execution of aspects of campaigns or to give advice and opinions, and also to be charged with local campaigns, therefore, an understanding of the logic of campaign is indispensable.

Definition

A campaign can be said to be a series of coordinated actions or activities intended to reach the same goal or objective. Chambers dictionary gives the following definition: *'an organized series of operations in the advocacy of some cause or object'*. Note the use of organized or coordinated – to imply that it is thought through, planned and has definite ends.

In military terms it might refer to a number of battles or movements to gain a specific objective – eg in the invasion of Iraq by coalition forces where the main objective was to force regime change. The campaign consisted of a series of movements of troops and heavy armour to take major towns and items of strategic importance, such as ports and aircraft landing strips. This was supported by 'special forces' operations and bombing and artillery salvos to destroy troops.

In business it is usually linked to either marketing - ie promoting awareness of products and finding out wants or selling – actual product penetration to customers.

The diagram below shows the major steps involved in a campaign:

- ◆ agree objectives
- ◆ agree success measures based on objectives
- ◆ decide type of campaign

- ◆ develop the components of the campaign
- ◆ plan the campaign
- ◆ execute the campaign
- ◆ obtain the results
- ◆ compare with the success measures
- ◆ deliver a verdict
- ◆ give feedback and re-visit objectives as appropriate

These aspects will be explored step by step.

14.2: Campaign management – flowchart

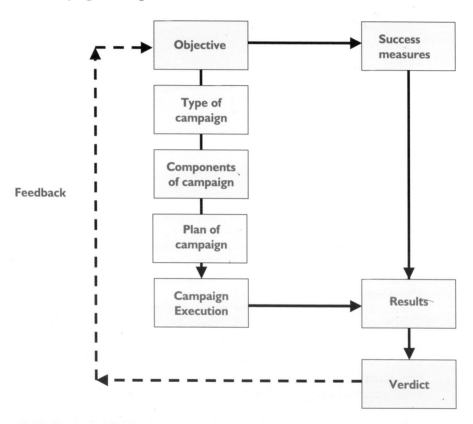

Why have a campaign?

The reason for having a campaign is to meet an objective. The diagram above shows the steps in a campaign, the first of which in planning a campaign is to agree what the objective is. This might be a specific objective or a more general objective, which may in turn have several supporting objectives.

Objectives

There are several different types of objectives including:

- ◆ Increasing awareness
  - Branding
  - Services range
  - Aspects of services (opening hours, cessation of branch closures etc)
- ◆ To inform them about something
  - change to status quo
  - anniversary of product
  - new product/service
  - new branches/partnership etc
- ◆ To sell something
  - products
  - services
  - ideas
  - third party services
- ◆ To find out about something
  - customer needs
  - financial state
  - preferences - market research
- ◆ To get them to contact you
  - to encourage them to visit a branch
  - to make them call you
  - by filling in a form or request for information
- ◆ As a base for a follow up calls – (very effective if properly executed)

For a sales campaign it is likely that you will need to set an overarching objective and then support it with subsidiary objectives to give better shape to the campaign. For example an organization might wish to increase its market share by x%. That is a general objective and whilst it will provide an overall framework for activity it is far too imprecise to serve as a guide for specific activities. This objective needs to be broken down into a set of more specific, concrete and understandable objectives relating to specific components of the market such as:

- ◆ To improve our product penetration to the point where each client has at least four products on average, eg
  - To increase our cross-sales of mortgages to current account holders by 25%
  - To increase our sales of life assurance to all customers such that at least 35% of our customers have a policy with us
- ◆ To reduce customer defections by 15%
- ◆ etc

Having agreed the objective(s) you are then in a position to agree the success measures.

Success measures

In order to be able to analyse the effectiveness of your campaign, you need to decide on measures for success right at the outset. These must be based on the objectives and also based on reality! It is obvious that you are only successful if you attain your objective – but you need to know exactly when you have got there – or at least how far along you did get. Success measures need to be specific and realistic. A stretch target is ok but a totally unrealistic target and measure is no good – you won't get there, everyone will be disheartened and you will have compromised your credibility with the stakeholders. The campaign may have low, medium and high targets and the measures and the data collected will enable you to see how well you did.

It is also a fact that people respond to the stimuli that you give them. If you set a target, and their own personal success is based on that target, then they will try to hit those measures. It is vital therefore that the measures chosen reflect the objective that you want to achieve. It is no good setting a target that examines how many calls made (although that may be a part of a measure), all people will do is make lots of calls and they are unlikely to be effective. You need to look at the success in converting those calls into products and services actually taken up.

Type of campaign

The type of campaign will range from those at the national (or international level), through regional and local, down to branch levels and will be shaped by the objectives.

National

These types of campaigns are usually run to meet specific corporate objectives as designated in the corporate plan and the supporting marketing plans. They are typically:

◆ Large in scope
◆ Benefit from economies of scale
◆ Give a consistent national message which can be supported locally and in branches
◆ Can use a wide range of media
◆ Are expensive!
◆ Need careful managing otherwise they can become expenditure with little or no returns
◆ Difficult to assess in terms of effectiveness
◆ Can get lost in the 'clutter' of every day media saturation as they are often impersonal.

Local

These campaigns by contrast can be more targeted on a selection of branches locally and typically:

◆ Focus on selected locations
◆ Can be pilot campaigns to test the water before committing to a national campaign
◆ Can be more tailored (eg run in Welsh in Wales)
◆ Use different media (local press and radio rather than national TV, press and radio)
◆ Have a different 'feel' to them as they are more 'personal' to an area
◆ Do not blanket areas where you may not wish to do business (eg for many regional building societies where they simply do not carry out business outside their designated area, national campaigns are a waste of time and money)
◆ Can be cheaper.

Regional

A regional campaign will be a hybrid between the two but might be, for example, focused on Yorkshire, Wales, Scotland or Northern Ireland, and be tailored so as to be sympathetic to regional usage, customs etc.

Branch

Lowest level of campaign – conducted wholly by the staff – with maybe some outside support and focused very much on the branch needs. Might be as part of a larger campaign but still tight in area of operations. Very tailored and focused and typically:

◆ Will involve local deals reflecting special situations (eg large factory closes and sympathetic branch banking is needed; south coast branch may focus on retired people as they may make the typical profile locally)
◆ Low cost – involving low tech media such as posters, leaflets and possibly telephone calls
◆ Can involve more 'physical' events – such as evening seminars, 'coffee mornings' etc
◆ May be a little amateur if staff have little experience of running them
◆ Should be highly personal as many customers will be known to staff.

For example a bank may decide that it wants to run:

◆ a general awareness campaign at UK national level
◆ a focused financial advice campaign for the Midlands, where it is undersold compared to its national average
◆ a mortgage campaign locally in South Nottinghamshire where penetration is particularly low

◆ a highly focused branch-based campaign in West Bridgford, Notts which is a new branch and trying to build up a mortgage base

and would plan accordingly, at the different levels.

Components of a campaign

The mechanisms used to support the campaign will be driven by the type of campaign being run. Items that are relevant here include:

◆ **Duration** - How long will it last? When will it start and end – any special considerations – holidays, religious events? Any other major campaigns that clash? Is it to be one 'hit' or several over an extended period? etc.

◆ **Budget** – How much do we have to spend, or alternatively how much will it cost to run the campaign? Can we afford it or do we need to trim the scope? What proportion should we spend on which type of media? What resources do we need? Do we have them internally or do we need assistance?

◆ **Audience** – On whom are we focussing – everyone, specific segments, localities? existing customers? new ones?

◆ **Products** – Which ones are we going to emphasize? Are they tailored to the segments we have chosen? Is price a factor or service?

◆ **Media** – There are many different media that can be used from TV and radio through telephone, local press and leaflets, branch posters. The table below shows where they might be most effective.

	National	Regional	Local	Branch
National TV/Radio	H	M	M	L
Regional TV/Radio	L	H	H	M
Local press	L	H	H	H
Telephone	L	L	H	H
Mailshots	L	L	H	H
Posters	L	L	L	H
Leaflets	L	M	H	H
One on ones	L	L	L	H
Physical get-togethers	L	L	M	H

Plan the campaign

This is about agreeing the components and then refining them in light of what is practicable and then linking all the aspects together to form a plan to be implemented.

This will typically be in the form of a Gantt chart – see Figure 14.3 – which lists all tasks, milestones, presentations etc and allocates responsibility to appropriate staff, outside parties and agencies etc, this will form the blueprint for action and for measuring progress.

14.3: Marketing plan – illustrative

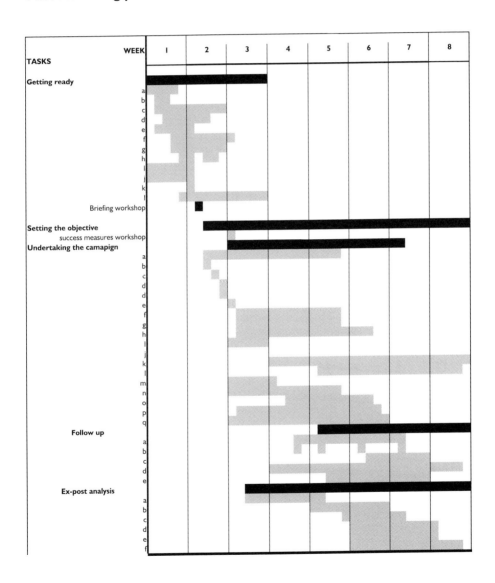

Execute the campaign

This is about carrying out the tasks in the campaign – actually contacting customers, sending out leaflets, follow-up, and then if that is the objective – selling services.

Obtain the results

The results of the campaign must be collected and then analysed to see what happened eg:

- how many calls were made
- how many appointments made as a result
- how many mortgages were sold,
- what value
- how did the customers break down by segments etc
- what did it really cost
- how much time
- and so on.

The information gathered should have been agreed at the outset and should be directly related to the success measures agreed at the start. This is to enable comparisons to be made to see how successful it was.

Compare with the success measures

The data collected is compared to the measures to see how the campaign went.

A gap analysis is carried out to see where expectations were exceeded and where they were not met. This forms vital feedback into future campaigns, and should be accompanied by analysis of possible reasons why.

Deliver a verdict

A report should be issued to interested parties giving an overall verdict on how successful the campaign was.

Give feedback and revisit objectives as appropriate

Once the report has been digested then feedback can be given to the relevant parties and changes can be made to future campaigns either to composition of the campaign – to capitalize on the good points – or to improve areas of shortfall. Perhaps even the objectives were not right and will need to be changed.

Tips

Regulatory issues - Any customer communication is subject to rules and standards. It is important that these are understood and adhered to. See chapter on Ethics.

Assistance – Talk to the in-house marketing department – the staff will have experience and advice for you, including contacts and probably special deals to reduce prices.

Research – Campaigns run for the purposes of research are different and must be run separately from sales campaigns. See chapter on market research. Do not mix up the two. It is called 'sugging' and it really upsets people and can damage relationships.

Campaign summary

A campaign can be said to be a series of coordinated actions or activities intended to reach the same goal or objective.

The major steps involved in a campaign are:

- ◆ agree objectives and agree success measures based on objectives
- ◆ decide type of campaign
- ◆ develop the components of the campaign
- ◆ plan the campaign
- ◆ execute the campaign
- ◆ obtain the results and compare with the success measures
- ◆ deliver a verdict and give feedback and re-visit objectives as appropriate.

Summary

Price is a major weapon in the armoury of any organization selling its wares, but care must be taken not too use it too bluntly or with a disregard for the consequences – either of competitor response, effect on profits or the perception of quality. While many prices are fixed centrally in financial services, there is still room for discretion in servicing the client and a little flexibility can go a surprisingly long way.

1 Price in general has a major effect on the volume of what you sell but profit is your revenue (what you receive) less your total costs; what you charge, therefore, affects this enormously.
2 Price is very visible and can give a powerful sign of quality and value. As such it can affect and, if used positively, reinforce your image.

3 There are five main factors that affect how you price:
- ◆ price range
- ◆ segmental differences
- ◆ strength and position of your offering
- ◆ the costs to deliver it
- ◆ the need for flexibility on pricing (market)

and the mix of these factors will greatly influence how you price your offerings.

4 Price-cutting or price competition is very easy to employ as a marketing weapon, but for precisely that reason it is also the easiest to respond to. In general you should not enter into a price cutting 'war' unless you can sustain the long campaign, have a sustainable advantage or are prepared to take the hits for a different purpose.

5 In the last few years there has been an increasing trend to commoditization of financial services and this, when coupled with greater price transparency, has lead to a greater focus on price competition.

Select bibliography

Mastering Marketing: FT Section 3: Lakshman Krishnamurthi, pp81 – 87

Value Pricing : Russell-Jones & Fletcher (Kogan Page)

Principles of Marketing: Kotler

Notes

1 Article in *The Times* 'World news' 14 Tuesday January 2003

Fifteen

Sales management

Topics in this chapter

Team selling

Targets and measures

Individuals, groups and teams

Introduction to this chapter

Managing a sales force is different from managing normal staff. This is because staff not engaged in sales normally constitute groups, which operate in ways that differ in many respects from teams; and teams and teamwork play a greater role in financial services than is generally recognized. Prior to meeting a customer a good salesman will review the current position and information available and then decide what needs to be done. Where appropriate he will seek help and advice from colleagues, possibly asking them to join the meeting, or be on standby should the need arise. This is teamwork at its basic level – cooperation for a common goal – that of selling more to customers. For larger corporate accounts there may be an account team that is already in situ – probably part time rather than full time, but nevertheless a team. The team will be charged with serving the client, and will meet regularly for defined purposes as well as on an ad hoc basis for specific occurrences. It will probably have a range of skills and experience within its members.

This can be contrasted with a sales team or sales force, which is a group of individuals brought together for management purposes or to attack a particular segment.

15.1   Individuals versus teams

The difference between an individual, a group of individuals and a team is that the latter has a dynamic of its own, and requires managing in a different manner from groups of individuals, to ensure that they work together to achieve results that are greater than the sum of the parts. People working in the same branch or department are usually a group not a team, although there may well be teams within the larger 'group'. If you put a group of clerks into a room with telephones – that does not make a call centre, because the key ingredients are missing. Most people often use the words 'group' and 'team' interchangeably and they are taken to mean the same thing. This is not the case and there are some key differences between them, as shown in the following table:

Criteria	Group	Team
Size	Any	*Limited*
Leadership/management	Autocratic/solo	*Consensual/share/rotating*
Selection	Irrelevant	*Critical*
Perception	Focus on leader	*Mutual knowledge and understanding*
Style	Convergence conformism	*Role-spread coordination*
Spirit	Togetherness/ persecution of dissenters	*Dynamic interaction*

Groups

A group is largely based around the individuals – ie they are accountable, motivated and rewarded on their own individual efforts. They usually nestle around a strong leader with the rest subordinated to her demands. Skills may be all of the same type or a general patchwork of skills with no particular selection.

Teams

A team by contrast still has individual goals and accountability but they are focused or placed in context by a degree of mutuality, collective responsibility and a large degree of self-management. They still require leadership but it is of the 'sharing' and 'delegating' kind rather than 'telling'. It will also have complementary skills. A good example is a cricket team. This is not a group of individuals (as may happen when it is played in school at play time) but a set of individuals specifically chosen for their skills and experience. It would be of no use having 11 bowlers in a team –

even if they were the best in the world – because then there would be no-one to score runs or field. It needs complementary skills such as a selection of bowlers, batsmen, wicket-keepers and fielders, as well as some leadership skills in the captain.

Group to team metamorphosis

There is a continuum between groups and teams[1] with five stages between them:

- **Groups** – a random collection of individuals
- **Psuedo-teams** – individuals that could perform better together if they were better organized
- **Potential teams** – a set of individuals making the effort to be more efficient
- **Real teams** – a set of individuals with complementary skills and commitment to a common purpose and goals
- **High-performance** – a real team that develops its members and out-performs the rest.

A good manager will drive the group to be a high-performance team; that is why in games such as football so much emphasis is placed on the manager. His skills are to make several, often 'prima donnaish', individuals play together to achieve that 'greater than the parts' result.

15.2 Team management

Not all managers make good leaders – and vice versa. It is important therefore that both roles are clear and that the right individuals take the right roles. Also not all superstars make good managers.

Peter principle

All too often, and particularly in sales, the 'Peter principle' comes into effect. This 'rule' states that people are promoted to the level of their incompetence. What this means is that, often, very good salesmen are rewarded by promoting them to the role of sales manager. This is usually done without any thought for their ability or desire to manage (as opposed to enjoying the salary, perks and status that often go with the job). Accordingly what happens is that a perfectly good salesman is destroyed as he struggles to manage a sales team, and also neglects his own customers and sales. This is detrimental to him, the sales force, the company and of course to the customers. This is often seen in sports teams (eg cricket or rugby) where a good player is given the captaincy but then can neither manage the team to victory nor achieve the performance levels he enjoyed prior to the promotion.

15.3   Leadership and management

Running a sales team requires two key skills – leadership and management – and these are different.

Leadership is not the same as management and is about:

◆ Vision
◆ Inspiration
◆ Honesty
◆ Credibility
◆ Communication
◆ DWYSYWD
◆ Trust
◆ Belief

Management on the other hand is about:

◆ Goals
◆ Expectations
◆ Rewards
◆ Feedback
◆ Teams
◆ Delegation
◆ Empowerment
◆ Deliverables

Sales people will arrange their own time to maximize their own benefit. A manager has to ensure that their activities also maximize the benefit to the organization.

There are some simple rules for running a sales force or team:

◆ objectives must be:
  ● fair
  ● clear
  ● achievable but stretching
  ● understood
  ● agreed by all parties in advance of reviews (ex-ante not ex-post)
  ● qualitative and quantitative
◆ teams should have objectives set that reflect a team and not a set of individuals (both team goals and individual)
◆ objectives need to reflect volume and value
◆ rewards must reflect the value generated to the organization
◆ communication is important:
  ● downwards
  ● across
  ● upwards
  ● outwards

◆ there can be no passengers because this creates bad feelings and is a disincentive to others (underperforming members with potential should be coached – others managed out, firmly!).

Metrics

In order to manage teams you must have some measure – but these should be chosen carefully and to hit objectives:

◆ metrics should be chosen that motivate the seller, but also align their actions with the goals of the organization.
◆ activity metrics do not equate to revenue (eg number of calls made is useless unless it results in 'hits which are then converted into sales).
◆ a few key measures are better than lots of unfocused measures.
◆ monitoring and feedback should be regular (at least quarterly formally and frequent informally) and properly constituted.

15.4   Successful sales teams

Not all teams achieve their ends, for many reasons, but successful teams exhibit several characteristics in common:

◆ tight performance management
◆ highly segmented offerings
◆ customer-value focus
◆ support for members
◆ excellent team organization
◆ first-rate management
◆ majority of time spent with customers or on customer-facing activities (activity analysis is particularly useful in this regard)
◆ cross-product selling and cross-handling incentivized.

15.5   Incentivizing staff

One of the key components of sales is that it usually demands a different set of incentives from the norm. This is best linked to a series of competency assessments where reward is linked to outputs and results.

If competence is what a salesman puts into a job, results are the outputs. This may seem a simple observation to make, but generally organizations place the emphasis on rewarding results without considering that it might achieve the same or better results by investing in people's inputs.

At a management level, companies frequently point to the usefulness of competency frameworks in equipping line managers to perform their people-management function more effectively. Competencies give managers the tools to understand the performance levels expected from their direct reports, how these can be measured and what needs to be done in the way of coaching, training and development to remedy any shortfalls. At the level of the individual employee, the benefit of competencies will be to provide role clarity, so that individuals are clearer about the demands of the job and what behaviours are paramount.

Note – People will always carry out the tasks that they believe will earn them 'rewards' however they define or perceive that. Whatever they say and whatever you ask them to do unless the remuneration system is geared to the behaviours that you want then you will not get it. For example, in a management consultancy the management wanted greater utilization of staff. They changed the remuneration basis, but also increased dramatically the utilization of the senior staff. As a result the senior staff filled jobs from the top down, thus using up budgets very quickly and leaving insufficient time for the rest of the staff to carry out their (more important) tasks. This resulted in rushed and poorly finished projects which caused unnecessary stress to staff, resulting in high turnover and bad client feelings.

Costs are important

Using competencies allows the organization and the sales force the means to improve sales performance by focusing in a systematic way on those skills that will give your business a competitive edge and greater-than-average returns. Without this structured approach it is difficult to address the hidden costs that make running a sales force (or relationship management team) so expensive:

- poor, unskilled recruitment, resulting in people with substandard skills being brought on board;
- failure to recognize the psychological contract and the implicit bargain between competence and recognition, leading to people feeling undervalued and de-motivated;
- blunt incentives which incentivize people at high cost to achieve a narrow range of results at the cost of colleagues and the customer;
- poor training, coaching and development which fail to address real competence shortcomings;
- salespeople who fail to live up to your brand image and the promise of good service and advice;
- finally, managers who are unable to manage.

The results of ignoring the people dimension include:

- high staff turnover
- unfocused training
- poor motivation

◆ blunt and wasted incentives
◆ unskilled recruitment
◆ poor values fit
◆ marred brand reputation.

15.6   Issues affecting sales teams

There are some issues that will point to the likelihood of a team performing poorly:

◆ Too much time spent with individual customers that is not justified by the outputs/value
◆ Sales forces not selling the full range of products (easiest sold most)
◆ Quote achievement results in slow of activity
◆ Mismatches between volume of sales and value to the organization
◆ Leads lost due to poor hand-offs or insufficient information
◆ High commission paid to salesmen generating low value
◆ High turnover in sales force
◆ Product penetration is poor.

Why have sales staff not always been effective?

Analysis of staff reveals that too often they spend the majority (80%) of their time on non-revenue related activities – a classic Pareto inversion – and only 20% on revenue generation. Clearly these two should be the other way round to stop them from being expensive administrators and filing clerks.

Figure 15.1: Sales force – too busy for customers

Activity analysis reveals poor use of time. 75% is non-revenue related – they are expensive clerks with poor time management

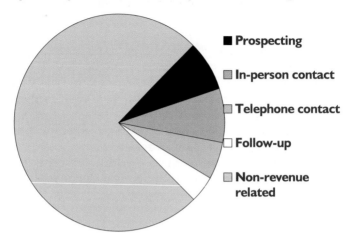

- ■ **Prospecting**
- ▨ **In-person contact**
- ▥ **Telephone contact**
- ▢ **Follow-up**
- ▨ **Non-revenue related**

Source: BBB Research

There are a number of reasons as to why they have been ineffective. These include:

1. Many authorization processes are inefficient/bureaucratic:

Sales

- ◆ usually insufficiently focused
- ◆ tasks to achieve sales goals not carried out well
- ◆ emphasis on new business 'hunting' rather than 'farming' existing client base
- ◆ cross-disciplinary efforts poor
- ◆ organizations' talents under-utilized

Authorization/Credit

Is often very expensive. Typical symptoms:

- ◆ slow approvals
- ◆ poor credit quality
- ◆ declining efficiency
- ◆ low levels of productive automation
- ◆ too many hand-offs

IBM Credit Corp, the finance arm of IBM, re-engineered its loan processing system and changed the turnaround from ten days to six hours.

Administration

- ◆ usually too much effort is wasted prior to the decision with form-filling or unnecessary data collection. Analysis of such processes has shown that up to 80% of activities in some processes represents wasted or non-value added time.
2. Poor usage of information systems:
   - staff need the right information at the right time to enable them to carry out their duties effectively (market, client, profit/costs)
   - MIS has been often ill-suited to real needs – and usually driven by history, system constraints (real or imagined) and poor user involvement in establishing the MIS
   - there has usually been poor sales tracking and other information
   - garbage in garbage out (GIGO) holds true here
3. Too many people in the chain, with poorly defined responsibilities
4. Menial tasks are often insufficiently delegated and/or support is often poor.

The best sales staff:

- ◆ make better use of internal resources – ie they know how to use and where to get information, they talk to the right colleagues who are able to give them the knowledge or information that they need to meet customer needs – networking across an organization is vital
- ◆ monitor their own activity more closely and understand where the down time is and how they spend their day and adjust activity accordingly
- ◆ have sharper-focused call objectives – single point or realistic
- ◆ adopt momentum sales plans
- ◆ plan sales goals
- ◆ use 'sales funnels' and manage them actively
- ◆ use cross-disciplinary skills where relevant
- ◆ delegate non-revenue tasks to other, more junior staff
- ◆ focus on the buying cycle of an individual or an organization and in the latter case understand who decision makers and personnel with real buying powers are
- ◆ track clients and build relationships
- ◆ set goals for themselves
- ◆ plan their days, weeks, months
- ◆ delegate administration work
- ◆ analyse the buying process
- ◆ never prospect without referral
- ◆ work fewer prospects

> 'We want to be regarded as the premier financial services firm bringing value added products to a limited group of major customers'
>
> *Bob Engel, J P Morgan*

15.7   Why sales team members are different from other employees

A sales force has a specific role to fulfill within an organization. This is about persuading customers to take up offerings rather than (usually) in delivering. Their objectives are to increase the organization's share of the customer's wallet. To this end they require a different set of **Knowledge**, **Skills** and **Attributes** from ordinary employees to be successful:

Knowledge

- ◆ Products – implications and requirements for success
- ◆ Organization – structure, cross-organizational issues
- ◆ Customers' needs and wants

Skills

- ◆ Negotiation
- ◆ Listening
- ◆ Decision-making

Attributes

- ◆ Numerate – to understand cashflows, NPVs and some complex products, depending on role
- ◆ Literate – able to write letters, develop presentations and write reports
- ◆ Presentable – so that the customers are comfortable with him in one-to-ones but also as a face of the organization
- ◆ Consistent – the same message to customers in the same way
- ◆ Able to put across complex issues in an easy format
- ◆ Focus (80% on existing customers – 20% on new)

Prioritizing time

It is vital that the time you have available is used in the most efficient and effective manner (efficient is doing things in the best way possible – effective is doing things that are focused on what you want to achieve). To do this it is necessary to understand what you do and why you do it.

The use of timesheets is very common in sales environments as well as professional services. It allows real time to achieve to be monitored, serves as inputs into future planning and allows you to understand the real costs of the business that you obtain. Care must be taken if allocating costs to ensure that they are 'real' because it can sometimes turn out that an unfair picture is given.

Then you need to categorize activities into four areas :

- ◆ first by timing and whether they need short-term or longer-term action
- ◆ second by type of activity response – whether they are initiated by you (proactive) or whether they come to you for action (reactive)
- ◆ third as to whether they are urgent
- ◆ fourth whether they are important.

Note – You need to understand the difference between the latter two – and also that tasks can be both urgent **and** important. A simple 2X2 grid can help here as shown in Figure 15.2. Here tasks are split by **Timing** versus **Type of response** and can then be marked to indicate importance or urgent.

Figure 15.2: Task/activity prioritization

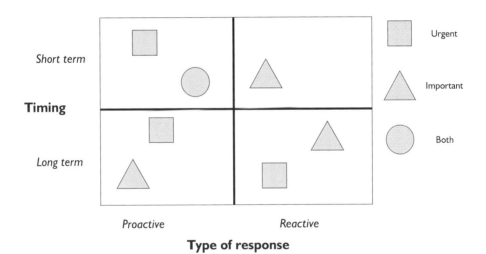

This allows you to expend the right amount of effort on the key tasks. Note that some activities can become urgent if you leave them too long!

Summary

Managing a sales team is very different from managing a department or a loose collection of staff. It requires a different approach, based around a group with complementary skills and experience, focused metrics that are fair and challenging, a clear view of organizational value and good motivation. Corollaries of these are good information, inspired leadership based on trust and sharing, good management of time and rewards that reflect both sales team efforts and organizational value generated.

1 A group is not (necessarily) a team – teams work for mutual goals and strive to be generate better results than groups.
2 Not all good sales people make good managers – recognize this and find other ways to 'reward' them – Peter principle.
3 Management and leadership are different.
4 Metrics should be clear, few and focused on value to the organization.
5 Sales staff have specific roles to fulfill within an organization. This is about persuading the customer to take your offerings rather than (usually) in delivering.
6 The objective of a sales team is to increase the organization's share of the customer's wallet.
7 Time management is critical – as is a focus on existing customers – 'farming'.
8 The organization needs to ensure that it has the right calibre of staff with the right skills and in-depth product knowledge.

Select bibliography

Organizational Behaviour: Huczynski & Buchanan – FT Prentice Hall

Notes

1 Katzenberg and Smith: *The Wisdom of Teams: Creating the high performance organization*, (Harvard Business School Press 1993)

Section summary

Sales is about getting a customer to buy from you – whether it is the first time or subsequently. In order to ensure that they continue to buy from you it is necessary to keep them feeling that the relationship is beneficial to them. This is called **retention**. Retention is in many ways as important if not more important than obtaining new customers because, unless you keep those customers with whom you have already had a sales relationship, any new customers are merely replacing the old defecting customers. Sales and retention have different drivers and the next section explores these differences as it considers customer service – ie how you handle existing customers.

III

Customer service

Introduction to this section

This section considers the third strand – customer service, ie that aspect of interaction with the customers that takes place after a sale has been contracted. In financial services of course it is a continuum and therefore new sales are taking place all the time so the service aspect permeates all transactions.

Three steps in the sales process

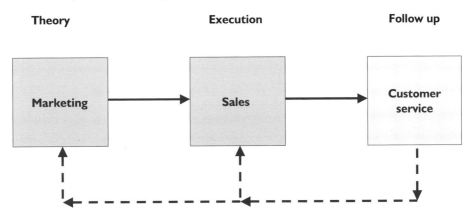

What is customer service?

Much research has been carried out into the nature of sales and service and a few paradigms have emerged:

- ◆ attention to clients is often ex-post rather than ex-ante – ie when something goes wrong (often too late);
- ◆ cross-selling is more cost-effective (product penetration) and income/profit streams are more predictable;
- ◆ development costs are amortized across a longer period therefore margins are better;
- ◆ it is much more expensive to acquire new customers because acquisition has an inherent cost:
  - ● marketing and sales to a new 'universe' of clients;
  - ● new account set-up costs;
  - ● low initial levels of transactions;
  - ● discounts and offers to attract them in;
  - ● as they have no established relationship upon which to build they are less likely to give you the benefit of the doubt and more likely to leave;
- ◆ there is a high correlation between retention and profitability and retained customers are much better in the long run because:
  - ● they buy more;
  - ● they pay more;
  - ● they cost less to serve;
- ◆ customers are more likely to stay with you the longer they have been with you. (NB Many organizations, however, misread the fact that customers have stayed with them for a long time for loyalty – when in many cases there was no other choice or customers were not aware of the options – and accordingly as their service deteriorated or competitors entered the market with attractive propositions, they paid the price when customers went elsewhere.)

Relationship management – objectives

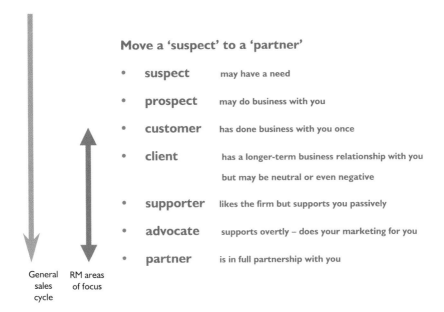

Move a 'suspect' to a 'partner'

- **suspect**   may have a need
- **prospect**   may do business with you
- **customer**   has done business with you once
- **client**   has a longer-term business relationship with you but may be neutral or even negative
- **supporter**   likes the firm but supports you passively
- **advocate**   supports overtly – does your marketing for you
- **partner**   is in full partnership with you

General sales cycle   RM areas of focus

◆ long-standing customers move from being 'customers' to being 'partners'; ie they:
  - ❑ bring an increasing share of transactions to you;
  - ❑ they bring others in their 'family' (business or personal) to you;
  - ❑ they become advocates of your services;
  - ❑ they 'sell' on your behalf.

Acquisition versus retention

Keeping existing customers is vital both to consistency of sales and to growth. Having sold something to a customer you have already entered into a relationship with him. Usually just after he has bought something he feels that the relationship is very beneficial and is happy to talk about other issues. Retention is about maintaining this good feeling and building on it to sell other products.

The following diagram shows that different issues drive acquisition and retention.

Acquisition and retention have different drivers

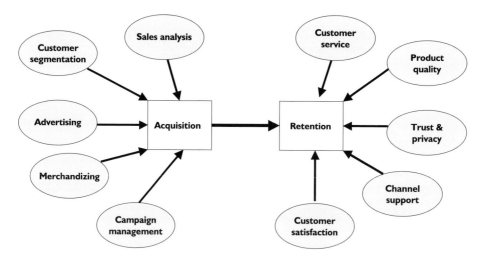

Acquisition of new customers is based on key issues such as:

- ◆ advertising – getting your message across to those who are unfamiliar with your organization and your products
- ◆ merchandizing – putting support collateral together and packaging it
- ◆ segmenting the customer base to ensure that your message is targeted and focused on their needs and wants
- ◆ analysing your sales force to make sure that they are efficienct and effective in what they do
- ◆ managing your campaigns to focus on targets and returns on monies spent.

Retention is, however, subtly different and rests on :

- ◆ customer satisfaction – keeping the relationship and enhancing it (in line with expected future returns)
- ◆ customer service – looking after the customers to ensure that they are satisfied with you
- ◆ trust – building up that trust from one-off acceptance of purchasing, to long-term relationship and multi-product penetration
- ◆ continuing product quality
- ◆ channel support such that they have the details of existing customers and can respond to queries and requests for information or products.

This is the foundation of cross-selling and it has many benefits. Principally, customers who have bought from you once are very much more likely to buy from you in the future, whereas those who have not bought from you are 'cold' customers and have to be persuaded of all the merits of dealing with your organization. You know (or should know) your customer and can therefore respond in a more focused manner.

Sixteen

Knowing your customer

Topics in this chapter

Customer value

Buying behaviour

Delivery differentiation

Features versus benefits

Introduction to this chapter

Understanding customers is very different, at the micro level, from knowing your customer. It is about understanding the propensities of a set of customers (see segmentation) to purchase services and what they will pay for them. The key components are:

Customer value

Customer behaviour

Customer satisfaction

These three items are closely linked and by taking all three into consideration when managing your clients the better the result will be for you. It is impossible to consider only one in isolation, at least it is not possible so to do effectively.

This is really about developing a set of performance metrics that enable you to measure these three items, conduct gap analysis, develop actions to close the gaps (for those customers that will generate value) and manage the customers to improve performance.

Satisfaction is an intangible but can have a major effect on your business. Highly satisfied customers are, on average, five times more likely to stay with your organization than those that are merely satisfied. Dissatisfied customers, however, tell others and it is estimated that they tell over 10 others! Moreover only about 5% complain – so for every customer complaint that you hear about another 20 have had similar experiences. Resolving a complaint satisfactorily, however, has a very beneficial effect on the customer's perception of the organization and as a result tends to increase loyalty.

Figure 16.1: Understanding customers – key components

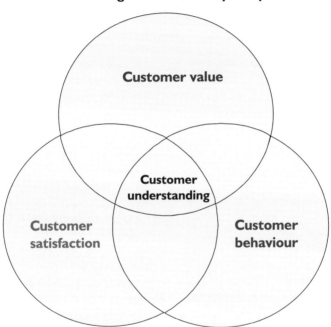

Customer value

This is the value to your organization of your customers. At the macro level it is revenue less costs and a proportion of losses incurred. At the individual level (lifetime) value can be loosely calculated as:

Value from transactions
(product purchase or usage)

times

Number of transactions per year
(extrapolated out and averaged)

times

Expected lifetime of relationship
(how long either you will be in business or how long you expect realiztically your customers to stay with you)

(Discounted down to NPV)

This can be a staggering sum, not only for corporates but also for individuals – particularly when you add in increasing product penetration, referrals etc (at a representative proportion of value) and brings home the message of understanding value.

Take a large food retailer

A typical customer probably goes in once a week and spends around £100, plus £200 say twice a year at Christmas and for other special occasions. This represents an annual value of around £5,400 per person! Over a 10-year period this would be (at constant values) £54,000. For every customer lost this represents a major disruption to cash flow – and they then have to replace them just to stay still. For every 1,000 customers that they lose the (annualized) value lost is £5.4 million and the lifetime value at constant values is £54 million!

However the lifetime value is of even greater importance when you consider the real benefits from good customer management. A small increase in retention has a massively disproportionate effect on the life-time value of a client. This is because the embedded value increases geometrically the longer they stay.

237

Take a bank

A typical customer might have:
◆ A mortgage of £150,000 on which you charge interest spread of 1%, plus fees
◆ A current account with charges of £100 pa – plus free cash
◆ A £10,000 loan for a car which earns you 2.5%

There may also be potential to sell him:
◆ A life policy
◆ Buildings and contents insurance
◆ F/X through you as well as travellers cheques say twice a year
◆ Credit card

By adding up all these up for your own organization – even an ordinary customer is of great benefit to the organization – and when annualized this value is even greater!

For example in personal insurance changing the retention rate from say 90% to 95% increases the customer life-time value by a staggering 84%! This is because with an average retention rate of 90% the customer stays on average 10 years but with 95% retention rate the average loyalty is 20 years!

Figure 16.2: Increasing the customer life-time value by retention

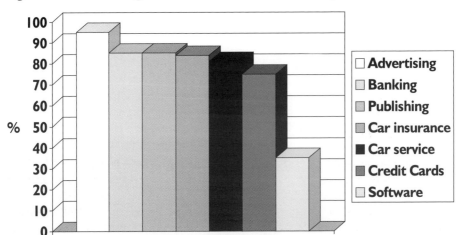

How much (%) a 5% increase in retention lifts lifetime value

The effects of increased retention rates are therefore spectacular. The objective of pro-actively managing your customer base is of course to effect this increase in loyalty and therefore value to the business.

Case study – An insurance company with 90% retention[1]

Has	100,000 customers
Average customer life-time value	£280
Business value	£28 million

But if it can increase its average retention to 95% it will

Have	155,000 customers
Average customer life-time value	£515
Business value	£80 million

It not only gains a net 55,000 customers because it has reduced its customer loss but they will now stay for 20 years instead of 10 (so doubling business), but in addition due to the longevity of embedded value they increase their value by over 80% to £515.

As a result business value virtually trebles!

It is therefore extremely important both to:

- maximize value from customers;
- maximize retention; and
- minimize the number of customers who are likely to deliver low value (or losses).

Customer behaviour

This is the way in which a customer 'doles out' his share of wallet or 'spend'. Does he put all his transactions through you? Or does he multi-bank (a more common phenomenon than hitherto)? If he has a life policy – do you also have mortgage protection policy, buildings and contents, or perhaps car and other insurance from him? Or is it spread across several companies (quite likely – especially if the lender for his mortgage has sold policies)? If the latter two situations are the case – why is this and what can you do to change it or influence him to reconsider – next time?

Clearly the more that you can influence him to put through you – then the greater his life-time value will be.

Customer satisfaction

What determines how much share of wallet you receive is largely the level of satisfaction that the customer in turn receives from you. Satisfied customers are the ones who continue to take your products and services. It is worth noting that just satisfying them is insufficient, because it will take only a marginally more attractive offer to entice them away – a better Customer Value Proposition. Note that for *very* dissatisfied customers – they may leave even for a worse offer!

Case study

Thomson, the holiday company, offer package tours to millions to many destinations. Package tours invariably involve issues of a multi-varied nature (poor hotel service, late transfers, late flights, trips that were not what was expected etc). The resort staff, however, are used to dealing with crises. The staff are trained to sort out problems in situ and to make recompense immediately wherever possible. For major issues they send compensation to the customers' home address so that it is waiting for them when they arrive home from their holiday. This creates a very favourable impression with customers and they have great loyalty from them with many repeat bookings. Many customers are paying for holidays up to a year in advance so it is vital that they are managed properly – the cashflow implications would be disastrous. Thomson takes customer loyalty and life-time value seriously.

People will trade much for convenience *as they see it* and if you are only just satisfying them then they will switch to somewhere else – often on a whim.

Customer service is about ensuring that your customers are **very** satisfied – or it is about finding out **why** they are not and *doing something about it*! This influences their behaviour so that you maintain customer value.

Figure 16.3: High benefits usually imply high delivery costs

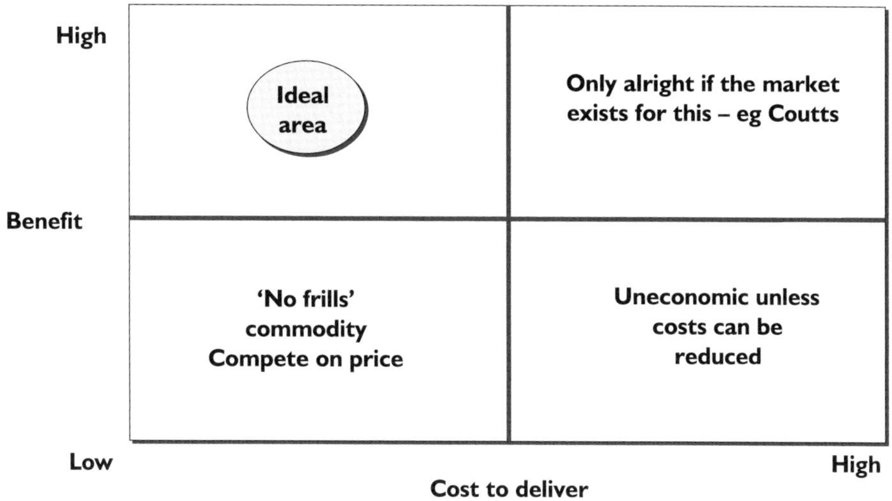

High	Ideal area	Only alright if the market exists for this – eg Coutts
Benefit	'No frills' commodity Compete on price	Uneconomic unless costs can be reduced
Low		**High**
	Cost to deliver	

What does a customer want? What does it cost to deliver? And how much will they pay?

It is equally important that you understand the cost to the organization of delivering that value. Where there is high benefit there is almost always a high cost of delivery. You must ensure that if you are in this market the income you receive reflects this higher cost – otherwise you will be subsidising your customers very handsomely. The ideal area is where you deliver high benefit at low cost. Unfortunately there are not many areas like that.

If the value delivered costs more to deliver than the income received, it begs the question as to why you are offering this level of service. Could you offer a lower level of service and a cheaper cost – or can you charge more for the premium service you are offering?

16.1   Understanding the customer

It is vital that you understand the customer in the context within which he is situated.

For a personal customer this includes:

♦ Lifestyle
♦ Place of work
♦ Type of work
♦ Income

◆ Future expectations
◆ Family status
◆ Residence

For a corporate this includes:

◆ The economy in which it operates
◆ Legislation
◆ Competition
◆ Environmental considerations
◆ Technology
◆ Culture
◆ Finance
◆ Operations
◆ Sector-specific issues
◆ Local/geographic issues
◆ Politics

…all tempered by the legislation that affects what you can do. Financial services is very heavily regulated and subject to all manner of legal and other restraints, which also need to be understood – eg capital adequacy, money laundering, best practice, best advice etc.

There is also a key difference between personal and corporates:

the latter also have customers.

If you can understand what they need to do for their customers and assist them in this aspect you will go a long way towards giving them a service that is better than the competition and helps them to help ***their*** customers.

By working with your customer to help him improve what he does for his customers you are forging a much tighter bond with him, increasing his loyalty and making it that much harder for the competition to take him away. A likely outcome is that he may introduce you to his customer as well – as he moves towards being a supporter. For example in some letters of credit there are provisions for pre-payments to the customers' customer to assist them in preparing the goods for export.

Figure 16.4 shows this and the key area of focus is to meet all three needs – yours, your customer's and his customers' needs.

Figure 16.4: Improve your customer's life

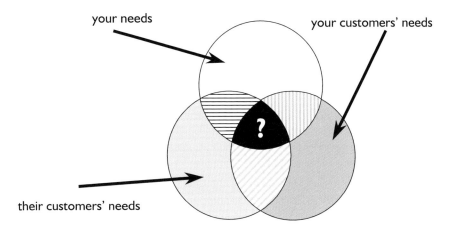

your needs

your customers' needs

?

their customers' needs

What can you do to improve his day and his customers' day?

The more that you can place your offerings in the central zone (**'?'**) then the greater the help that you will be giving to your customer. By helping them to satisfy their customers' needs you are making them feel that you are in partnership with them and progressively moving them up the ladder of satisfaction.

16.2   Base your understanding on facts

All organizations are full of myths and folklore about customers. These will influence behaviour of staff to meet perceived customers and often result in initiatives that are wholly wrong. It is best to tackle these head-on and disprove them so as to ensure that behaviour is correct and customer-focused.

> ### Case study
>
> An insurance company that sold only life products through a self-employed direct sales force was convinced, despite general sector analysis to the contrary, that its customer base was largely AB, C1. This was in the face of low premiums, and low persistency. Only when a comprehensive analysis of the customer base was carried out and hard evidence presented did management come to see that their its base was largely C2, DE and, therefore, representing much lower value per policy and typically with premiums that were too high to be sustainable, so they changed their approach (too late unfortunately).

An understanding of your customers is vital in order to target products and effort effectively. It is impossible to sell the products that you wish to sell if you do not understand who your customers are and, more importantly, what they want.

This must be linked with the benefit that you receive – customers will always take 'free' benefits from you and this incurs a cost. You must evaluate what you are delivering and ensure that it is cost-effective and focused on the areas that will maximize the return.

Where loyalty schemes are established it is vital to understand if they are delivering adequate value back and that the right customers benefit from them – eg frequent-flyer schemes usually award points for distance travelled – which may not necessarily reflect cost and profit to the airline.

Case study

Delta had an airmiles scheme based on traditional lines – ie distances flown. By matching revenue earned to frequent flyers it noticed that the two were not the same; and in fact there was a tendency towards an inverse correlation. It therefore redeveloped the scheme to reward those flyers who generated revenue and not necessarily those who fly regularly.

16.3   Key commandments

- ◆ Understand your customer base
- ◆ Understand your customers' requirements/business
- ◆ Prioritize your customers
- ◆ Manage out unpopular customers
- ◆ Sell a larger range of products to existing customers
- ◆ Target new customers in profitable sectors/segments
- ◆ Seek to move into new segments where you can make money.

Summary

Without customers you have no business and they are not obliged to take your products – therefore you must sell your products to them. To do this you must set targets:

- ◆ For revenue
- ◆ To convert leads

◆ To drum up more leads
◆ To manage existing customers.

Having set the targets you must then align remuneration with the targets to encourage behaviours to change and establish the mechanisms for measuring and monitoring progress.

1 The key components of customer understanding are:
    Customer value
    Customer behaviour
    Customer satisfaction.
2 A small increase in retention has a massively disproportionate effect on the life-time value of a client. This is because the embedded value increases geometrically the longer they stay.
3 Satisfied customers are the ones who continue to take your products and services.
4 There is also a key difference between personal and corporates: the latter too have customers so you need to work with them to help them help their customers.
5 Without customers you have no business and they are not obliged to take your products – therefore you must sell your products to them.

Select bibliography

Loyalty rules: F Reichheld

Principles of Marketing: Kotler

Value Based Marketing: Peter Doyle

Notes

1 **Peter Doyle**: *Value-Based Marketing* (Wiley 2000)

Seventeen

Building relationships

Topics in this chapter

Understanding and managing customer expectations

Developing customer confidence

Cost-effective value adding

Planning and delivering propositions to customers

Managing face-to-face customer contacts

Managing remote contacts

Managing multi-contacts

Introduction to this chapter

Establishing a relationship with a customer takes time and develops over the life time of the relationship. It is a function of the number of transactions, the quality of service received and costs associated with it. Good management can improve both the rate of relationship development and the likelihood of customer retention.

The challenge for any organization is to ensure that its efforts are focused on those customers who deliver the revenue and profitability that it desires. Relationship management is costly and therefore is not to be wasted on customers that lose you money.

17.1   Cost-effective value adding

The link between revenue and profit is often assumed but it is not usually true that those generating revenue generate profit. First Union in the USA undertook an analysis of its customer base by splitting its customers into ten segments for profitability. It received a shock when it found that those in the bottom segment generated most revenue, thereby demonstrating an inverse correlation between revenue and profit[1]. This means that staff are recruiting customers that destroy value to the bank!

In Figure 17.1 different customer segments have been plotted to show whether they are generating value or destroying value for the organization. Of the six segments:

◆ two generate the value
◆ two consume as much capital as they generate and
◆ two actually destroy value!

Figure 17.1: Managers should identify the contribution customer segments make to value

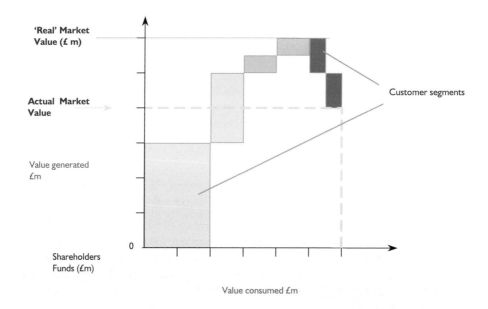

From this (simple example) analysis the organization needs to manage out the poorly performing segments and try to improve the medium segments by increasing charges, or reducing costs. Business often calls for tough decisions and this is a case where the need for these is amply demonstrated.

Pareto's law holds true with frightening accuracy in banking. Several recent studies showed the following[2]:

◆ For one bank 15% of its customers were responsible for 85% of profit
◆ In small-business banking less than 10% of the clients generated 90% of profit
◆ For a typical portfolio of retail customers 20% of accounts generated 200% of the overall return and up to 50% of accounts generated losses (destroyed value to the bank).

It is critical therefore that relationship management focuses on that top 20% of 'Pareto' customers. Clearly the major prize for an organization is to manage out the unprofitable ones and move marginal customers further up the profitability ladder.

17.2 Understanding and managing customer expectations

There are several types of customers and they will all have different needs. These include:

◆ new
◆ renewing
◆ spasmodic
◆ inactive

and within these categories they may be:

◆ low-value
◆ low-volume
◆ high-value
◆ high-volume

and some will be:

◆ lapsed/inert

It is clear that in general you want high-value customers – but of course in the broad sweep of things your customers will be a mix. The critical element is ensuring that your accounts receive the level of service that their value to the organization merits.

This means that low-value accounts do not receive high levels of personal service – or if they do then they will pay for them. In fact you should give low level of service (but not quality) for low-value clients and also manage some of those out. For inert or inactive clients you can just write them off after a while – and if they re-activate, re-animate the account.

Figure 17.2: Differing priorities by segment

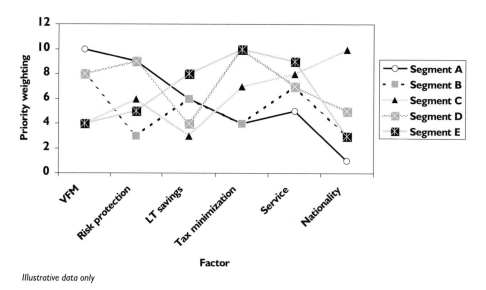

Illustrative data only

Figure 17.2 shows how different customer segments have different priorities with the same product – depending on their needs. Some value tax minimization highly whereas others are looking for good value. Meeting these needs is a major challenge but one that is made easier when the underlying needs are understood.

When meeting customers it is important to manage their expectations. This involves understanding their needs and expectations and then making it perfectly clear to them what they will receive as a customer. This means that prior to the meeting – or if it is an exploratory meeting immediately thereafter – you need to develop an account plan. Depending on the type of customer, this may be a detailed document or merely a few general jottings to serve as a framework for informing them.

When meeting customers – remember that you are both negotiating. The customer is under no obligation to take your offering and, similarly, you are under no obligation to supply him. The best solution is a win:win where both parties feel that they have got at least part of what they want. Figure 17.3 shows the possible results from a meeting.

Figure 17.3: Negotiation

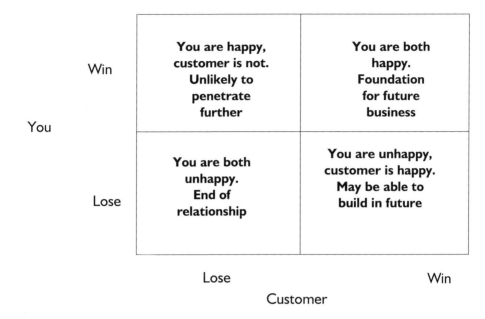

If you are unable to achieve a win:win, the next best is customer wins – as long as it is not too bad for you. This at least allows you to have another crack at his business and change the terms to be more favourable next time.

Part of achieving the win:win is by managing expectations so that what you can do for your customer becomes the 'expected' and therefore fits.

17.3   New customers

There are some key objectives that you must have when meeting new customers.

Gain understanding

- ◆ Introduce your organization and its total capabilities to them; even if they are not all relevant at this stage, you do not yet know his likely future needs
- ◆ Assess the potential short-term revenue
- ◆ Assess the longer-term revenue opportunities
- ◆ Review possible offerings that may be useful to him
- ◆ Ascertain what the competition is and what they are offering
- ◆ For a corporate:

❑ Understand the structure
❑ Establish who the decision-makers are
❑ Learn the decision-making process
❑ Understand the buying cycles
❑ View premises (if the first visit does not take place there)
◆ Arrange a follow-up meeting

Understand requirements

◆ Respond to a particular request
◆ Identify issues
◆ Offer a service or a series of services
◆ Further build on the relationships

Presenting a proposal

◆ Prepare the proposal – core/basic
◆ Prepare variations
◆ Identify negotiation points
◆ Present the proposal
◆ Check focus of the proposal
◆ Obtain feedback/reactions
◆ Negotiate the terms
◆ If necessary fix the next meeting

Doing the deal

◆ Obtain the purchase
◆ Sign the contract
◆ If necessary introduce other personnel
◆ Further build the relationship
◆ Sort out any immediate issues
◆ Look for other opportunities
◆ Establish start dates
◆ Agree next steps
◆ Fix next meeting

Orphans

These are customers who have nobody looking after them. This is usually because there has been a change in personnel. They are often a very good source of business because picking them up and managing them can pay dividends. Depending on the time since they were properly managed this can sometime be difficult and the life-time value needs to be considered to judge whether these types are worth the effort.

Diaries

These are critical aids in customer service. Time is money in the old saying and this was never more true than for a relationship manager. To maximize the benefits from dealing with clients it is important that time is prioritized. This means planning well in advance. The things to plan include:

- ◆ Recurrent items that always take place – such as annual or semi-annual reviews
- ◆ Visits – to be correlated with other activities to minimize time lost in travelling
- ◆ Internal reviews of profitability
- ◆ Board/executive presentations
- ◆ Telephone calls/meetings

You cannot manage the past – it has happened so you need to be continually looking forward.

With electronic diaries now available to virtually everyone it is possible to run a real-time diary that others in the organization can have access to as well and so they can see when you are free and use it to ask for meetings etc.

Effective usage of diaries is an important element in managing client relationships. By continually demonstrating that you are on top of his needs you cement the relationship further.

The database should also be used for generating automatic diary reminders and linked into personal diaries to ensure nothing key is missed (loan anniversaries or maturities, important events – children attaining majority etc) so that meetings can be planned in a timely fashion.

Sales funnels

Using a sales funnel is a very useful way of managing sales pipelines because it serves as a diagrammatic way of showing where you are with your proposals. You can use it to focus your attention on those that are closest to completion and also to demonstrate progress to superiors. It will also highlight where extra help is needed in good time so you can manage the lead through. By using reasonable discount factors for the different levels of proposals you can put a 'discounted' or realiztic value on your work and demonstrate that you are adding value.

Taking a simplistic example where a relationship manager has three levels of business – suspects, prospects and proposals – he could place discount factors on them of say 25%, 55% and 75% to give values of business:

No.	Type	Value	discount	Expected value
		£	%	£
45	suspects	2.8m	25%	0.7m
30	prospects	1.8m	55%	0.9m
18	proposals	1.2m	75%	0.9m
93		5.8m	43%	2.5m

This also enables everyone to see the value of the leads and what proportion are taken forward to close.

Figure 17.4: New sales model

3D Sales funnel

Outer ring= suspects
Inner ring = prospects
Centre   = proposals

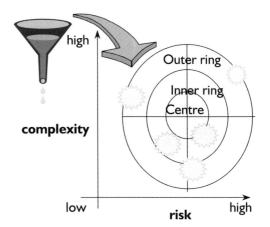

- ◆ Place opportunities on funnel with size representing size of opportunity
- ◆ Quadrant equals risk/complexity of opportunity to bank
- ◆ Gradually guide the opportunity down the funnel
- ◆ Minimize the risk where possible
- ◆ Use funnel to 'self-coach'

The information from the sales funnel can then be translated into a report. For example:

Stage in sales	Deals	Revenue	Need management input	Need specialist input
OUTER	24	N/A	7	6
INNER	12	£7.0M	4	5
CENTRE	6	£5.4M	2	1

This allows management to see likely trends, to map progress and to take action to support sales staff. By plotting the business on the sales funnel in terms of risk and complexity it further allows a detailed analysis of ancillary issues to assist in closing them.

Summary

1 It is not usually true that those customers generating revenue generate profit and this needs to be analysed and understood, with effort allocated accordingly.
2 Relationship management is costly and therefore is not to be wasted on customers who lose you money.
3 Part of achieving the win:win is by managing expectations so that what you can do for your customer becomes the 'expected' and therefore fits.
4 It is important to manage sales leads very hard to ensure that you reap the benefit of your efforts.

Notes

1 **Jerry Cover**: *Profitability Analysis – a necessary tool for success in the 21st century* (ABA Banking journal 1999)
2 ibid

Eighteen

Information

Topics in this chapter

What is information?

Why do you need it?

Characteristics of information

Laws governing information

Data mining/warehousing

Data protection

Introduction to this chapter

It may be said categorically that information is the oil that keeps the engine of an organization going. Whether it is the daily balance of a client, the transactional analysis of a branch, the profit and loss accounts or the aggregated balance sheet numbers produced annually. Without it everything would stall and stop so it really is indispensable. There are however some issues – nowadays there is so much around that you can 'drown' in information, and of course much of it is useless.

Figure 18.1: Information relative to magnitude of decision

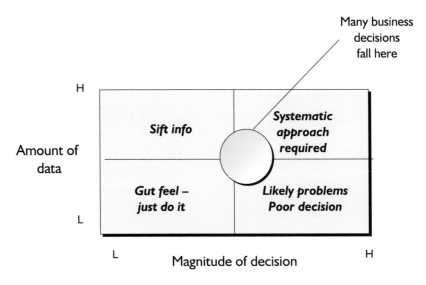

It is a balance between the **magnitude of the decision** and the **amount of data** you have to enable you to analyse the risks – but data should be turned into **information** that supports decisions.

18.1   When do you need information?

There are several occasions when you need information. It is always for decision-making purposes – whether immediately or subsequently following discussion – and includes:

◆ Before meeting a client – to prepare yourself for discussions and to enable you to fill gaps
◆ During meeting – to flesh out points or to probe for answers
◆ After meetings – linking in to the discussions
◆ For periodic reviews – to enable you to see how the customer has performed, profitability etc
◆ For marketing purposes – what should we offer her?
◆ For day-to-day management of customers, staff branches or organizations.

Case Study – British Airways (BA)

British Airways (BA) is overhauling its customer information into a single, group-wide database in an effort to cut costs and improve its knowledge of individual flyers. BA has previously been storing all customer and commercial data on multiple, disparate databases, but the new system – also used by airlines such as American Airlines and Qantas – is also aimed at bolstering BA's Web strategy.

Higher-impact marketing initiatives are in the pipeline and are due to be rolled out when the new system is fully implemented.

'It is essential to have access to a single, consistent view of each customer, and each product they buy, if we hope to offer our customers the services and products they want as best we can,' says BA head of customer information Rob Thorne. 'This is why we took the decision to move to a single, cross-enterprise data warehouse. It will underpin our future growth.'

Source: Precision Marketing, 8 January 2002

18.2 Information axioms

There are a number of laws or axioms that govern information:

- ◆ Diminishing returns
- ◆ Praxis
- ◆ Perpetual mobile
- ◆ Data hunger
- ◆ Indispensability
- ◆ Familiarity

These are expanded on below.

- ◆ **Diminishing returns** – It is a fact that, rather like the statistically significant number in market research, after a certain point more information does not add value. In fact the value of the extra information is usually incremental at best and often involves a disproportionate cost to get it. Paralysis of analysis not only slows down any decision, it can also adversely affect it by reducing its effectiveness. Too much data clouds perspective and leads to errors unless it is handled properly. Conversely confidence in the (less accurate) decision increases with the amount of 'evidence' – piles of data give a warm feeling. This leads to overconfidence in the decision and poor decisions. It is therefore essential that the information you use to make a decision is no more than you need.

Figure 18.2: Overanalysis

As information increases, the relative accuracy of analysis decreases while the confidence in the decision engendered by the greater information increases.

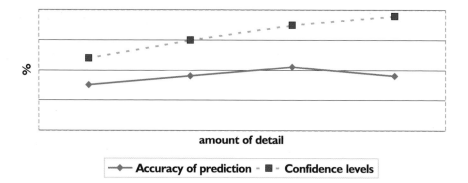

◆ **Praxis** – Information tends to be specified by how things are usually done, rather than by what we really need to take decisions or carry out our work. For example some financial institutions systems were constructed so as to allow specific views of information that seemed very important at the time, but as a result rendered meaningful analysis of different views extremely time-consuming because data had to be re-analysed, or impossible as the data held was insufficient for current, changed circumstances. Many systems did not hold simple data such as date of birth or gender, which is so vital for marketing.

◆ **Perpetual mobile** – Once data has been requested it keeps coming unless proactive steps are taken to stop it.

Case study

Each third Wednesday of the month an international UK bank asked for Sterling overseas liabilities of German banks to be returned to HO. One day in the 1970s a bright young clerk queried this because the return was always nil. After a long time he was told that in 1914 when Sterling was a reserve currency and war with Germany broke out (WWI) it was thought to be useful. It had been collected ever since and all over the world clerks had been sending in returns which were duly filed and ignored. The practice was subsequently stopped.

◆ **Data hunger** – There is a tendency for data to adopt the maxim of 'more is more'; occasional analysis becomes the norm and more is requested. This is costly and often used to defer decisions.

◆ **Indispensability** – Once data has been requested there is an expectation that it will continue to be produced – costs and usability notwithstanding.

◆ **Familiarity** – Information that is used, even if difficult to use, once accepted, becomes the norm. As a result there is a hidebound reluctance to use a different type or format (not-invented-here syndrome) even if it is more relevant because that involves moving out of people's comfort zones.

18.3   Data versus information

Analysis must be based on information not data. Data is equal to facts; to become information it requires the context.

Figure 18.3: Understanding the context

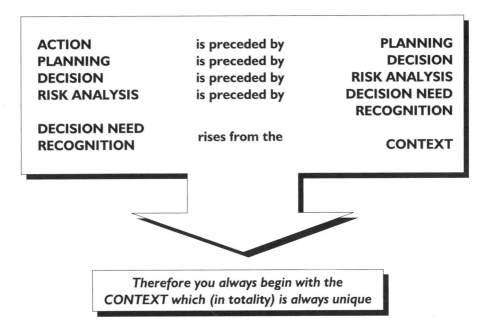

A list detailing the ages of every householder in a given locale over the last 10 years is data not information. An analysis of the changes over time, however – the trends – is information not data which allows an understanding of the context or situation and can form a valuable input into, for example, decisions as to how to market services there.

Remember DRIP when analysing:

Data Rich, Information Poor

Volume does not equal Quality

Data usage

Information is there to enable you to carry out your daily tasks both efficiently and effectively. This will range from checking a balance to decide if there are sufficient funds to enable a cheque to be paid, looking at a customer's expenditure patterns and lifestyle when deciding what product opportunities there are or analysing the entire organization to decide new product development or for setting strategic objectives. All lead to a decision-making point and therefore you need to follow the following steps.

18.4   Why do you need information?

Information is needed for several reasons including:

◆ **Decision-making** – should we lend £1,000,000 to this man or not?
◆ **Planning** – what should we do, when – should we launch this new product in January after the sales, in summer when purchasing is low, or in time for the Christmas rush?
◆ **Control** – to pay the cheque or not to pay – that is the question.
◆ **Enabling** – what are my limits, can I authorize the loan myself or do I need to refer it? How long is a temporary excess on an overdraft?

For information to be useful therefore it must help in these types of situation. As a result it must demonstrate certain characteristics. It should flow to us and therefore the mnemonic 'CURRENT' can help:

C	**COST EFFECTIVE**
U	**USABLE**
R	**RELEVANT**
R	**RELIABLE**
E	**ERROR FREE**
N	**NORMAL**
T	**TIMELY**

◆ **Cost effective** – it should not cost more than the value that the information will generate to the user
◆ **Usable** – it must be in a form that facilitates it being used (an accurate output in French would be of limited use in Latvia)
◆ **Relevant** – it should contain what you need to support your work
◆ **Reliable** – it must have data integrity
◆ **Error free** – it must be accurate – zero tolerance in some cases (balances or data for assessing branch performance), although some errors may be acceptable in other cases – eg data for marketing purposes
◆ **Normal** – it must be consistent with itself
◆ **Timely** – it must arrive in time to be useful – last week's balances are of no use in making decisions on cheques today.

18.5 Results of the information age

We live in what is called the information age – there is so much available to everyone that it is not possible to understand it. It also has benefits and drawbacks.

Benefits

◆ It has facilitated transaction banking, which has enabled a wide range of services to be made available easily.
◆ There is faster processing of increasing types and volumes of transactions, which has enabled the way that banking is carried out to change – eg on-line banking.
◆ There is greater facility for managing monies more easily and remotely.

Drawbacks

◆ The corollary of this is that the art of banking has become de-personalized and reduced the link to the customer (few people venture into their bank any more).
◆ It is far easier to transact remotely and therefore many now question why they need a physical branch any longer (and many no longer bank at 'physical banks').
◆ The propensity of customers to change banks has therefore increased.
◆ IT issues can result in difficulties in dealing with customers – eg if the system goes down or entries are incorrectly posted.
◆ Auto-decision making (eg credit scoring) may omit important non-quantifiable information that may impact on the decision – such as local knowledge or relationships.

18.6   Data warehousing

What is a data warehouse?

In order to maximize usage of data – ie by turning it into information that can form the basis for decisions and conclusions – it needs to be stored and analysed. The usual method of this is to store it within a special part of the system known as a data warehouse (sometimes it can be a stand-alone system).

It has been defined as '...*the logical link between what the managers see in their decision support EIS applications and the company's operational activities.*'[1]

In other words data warehousing allows data that has already been transformed into information to enable decision support and executive information production.

A data warehouse is a relational database management system (RDMS) that stores the data in such a way that it can be interrogated (slicing and dicing) for business reasons and by business users. Data warehousing makes it possible to extract operational data and overcome inconsistencies between different legacy data formats. As well as facilitating the integration of data throughout an organization regardless of location, format, or communication requirements it is possible to incorporate additional external or even expert information.

In other words the data warehouse provides data that is already transformed and summarized which when extracted can form the basis for management information.

There are generally some key characteristics (after Bill Inmon[2]) ascribed to a data warehouse:

- **subject-oriented** – data is organized according to subject instead of application eg a bank using a data warehouse would organize its data by customer, DOB location etc, instead of by different products (O/D, loans, mortgages etc). Data organized by subject contains only the information necessary for decision-support processing;
- **integrated** – when data is kept in many separate systems or applications in an organization, encoding of data is often inconsistent. In one system gender (or sex) might be coded as 'm' or 'f'; in another by 'male' or 'female'; and in yet a third by 'man' or 'woman'; and in some (binary thinking) 0 or 1. When data is transferred into a data warehouse it is 'cleaned' so that it assumes a consistent format and coding – therefore enabling easier analysis;
- **time-variant** – a data warehouse usually contains a location for storing old data, eg from 5 to 10 years ago, and in some cases even older, to be used for comparisons, trends, and forecasting. This data is not updated;
- **non-volatile** – data is not updated or changed in any way once it is in a data warehouse, but it is only loaded for subsequent access;
- **consistency** – data warehouses are designed for query processing as opposed to transaction processing and, as a result, those databases that are linked to, or

designed for, On Line Transaction Processors (OLTP) are unsuitable for data warehouses.

The structure of a data warehouse

There are five areas of a data warehouse as shown by Figure 18.4:

◆ Summarized data
◆ Collated data
◆ Current data
◆ Older/archived data
◆ 'Metadata'

Summarized data is compact and easily accessible and can even be found outside the warehouse.

Collated or slightly summarized data is that which has been synthesized and slimmed down from lower levels of data within the warehouse. An important question when constructing a data warehouse is what period is *time-critical* as well as the characteristics of the collated data when presented.

Current data is central in importance because it:

◆ reflects the most recent happenings (however you have defined that), which are usually the most interesting;
◆ is voluminous as it is stored at the lowest level of granularity;
◆ needs fast access, which usually means that it is expensive and complex to manage.

Older/archived data is infrequently accessed and stored at a level of detail that is consistent with current detailed data. (It is usually stored in some form of mass storage.)

Metadata is the final component of the data warehouse and is really of a different dimension in that it is not the same as data drawn from the operational environment but is used within the system to locate the contents of the data warehouse, as a guide to the mapping of data into the warehouse, and as a guide in transposing between the current data and the collated data and then the collated data and the summarized data, etc.

Figure 18.4: Data warehouse – structure

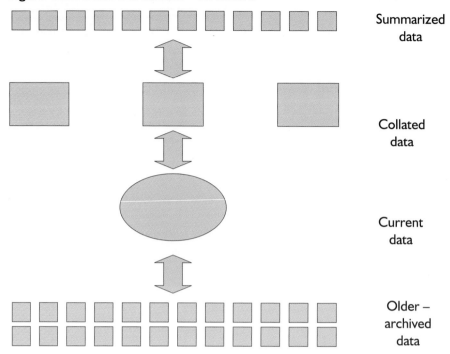

Summarized data

Collated data

Current data

Older – archived data

Figure 18.5 shows how this might work in practice – eg for a building society. If we assume that the date is 25 June, year is 2001, then the current data is 25 June 2000 to 24 June 2001. Sales data does not have to be real-time because it is unnecessary for this type of analysis and will enter the warehouse only once all processing is completed.

Details can then be summarized – sliced and diced – as you wish.

Figure 18.5: Data warehouse – example – mortgage sales

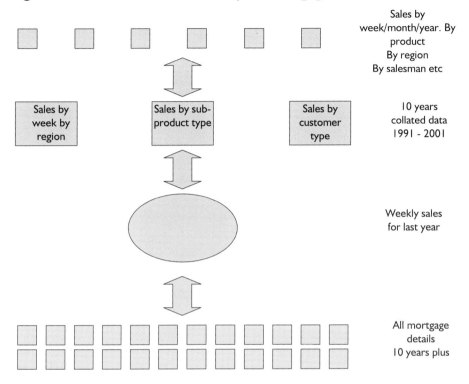

	Sales by week/month/year. By product By region By salesman etc
	10 years collated data 1991 - 2001
	Weekly sales for last year
	All mortgage details 10 years plus

To maximize on the data warehouse you must then use a technique called data mining.

18.7   Data mining

What is data mining? The analogy comes from the mining industry and it is essentially about pulling data out and manipulating it to deliver useful information. It is also known as 'knowledge discovery in databases'.

Some definitions of data mining are:

> '...the nontrivial extraction of implicit, previously unknown, and potentially useful information from data. This encompasses a number of different technical approaches, such as clustering, data summarization, learning classification rules, finding dependency networks, analysing changes, and detecting anomalies.'[3]

> '...the search for relationships and global patterns that exist in large databases but are `hidden' among the vast amount of data, such as a

267

relationship between patient data and their medical diagnosis. These
relationships represent valuable knowledge about the database and the
objects in the database and, if the database is a faithful mirror, of the real
world registered by the database.'[4]

Data mining is about analysis of data using sophisticated software techniques to
identify patterns and regularities in structured data (which is usually held in
'warehouses'). The software is responsible for finding the patterns by analysing the
data and pulling out relationships and correlations. Using sophisticated analysis
enables patterns to be recognized that were not previously discernable or which
would take too long by normal techniques. The analogy with mining comes from
the fact that you might – and indeed hope to – strike a 'lode' of lore or knowledge,
which you can then exploit.

Data mining enables vast quantities of data to be manipulated and then analysed and
as such it works upwards from the lowest pieces of data. This is further analogous
to a mining operation where, frequently, a machine or miners sift large amounts of
material in order to find something of value (coal, silver, diamonds etc).

Issues with data

Data-mining systems rely on databases to supply the raw data for input and this
raises problems in that databases tend be dynamic, incomplete, 'noisy', and large.
Other problems arise as a result of the adequacy and relevance of the information
stored.

Limited information

Databases are often designed without taking data mining into account and as a result
issues arise. Typically is the fact that not all data required is present. A good example
for many customers is that simple data (such as date of birth) is not held as it was
considered unnecessary at the time when the (typical) product was developed. For
meaningful analysis of patterns of behaviour and product relevance – eg if looking at
customer life cycles – it is often critical.

'Noise'

Databases usually contain errors which contaminate the data they contain and at
the same time the data has attributes that rely on subjective or measurement
judgements which can cause errors, resulting in some items being mis-classified
(for example if staff guess at gender or socio-economic class). Error in either the

values of attributes or class information are known as 'noise'. Where possible the 'noise' should be eradicated or eliminated to improve the accuracy of the data. This is often known as 'data cleansing'.

Duplication

This is frequently an issue for financial services organizations where they have moved from a product-based structure to a customer-based structure and they hold several records of one customer – often containing different or conflicting data. This too needs cleaning to ensure robust and meaningful analysis.

Missing data

Missing data can be dealt with in a number of ways, such as;
- ◆ ignoring missing values
- ◆ omitting the corresponding records
- ◆ inferring of missing values from known values
- ◆ computing and using averages for the missing values.

Uncertainty

Uncertainty refers to the severity of the error and the degree of noise in the data. Data precision is an important consideration.

Size, updates, and irrelevant fields

Databases tend to be large and dynamic in that their contents are ever-changing as information is added, modified or removed. The problem with this from a data-mining perspective is how to ensure that the rules are up-to-date and consistent with the most current information. Also the learning system has to be time-sensitive because some data values vary over time and the results and conclusions can be affected by the 'timeliness' of the data. Another issue is the relevance or irrelevance of the fields in the database – eg post codes are fundamental in many sets of analyses such as linking local market share to footfall or penetration of a branch in an area.

Uses of data mining

Data mining has the ability to assist in many areas of analysis, including:
- ◆ identifying buying patterns of customers

- ◆ associating buying behaviour with certain 'classes of characteristics' (segments, demographics)
- ◆ analysing responses to advertising or mailing – and therefore enabling predictive analysis of future responses and facilitating greater focus
- ◆ fraudulent credit card use
- ◆ fraudulent mortgage patterns (between customers, solicitors etc)
- ◆ loyalty analysis
- ◆ credit card spending and cross-correlation to classes of customers
- ◆ product penetration by types and classes of customers
- ◆ risk analysis
- ◆ branch network product sales.

Comparison of OLAP and OLTP

Nowadays data is stored electronically and then interrogated to enable us to extract and analyse (process) it to provide information. This usually involves both analytical processing (OLAP) and transaction processing (OLTP).

OLAP is short for On-Line Analytical Processing and focuses on the analysis of data to provide information (typically EIS/MIS). This data is analysed from databases and then transposed usually into pre-set formats, either to produce reports or to allow staff to access and produce their own reports for management purposes. The database itself is organized so that related data can be rapidly retrieved across multiple dimensions.

OLTP is short for On-line Transaction Processing in which the system retrieves and updates a small number of records. For example, with a typical customer order entry for a change of address, the OLTP transaction might retrieve all of the data relating to a specific customer and then insert a new address in the appropriate fields for the customer. Information would be selected from fields concerning the customer, customer number and detail lines. The relationships between the records are simple and only a few records are actually retrieved or updated by a single transaction.

These two types of processing are usually contained on different servers.

OLAP

OLAP database servers support common analytical operations, including: consolidation, drill-down, and 'slicing and dicing'.

- ◆ Consolidation – involves the aggregation of data such as simple roll-ups or complex expressions involving interrelated data. For example, sales offices can be rolled-up to districts and districts rolled-up to regions.

◆ Drill-down – OLAP data servers can also go in the reverse direction and automatically display detail data that comprises consolidated data. This is called drill-down. Consolidation and drill-down are an inherent property of OLAP servers.

◆ 'Slicing and dicing' –refers to the ability to look at the database from different viewpoints. One slice of the sales database might show all sales of product type within regions. Another slice might show all sales by sales channel within each product type. Slicing and dicing is often performed along a time axis in order to analyse trends and find patterns.

OLAP queries are typically transactions which, on-line:

◆ Need to access very large amounts of data, eg several days/weeks of account movements.

◆ Analyse the relationships between the elements – withdrawals, deposits, cheques, DDs, standing orders etc.

◆ Involve aggregating data.

◆ Compare that data over (hierarchical) time periods – daily, weekly monthly, quarterly, yearly.

◆ Present data in different perspectives, eg values by customer, by branch, by product, by channels, by location.

◆ Involve complex analysis – eg lifetime value of a set of customers by branch and variances to the norm.

◆ (in theory) offers fast response so that analysis can take place in order to provide timely information that will enable decisions to be taken that are time-critical and relevant.

OLAP servers can hold complex and multidimensional data in a compressed form. This is accomplished by using special storage arrangements and compression techniques that maximize space utilization. 'Dense' data (where there is data in existence for a high percentage of components cells) is stored separately from 'sparse' data (where a significant percentage of cells are empty). By optimizing space utilization, OLAP servers can minimize data storage needs, thus making it possible to analyse exceptionally large amounts of data within the server. (Anyone who has used 'defrag' in Windows on a PC will have seen this type of compression and optimization in process.)

OLTP

A database that has been constructed to support OLTP will be unsuitable to support OLAP. This is because the requirements are different. OLTP has different objectives such as maximizing transaction capacity and typically having hundreds of tables in order not to lock out users etc. OLAP needs to support queries.

OLTP systems are used to process data continually. When the data has been processed it is then placed back in the repository – from whence it can be analysed. It is therefore impossible for it to be used to pull off queries because the data is inconsistent and changing, duplicate entries exist, entries can be missing and there is no historical data within it, which is necessary to support trend analysis.

The OLTP data must be kept separate from any OLAP data and indeed it is usual for the OLAP data to be sourced from several places.

Data in an OLTP must therefore be transferred into the OLAP database to facilitate the analysis. It must first of all be 'cleansed'.

Cleansing data

Data cleansing is an important aspect of creating an efficient data warehouse in that it is the removal of certain aspects of operational data, such as low-level transaction information, which slow down the query times. The cleansing stage has to be as dynamic as possible to accommodate all types of queries – even those that may require low-level information. Data should be extracted from production sources at regular intervals and pooled centrally, but the cleansing process has to remove duplication and reconcile differences between various styles of data collection.

18.8   Sources of information

Information is the key to making informed decisions and to being master of a brief before meeting customers. You need information to enable you to understand your customers, your own organization's capabilities, what is happening in the world, what your competitors are doing and many other things beside as well as supporting the decisions you have to make every day. Otherwise you will be guessing or working under false assumptions.

There are many ways of obtaining information – you can use internal and external sources and of course one of the greatest sources of information about your customer is the customer himself. As Figure 18.6 shows information is an integral part of marketing.

Figure 18.6: The marketing process – overview

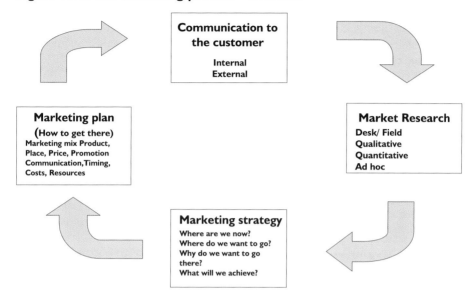

Information can come from many sources and therefore also in many formats. You must therefore pull information into a consistent format and this requires a consistent framework for collating information. It is also important to understand the difference between a vast unstructured 'dump' (data) and the salient points that enable you to understand your subject (information).

Key issues for consideration are:

◆ For what **purpose** do I require the information (background, to support a decision, to answer a specific query etc)?
◆ By **when** do I need it?
◆ What **sort** of information do I need and in what format?

This will then enable you to collect the right amount of information in the right level of detail and to focus your efforts on the right or optimal manner of collecting it. Collecting and analysing information that is relevant enables you to make informed and robust decisions as input into subsequent action. (See market research chapter for details of different types of research.)

18.9   Interviewing customers

One of the greatest sources of information about a customer is the customer himself. A well-planned interview can elicit much relevant information which will allow you to understand a lot about him and also to populate your database. Interviewing is a key competence for a relationship manager. An interview is a structured conversation with a purpose and may take place on your premises, on your client's premises or sometimes at other locations. Interviews are both effective at information gathering, for understanding issues and relationship building. It is worth noting that a meeting with a client to discuss anything is in effect an interview.

Interview techniques

There are some very clear pointers to successful interview techniques and, because people's ability to articulate or describe their thoughts and ideas varies, it is essential to use good questioning techniques because this makes you more likely to obtain quality answers.

Ten commandments:

1 **Establish good rapport** – this can be achieved by establishing some slight common ground of interest, recognizing their responses, and respecting opinions. This can also be shown by the tone of voice, expressions or even gestures. Good contact can be established by demonstrating attentive listening, with the interviewer showing interest, understanding, and respect for what the subjects say; by allowing them to finish what they are saying, and proceed at their own rate of thinking and speaking – within the constraints of the timing and objectives.

2 **Ask clear questions** – use words that make the questions easy to understand and that fit within the individual's frame of reference and that are short and jargon free.

3 **Ask single questions** – too often there is a tendency to mix several up and accordingly the answer only partly meets your needs.

4 **Use open questions** – these allow people to respond in their own terms using their own words and to elaborate on an idea. A closed question usually elicits a yes or no response.

5 **Ask experience related questions before opinion questions** – because the former set the context for the latter (eg where you are dealing with a customer complaint about staff handling: 'Describe the events that took place' followed by 'How do you feel about it?') and gets facts before emotion.

6 **Place the questions in sequence** – this refers to using a special kind of questioning technique called 'funnelling', which means asking from general to specific, from broad to narrow.

7 **Probe and follow up questions** – to broaden the response to a question, to increase the depth of the data being obtained, and to give clues to the interviewee about the level of response that is desired. This can be done through a direct link to an answer – 'Could you elaborate on that point?' or 'Do you have further examples of this?' – Note that sometimes non-verbal signs can encourage the interviewee to go on – a mere nod or just a pause. Repeating

significant words from the answer can also lead to further elaboration – eg 'exporting to Indonesia?' or '…so you switched to invoicing in euros?'

8 **Avoid questions that might be sensitive** – it is advisable to avoid deep questions that may irritate the informants, possibly resulting in an interruption of the interview or a closing down.

9 **Keep control** but encourage wide-ranging answers – sometimes you have to let the interviewees 'travel' wherever they like, but a rough checklist of ideas or areas the former want to explore is useful – experienced interviewers should be always in control of the conversation which they guide and re-orient as necessary.

10 **Interpret the answers** – throughout the interview you must clarify and extend the meanings of their answers to avoid misinterpretations on their part. This is often achieved by repeating and summarizing what has been said – eg 'So you did that and then that?' or 'So you need working capital finance of £5 million to cover exports to Afghanistan?' This allows them to confirm your understanding or to clarify your misinterpretation.

Key steps in preparing for an interview

Before the interview

- be clear as to the purpose and objectives of your interview.
- carry out all relevant research:
    - ❏ customer history
    - ❏ products
    - ❏ economic analysis
    - ❏ current restrictions on customers etc.
- if you are the one who prepares the setting for the interview make sure that the venue and time is satisfactory. Ensure that you remove any physical or psychological barriers and that you have privacy – discussing overdraft requirements or discussing unauthorized borrowings in an open office or a public area is not conducive to effective interviewing!
- if you are visiting a client for an interview make sure you have communicated effectively with your client about the point of the meeting and the timing and duration. Diarise it! (NB As a general rule you should only have **one** diary!)
- dress fittingly for the interview but be comfortable.
- ensure you have prepared for the interview, ie you clearly understand the purpose of the interview; you have researched the background needed for the interview; and you have an interview plan and prepared questions/offers etc.

The interview itself

- be on time if you are travelling – if you are meeting the customer at your premises then also be on time!

◆ introduce yourself and your role properly. Make the customer feel welcome – despite the nature of the interview. Shake hands and smile and pass the time of day with small talk. Establish rapport quickly and easily – be warm and natural.

◆ re-confirm the objectives and structure of the interview as well as the timings – confirm that that is the client's understanding too and that they do have the time required.

◆ establish any rules of 'confidentiality' if these are clearly important.

◆ take notes and explain that you will send written confirmation afterwards as appropriate.

The main body

◆ move into the main part of the interview clearly and professionally. Keep your objectives in mind and work to your plan.

◆ introduce the main topic early to ensure that you achieve your objectives.

◆ use an effective questioning technique – with well-structured open-ended questions (see above).

◆ when you have opened up an area of questioning then use shorter probing questions to penetrate the area. Stay with the topic until you have the information you want. Be sensitive, however, to your client's feelings. Do not over-pressurize him.

◆ avoid closed questions which prompt a yes/no answer – or use them to good effect! '… so what you mean is that you need a loan of £100,000 for 6 months?' – either a yes or no clarifies the position.

◆ do not use leading questions or the answer you receive may not be accurate or complete.

◆ summarize periodically to confirm understanding and to keep to your plan.

◆ control the pace of the interview.

◆ observe and use silences or pauses intelligently. Some people need longer to answer and collect their thoughts than others – give them that time. Listen by active listening, ie good body posture, eye contact and logical progression of answers and next questions.

◆ keep the rapport going – smile, offer tea etc.

◆ be sensitive and flexible. If your original interview plan is clearly off track – then clarify the area for discussion. If you lose the thread do not waffle, acknowledge it, move onto another topic and ask if you may return to the original line later.

◆ invite questions and answer them or agree to find out the information.

Closing

◆ finish on a high note wherever possible

◆ summarize and explain the next steps

◆ close the interview nicely
◆ arrange the date of next meeting and/or lines of communication if you need to follow up
◆ thank your client
◆ shake hands and depart or conduct them off the premises.

Interview reports

Straight after the interview write up your interview notes while the meeting is still fresh in your mind – it is amazing how points fade rapidly. Do whatever you said that you would do – eg write at once to confirm key points. Put in hand research or proposals for permission.

Common faults with interview technique

◆ lateness because of poor planning or incompetence
◆ letting initial impressions colour your thoughts – HALO or HORNS effect
◆ interviewer talking too much and allowing insufficient 'airtime' for the interviewee
◆ allowing the interviewee to take control of the interview
◆ waffle or rambling sentences that lead nowhere – from either side
◆ unspecified, confused objectives
◆ bias and prejudice – the influence of your dislikes or stereotyping
◆ unsystematic/poor planning, eg having too many questions for the time available
◆ failure to establish rapport.

18.10   Data protection and security

As information and data held have increased so too have concerns about it. These fall under three headings:

◆ **Availability**
◆ **Integrity**
◆ **Privacy**

Availability

The first – availability – is about keeping the data safe and making sure that it can be accessed by those who need to easily, and in a timely manner.

Integrity

To be of use it must be correct and this raises the second concern – that of integrity. The data must be kept such that access does not affect the data (unless that is meant to happen with, for example, account postings or contact details updates). Data that has been changed incorrectly is corrupted and of no use.

Privacy

The final area is that of who exactly does have access to the information. It is confidential to the holder and in many cases commercially sensitive so both the provider (customer) and holder (financial institution) have a vested interest in ensuring that the data is private, unless the express consent is held.

To ensure that these three areas are maintained to the satisfaction of all a number of laws have been passed covering this. They include:

- The Consumer Credit Act (1974)
- Data Protection Acts (1984) and (1998)
- Computer Misuse Act (1999)
- Civil Evidence Act (1995)

There are also internal rules in each organization covering this area which must also be adhered to – but they cannot override legislation.

Summary

Information is increasingly critical to support us in decisions, whether they be marketing analysis or selling products to clients. It must be in a format that enables us to make the right decisions and carry out our duties effectively. Successful selling, marketing and customer service is wholly reliant on good, timely, accurate information. There are three ways to find information – internal analysis of data held, external research and from customer interviews. Security and integrity are key to maintaining confidence in the data retention and usage.

1 For information to be useful it must demonstrate certain characteristics. It should flow to us and therefore the mnemonic 'CURRENT' can help.
   C COST EFFECTIVE
   U USABLE
   R RELEVANT
   R RELIABLE
   E ERROR FREE
   N NORMAL
   T TIMELY

2 Information is the key to making informed decisions and to being master of a brief before meeting customers. You need information to enable you to understand your customers, your own organization's capabilities, what is happening in the world, what your competitors are doing and many other things beside as well as supporting the decisions that you have to make every day. Otherwise you will be guessing or working under false assumptions.

3 Remember DRIP when analysing:

Data Rich, Information Poor
Volume does not equal Quality

4 One of the greatest sources of information about a customer is the customer himself. A well-planned interview can elicit much relevant information which will allow you to understand a lot about him and to populate your database.

5 As information and data held have increased so too have concerns about it. These fall under three headings: **Availability, Integrity, Privacy.**

Select bibliography

Managing Information : Phil Fawcett – **ifs** Publishing

Notes

1 **John McIntyre**: SAS Institute Inc.
2 **Bill Inmon**: *Building a Data Warehouse*
3 **William J Frawley, Gregory Piatetsky-Shapiro and Christopher J Matheus**
4 **Marcel Holshemier & Arno Siebes** (1994)

Nineteen

Presentations

Topics in this chapter

Preparing presentations

Effective customer meetings

Introduction to this chapter

In dealing with customers many occasions will present themselves where you are required to present facts to an audience. This could be the customer herself or your peers and superiors to obtain agreement to suggestions and options. It is critical that you are able to present logically and succinctly, and to clearly articulate the message. These may be of several types:

- ◆ In plenary session to many
- ◆ To a small group from a corporate customer
- ◆ To an individual either in her private capacity or perhaps as a representative of a corporate.

19.1   Preparing presentations

Although presentations are all different in one way, given the nature of the event and the audience, and you must tailor your presentation accordingly – in essence there are a few rules that apply to any presentation and the following questions should always be your frame of reference when considering and preparing a presentation.

◆ What are your objectives?
◆ How long do you have/need?
◆ Where will it take place?
◆ What media will you be using?
◆ Who is the audience?
◆ What should the content be?
◆ How will you structure it?
◆ How long will it take to put together?

Remember that a presentation is like an iceberg – 90% is unseen (below the water line) and is in the planning and preparation. The delivery, although important, is only the tip.

Below these are explored in detail.

What are your objectives?

Why are you making the presentation in the first place? You should be extremely clear as to why you are doing this. Is it to explain about your product? Is it to explain a new structure that is being put in place for customers? Are you asking them for a decision? If so:

◆ is the objective clear?
◆ have all options been identified?
◆ has data been gathered to support the analysis?
◆ has the analysis been carried out and a brief prepared explaining:
    ◆ the impact from each option
    ◆ the risk of the option
    ◆ the likelihood of the risk occurring
    ◆ the cost of doing it
    ◆ the implications of not doing it
    ◆ timing

Unless you have the answers to these questions your audience will not be clear as to why they are making the decision and therefore they cannot hope to make the right one, nor to understand the real drivers of the need to make the decision. Accordingly either you will not achieve the desired result or you will get a partial or incorrect decision.

How long do you have/need?

The time that you have been allocated is critical – either you will have to cut the presentation to fit in with the time or you need to ask for longer – but be sure that you have a good reason and a good argument for so doing. Note that the type of media used affects the timings – a series of power-point/freelance slides with builds can take much longer to get through than paper handouts of the same thing when talked through informally round a table.

Where will it take place?

This will affect what you can say, and how you say it. Presenting in a plenary session is different from a small group and different again from a intimate one-to-one. If you choose to use electronic media you should really check the venue for what is available and to make sure everything is compatible and works (is their software OK, is there a spare bulb for the OHP, can you link into the Lite-pro with your PC? Are the acoustics alright – what is the configuration of the room – are the seats OK – is it right for a presentation or a informal talk through etc? There is nothing worse than turning up with a PC presentation to be presented with a battered OHP.

What media will you be using?

(Paper, OHP, powerpoint/freelance slides etc.) The media should be chosen to suit the type of meeting and what is easily available. It is clearly inappropriate to use paper handouts for a large group – apart from anything else the wrong media look unprofessional, especially if the audience used to receiving presentations.

Who is the audience?

This is critical. If you are looking for a decision then unless the decision-maker(s) are present you are wasting your time. Knowing who will be there is the first step – of more use is knowing their own agendas and objectives. Any personal information you have will also pay dividends when you engage in small talk or relate an answer to a question to their own particular circumstances.

What should the content be?

Clearly the content must support the objectives. It should be presented in a logical flow to lead the listeners to your conclusion and to ensure that the message has been put across.

It is often useful to leave behind paper printouts of any presentations – or even to give them out in advance so that they can follow what you are saying and make notes as they go along. Depending on what is in it you might want to give them an 'edited' version if confidential information is involved.

What actions (research etc) do you need to put in hand to obtain the information that you need in the presentation – how long will it take – where should you go to get it – do you need help?

If possible tailor any information to the audience. If giving examples make sure that they are relevant and reinforce the points that you wish to make in their context. It is pointless referring to a situation in a global oil company's operations in the Middle East when talking to a small manufacturer of socks – unless there is a very useful lesson or parallel that makes a good point. Similarly it is of little value talking about equity release to a first-time buyer.

How will you structure it?

The structure is important and here it is very useful to remember the old adage

KISS – Keep It Simple Stupid

It should contain the following – without exception!

◆ An introduction to you and the session, as well as to the objectives of the presentation (yours and theirs). If appropriate they can also introduce themselves briefly
◆ An agenda containing the details of what you are going to cover
◆ A short background section if appropriate
◆ An executive summary of the key points
◆ The detail
◆ A summary of what you have said and conclusions if appropriate
◆ Next steps if appropriate
◆ Close and questions

Prior to presenting get someone else to look at it critically – does everything you have put on it pass the 'so what?' test.

Logic in structure

Use the following template developed by Barbara Minto[1] to get arguments across. It uses logic and understanding of people's thought processes to order information logically to persuade them to agree to the decision (that you require).

First describe the **Situation**

Then the **Complication** (what we do not like about it)

Then the **Question** you are trying to answer

Then the **Answer** to the question

The first three points should be familiar to the audience already because they form the basis of the presentation. You then give them the answer and support it with facts and they are already most of the way there to agreeing.

For example:

You are a company that manufactures xx. **(situation)**

You have received a major order from overseas that requires a major investment in working capital. **(complication)**

How shall this be financed? **(question)**

We can provide you with O/D, export finance, foreign exchange contracts, letters of credit etc. **(answer)**

This is then followed by facts and figures etc supporting the answer and demonstrating why it is a good answer and that they should agree.

19.2   General points

DO

- ◆ Use diagrams to illustrate points – but make them simple. For complex diagrams and if it is appropriate build them up
- ◆ Explain diagrams and tables – and give them time to absorb them
- ◆ Get your numbers right – it destroys credibility if there are errors in a presentation
- ◆ Welcome people and thank them for attending – at the beginning and at the end
- ◆ Think of the presentation from the audience's perception – what are their frames of reference – what will they understand?
- ◆ Make lots of eye contact – critical – do not look at your notes and read them out
- ◆ Face the audience – but have good movement
- ◆ Make it lively – use different voice tones and nuances – inject humour where you can and if appropriate
- ◆ Project to the back of the hall
- ◆ Rehearse – especially if you are unfamiliar with presenting
- ◆ Refer questions to colleagues if they are present – but do not give out 'hospital passes'
- ◆ Where appropriate, ask the audience to answer a question
- ◆ Try to make it as interactive as possible wither by asking questions instead of making statements or using them in the presentation to confirm points etc
- ◆ Take supporting documentation with you if appropriate.

DON'T

- ◆ put too many points on a slide. Around five or six is acceptable – but be sensible – if you need eight points on one slide then put them on but make them easy to understand
- ◆ use jargon – or explain unfamiliar terms or abbreviations
- ◆ mumble
- ◆ speak too fast
- ◆ fiddle with things in your pocket
- ◆ be nervous (easy to say)
- ◆ play with objects in your hands (pens pointers etc) – put them down if you are not using them
- ◆ talk down to the audience – eg '...it is perfectly clear that...' '...or it is obvious that...' – it may not be to them
- ◆ ignore questions – answer them, and ask if you have answered the question
- ◆ give an inadequate answer – say rather that you will get back to them – and do so.

Ask if they can hear you and can see clearly.

How long will it take to put together?

When planning a presentation it is useful to consider how long it night take to prepare. It can take a long time to research and then prepare presentations. Setting timescales and resource limits can help enormously.

19.3   Effective customer meetings

Although interview techniques have been discussed earlier there are some other useful issues for consideration. To make meetings or interviews truly effective you must conduct them properly. This means understanding the nature of human interactions. People operate on three levels in meetings[2] – they are called:

- ◆ Chatter
- ◆ Intellectual
- ◆ Emotional

Understanding these three levels and the differences between them is important – because moving into the wrong style can close down a meeting before it has even started.

Chatter is the meaningless talk that just fills time – eg 'how are you?' – 'did you see the game last night?' – 'did you have a good trip up?' – 'would you like a cup of tea?' etc. We do it unconsciously all the time but it is an important non-threatening way to start off a meeting. This phase is a very important part of creating the environment where the customer feels at ease and is willing to talk. You then gradually move into the next phase.

Intellectual is the phase where questions cause the respondent to think about his answer and develops mutual understanding of the objectives and ultimately a resolution. Good meetings should never pass beyond this phase. Unfortunately many do and often very quickly move into the third phase.

Emotion is where the respondent starts to feel very uncomfortable with the questions because they feel that she is being pressurised or that you are asking the wrong, irrelevant or personal questions. This has only one ending – the customer is unhappy. 'Hard' selling often ends up here.

Figure 19.1: Questioning intensity curves

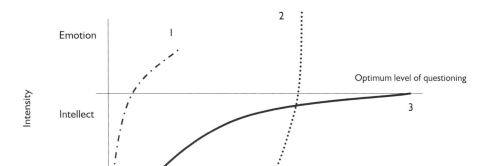

Figure 19.1 shows the three types of questioning. The best types of meeting never progress beyond the intellectual phase. In meeting 1 it has quickly progressed into emotion (an interrogation). In 2 while the meeting started off well it gradually slipped up into the emotional area – ie the questioner went too far. Number 3 is a well-structured and run meeting that will achieve its objectives. Note – too much chatter can result in not getting to the point!

Imparting difficult messages

Some meetings of course have different objectives – for example where you need to close an account or let a customer know that his facilities will not be made available. These require just as careful handling although perhaps a little more firmness is needed. Any organization that is managing its customers for value will have to manage out the accounts that do not fit with its profitability profile. There is no difference in handling the meetings except that you must be even more careful not to drift into the emotional areas.

Summary

Presentation skills are critical when dealing with customers or colleagues. Prepare for each one with the same care and detail.

1 There are a few rules that apply to any presentation and the following questions should always be your frame of reference when considering and preparing a presentation:
   ◆ What are your objectives?
   ◆ How long do you have/need?
   ◆ Where will it take place?
   ◆ What media will you be using?
   ◆ Who is the audience?
   ◆ What should the content be?
   ◆ How will you structure it?
   ◆ How long will it take to put together?
2 To make meetings or interviews truly effective you must conduct them properly. This means understanding the nature of human interactions. People operate on three levels in meetings[3] – they are called:
   ◆ Chatter
   ◆ Intellectual
   ◆ Emotional

Select bibliography

F Reichheld: *Loyalty rules*

Kotler: *Principles of Marketing*

Peter Doyle: *Value Based Marketing*

Notes

1 **Barbara Minto**: *Pyramid Thinking* (Pitman)
2 **Dwight S Ritter**: *Relationship Banking* (Bankers Publishing company – Chicago USA)

Twenty

Complaints handling

Topics in this chapter

Problem path

Rescue opportunities

Service recovery

Dealing with defectors

Introduction to this chapter

Problems occur in all industry sectors and in all players – the key difference is how they are handled. This is not only at the individual level when a customer is standing in front of you or shouting down a telephone – but also at the corporate level in terms if setting the complaints-handling culture and in establishing an effective mechanism for collating complaints and then doing something about the recurring ones.

A recent survey report (Julius) stated that in 2001 some 4 million people were considering or had considered changing their current accounts. This is a very high number and in addition around half were estimated *not* to have complained to their bank! Furthermore around 1 in 10 customers are dissatisfied with their bank but had not switched (see Figure 20.1). This reflects that great asset to banks and financial services everywhere – apathy (or inertia). One of the main reasons cited is difficulty – in changing/hassle/stuck with it [around 30%] – supporting the myth that hassle supports inertia. Interestingly enough a similar survey conducted by NOP for the Banking Code Standards Board found that 96% thought that it was easy to change bank and building society accounts. The fact that most do not, further supports inertia as a factor.

Figure 20.1: Reasons for not changing current account

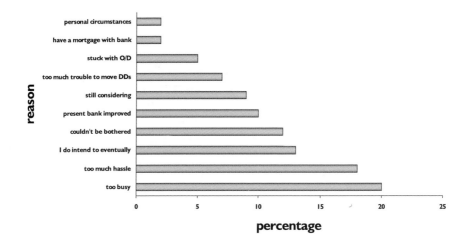

Source: Financial World November 2001

20.1 Problem path

There are several stages involved when a problem arises. In many cases, which are usually not documented and unrecognized, they are handled successfully and quickly. Sometimes however they are not and a lot of 'noise' can be generated.

The stages can be thought of by using the acronym 'CREDIT':

C Communication
R Response
E Emotion
D Decision
I Informs
T Termination

Communication – the problem arises and the customer tells the organization. However in many cases the customer **does not** tell the organization, especially if the issue is not particularly grave (eg duplicate statements). He is more likely to fulminate against a waste of my money and tell his friends, family and work colleagues. Where he finds a major error – such as a payment not made, credits not processed or 'phantom' withdrawals – they are much more likely to complain.

Figure 20.2: Nature of complaints

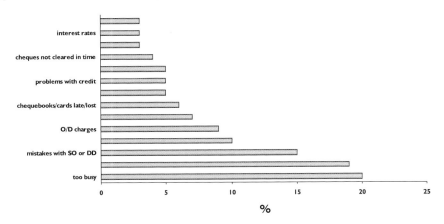

%

Source: Financial World November 2001

Response – the organization responds to the customer. Or in many cases does not. This may result in further communication or nothing but a sense of injustice.

Emotion – the customer reacts to the response. He may feel elated or angry at the response. He may also be neutral. He may contact the organization again, or may let it fester.

Decision – the customer considers whether the response is adequate (or worse or better than he expected). If he feels that the response is substantially below his expectations, and especially if it is not the first occasion, he may decide to take his business elsewhere. He will take into account other factors in weighing the response such as: past history, the magnitude of the error (in his eyes) and this incident may act as the trigger – or straw that breaks the camel's back.

Informs – if he decides to go then the customer informs the organization of his decision. This presents another opportunity to talk to the customer and try to persuade him not to go. This only happens where there is a relationship. Where no such relationship exists – eg a food retailer – the customer will simply stop using the outlet and go elsewhere. In that case there is little dialogue.

Termination – he ends the relationship and goes elsewhere, carrying a deep prejudice against the organization that he will usually express at any opportunity.

20.2   Rescue opportunities

There are two critical stages here – the first is the quality, timeliness of the response and the second is how the termination is handled. Too often the response is inadequate, or computer-generated and fails to satisfy the customer. This is a pity because in most cases only a slight effort will repay large dividends. Customers who have complained and had their complaint dealt with satisfactorily have a huge amount of loyalty to the organization and become advocates – whereas those who have had a poor experience will leave or become 'grognards' who have a deep dissatisfaction or in the worse case 'saboteurs', bad-mouthing the organization.

Services, by their nature, are people-related – and people are 'dynamic' and fallible. It is important therefore that the strongest procedures are in place to deal with complaints – sometimes referred to as 'empathy plus one'[1] – fix the problem and overcompensate by doing something over and beyond normal expectations. Staff must deal with complaining customers – even rude ones – and not reciprocate, to move as many as possible down the satisfaction continuum.

Figure 20.3: Customer satisfaction – continuum

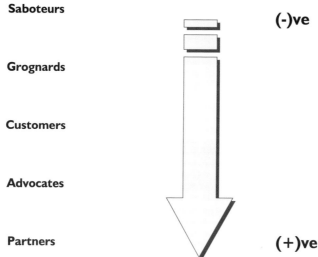

Saboteurs

Grognards

Customers

Advocates

Partners

(-)ve

(+)ve

Satisfaction versus dissatisfaction

Many organizations place a great deal of emphasis on trying to improve service continually. Research has shown that beyond a certain point the returns are very small and disproportionate to the effort[2] and after a time yield diminishing returns. It is far better to focus on dealing with dissatisfaction and attack this because it yields very positive results, often for little effort, and matters more than improving service for satisfied customers.

The research also indicates that the greatest danger to efforts to increase customer base and of course product penetration comes from losing customers because you are losing a relationship, which will take time to build with any replacement customer – and that replacement is merely that, not incremental business. The research suggests segmenting customers according to their propensity for dissatisfaction!

'Customer loyalty is the single most important driver of long-term financial performance' – Dave Illingworth: Lexus UK

Figure 20.4: Marketing cycle (III)

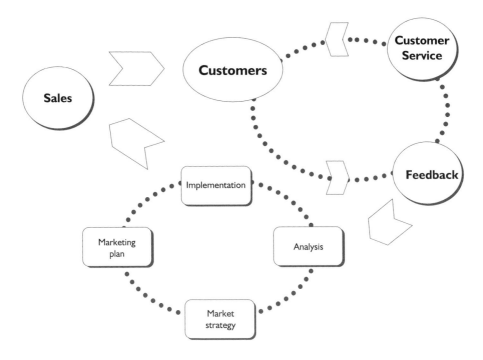

In Figure 20.4 feedback and customer service have been added to the marketing model. This is a prerequisite because it is their feedback about the good – and the bad – the complaints that have a vital input into the marketing planning cycle.

Marketing is of course a theoretical exercise – it is only when customers buy the offerings and comment that you receive any real market and customer-related feedback that tells you whether you have got it right. Complaints then, while not good, should be viewed as an opportunity to build the relationship with the customer.

20.3   Service recovery

No matter how good your staff and procedures mistakes and errors will occur. The financial services sector is heavily reliant on people and as a result there is a high propensity for errors to occur wherever there is a human interface.

Good procedures and training will go a long way to minimizing this but nevertheless they will still happen. One of the hallmarks of an excellent organization is how it deals with these errors when they do happen. They should be viewed as learning experiences and used to illustrate what needs to be done – as well as taking steps to fix them.

Complaints cost you money from two sources: the cost of rectification – which usually increases with time – and the potential business lost from the complainant. It is important therefore to ensure that complaints are handled quickly but sensibly.

Case study

A building society had a policy of investigating all phantom withdrawals from ATMs. This was to ensure that customers' complaints were dealt with adequately. It was slow and in the majority of cases the withdrawals were found to be false or internal errors. Money was only repaid at the end of the process. Customers were highly dissatisfied with the process and as well as complaining about the withdrawals were complaining about the delays in fixing them.

The process was reviewed and not only was the dissatisfaction found to be very high but it was very expensive to carry out the checks. As a result a new policy was adopted of paying out on all claims immediately with subsequent investigation where necessary (as many resolved themselves subsequently), with the proviso that where more than a set number occurred (3) within a given period they would not be recompensed until they were investigated fully. This greatly improved customer handling and also enabled staff to get on with day-to-day operations without constant queries and complaints about the process.

Organizations that have examined their complaints-handling process have usually developed a new set of procedures with one or two key paradigms – resolution should take place as near to the customer as possible, and as quickly as possible.

This is supported by an escalation process which is transparent to the customer so that they can have the confidence that any complaints will be taken seriously. Complaints should of course be recorded and that data fed into the database to allow patterns of issues to be identified and subsequently resolved. Dealing with complaints is a skill that not every body has. There are some key issues that are helpful.

Do:

- give your name
- let the person decide if he wishes to pursue his 'complaint' as a complaint
- tell the person what will happen next and the stages of the procedure
- act quickly once the complainant has left
- get his details, eg name, addresses, telephone numbers, dates
- get the facts/make notes
- listen
- accept complaints even if they are not about your section/department
- stay calm even if the person gets angry
- be sympathetic
- take the person seriously
- be honest
- let the person have their say.

Don't:

- argue with the complainant
- get angry
- get into a blame conversation
- undermine the organization
- pass the complainant on to someone else
- accept abuse from a complainant, eg swearing
- ask them to complain in writing or in person or come back later
- deter people from making a complaint
- consider the complaint as a personal criticism
- use jargon when writing back to the complainant.

Dealing with complaints is quite normal – but of course action should be taken to minimize them.

Case study[3]

UCI is a major cinema operator. it deals with 80 million customers annually in the UK alone as well as operating overseas, and found it difficult to keep track of them all. It was also dealing with complaints on an individual basis and missing the big picture. It installed a new complaints-handling system as part of customer relationship management into its cinemas and found it was able to identify key issues such as popcorn packets leaking and thus causing it to pay for dry cleaning. Changing the bags saved it a fortune. The new process also allows them to filter out 'persistent or professional complainers' and thus save time and money.

20.4   Corporate responses to complaints data

Once a complaint has been dealt with – and hopefully resolved – the details should of course be captured in a complaints log. The organization needs to review this periodically for recurrences and major issues and costs. While it is true that one complaint represents several and several may represent very many – it is not always so and it does not mean that the entire customer base is unhappy.

The complaints may only be representative of the feelings of an isolated individual or a small group of customers. You cannot please everyone all of the time and you are probably pleasing most customers (who you do not hear from). You do not have to change your policies to accommodate a few customers – especially where it is outside of your CVP.

> ## Case study
>
> South West Airlines, which pioneered low-cost flights, started out operating in Texas, USA. They flew only between towns in the state of Texas and offered no frills and very cheap flights. Each year they receive many complaints from passengers who want, *inter alia*, food served on the flight, the ability to check in baggage to other airlines, allocated seating and so on. South West does not change its policy because of these complaints because its stated policy is not to offer these things. That is why its flights are so cheap because it does not have to ticket baggage, wait for flights to come in etc. Those sort of complaints are outside of its CVP and so it does not address them. Of course a complaint about staff or other relevant areas would be addressed.

It is important to make this distinction before making changes in response to a complaint. Once you have determined that a complaint that recurs is serious, however, you must address it immediately and make the necessary changes.

Negative customer feedback and complaints should always be viewed as an opportunity for improvement. The serious evaluation of customer complaints and questions is a necessary and effective way of learning from mistakes, and ultimately enabling you to increase sales by taking action whether to resolve an error – customer satisfaction increases dramatically after a successful resolution of an error – or by obviating future occurrences.

Some extracts from organizations' websites on complaints. These have been chosen at random and do not necessarily contain all detail. Note that for some organizations not listed here it was difficult to find the right section and that in general it is harder to find out from insurance companies' websites, indicating that they have not quite thought this issue through.

Lloyds/TSB
Voicing your concern

We want to put things right as quickly as possible, so we've set up a 3 step procedure to resolve your complaints

step 1: approach your usual point of contact. You'll need:
◆ your full name & address
◆ full details of your complaint
◆ your account number, branch sort code and any policy numbers (do not include this information if you are contacting us by e-mail)
◆ what you think we should do to put things right
◆ photocopies of any relevant paperwork

We always aim to resolve your complaint at this stage.

step 2: refer to a complaint support unit
◆ If you are not satisfied with our response, we may refer you on to an appropriate manager or department for further investigation.

step 3: ask the support unit to issue you with a 'final response'
◆ If your complaint has not been resolved to your satisfaction, we will give you a 'final response'. This outlines your complaint and our response. We'll also provide you with details of the Financial Ombudsman Service.

If we haven't sent you a final response within 8 weeks of first raising the complaint, you may approach the Financial Ombudsman Service directly.

HALIFAX

Stage 1 – Where you first make your complaint

We aim to resolve your concerns within 24 hours. Sometimes it may take longer to look into the matter fully. If this happens, we will let you know within 5 working days, who will reply.

Often the people you first raise the matter with are able to help, but there may be occasions when it needs a specialist area to be involved. If you don't know who to contact you can:-

telephone Customer Relations on:
0845 600 8000

or a textphone is available for you if you have a hearing impairment on:
0845 600 1750

write to us at:
Halifax plc
Halifax Customer Relations
Trinity Road
Halifax HX1 2RG

We will then arrange for the right person to look into and respond to your concerns.

Stage 2 – Customer Relations

In the unlikely event that you remain unhappy, you can ask for your complaint to be referred to a Customer Relations manager for further review. If you are still not satisfied you can, at this stage, ask the Financial Ombudsman Service to help, or for service related complaints about Halifax Estate Agencies Limited, the Ombudsman for Estate Agents.

The Halifax supports fully and is a member of both the Ombudsman Schemes. These are impartial and conduct independent investigations.

20.5   Managing defection

In order to retain customers you must attack defections. With the emergence of a customer base that is both increasingly more financially aware and increasingly more financially 'promiscuous' they are, therefore, more likely to change. It is important, therefore, that the underlying reasons for those defections are understood and that you put in place processes to manage and where possible and appropriate to obviate the customer's leaving.

You need to find out why customers either leave or are tempted to leave.

Accordingly you must:

- ◆ Measure the defection levels (in Insurance this is known as persistency or lapse rates) to ascertain how bad the issue is for you
- ◆ Analyse the defections by category
  - o type of defector
  - o reason for defecting
- ◆ Split them into:
  - ● a] the types you wish to keep
  - ● b] the types you are happy to lose

◆ Develop a plan to attack the leaving causes of those customers in category a]
◆ Pilot the plan
◆ Get feedback from customers
◆ Implement fully
◆ Carry out comparative analysis for improvements in leaving trends

Types of defector

There are several reasons why customers defect. There may be one reason, or a combination. Usually it takes something quite robust to make them go, because inertia is still nevertheless a powerful force in customer choice. The major types of reasons to make a financial services customer into a defector are:

◆ **Poor service** – the most common reason for a customer defecting, but paradoxically the one reason that offers the best opportunity for long-term sustainable recovery. Where service deficiencies are uncovered – often due to customer complaints – then if action is taken to attack the problem(s) recovery can be made. It is well documented that in instances where customers have complained and the issue has been resolved their loyalty to the organization increases because they perceive that it listened; took their complaint on board; and then did something to rectify it.

◆ **Price** – easy to compete on price – you can sell anything by dropping the price. The questions are whether it is sustainable in the long term and if you can either increase the price later on – or recoup it some other way. Too often price wars lead to reduced profits for all and often force some organizations out of the market. The consumer usually benefits in terms of costs, but may lose out in terms of choice. Price reductions are also the easiest to match and, in view of the lack of sustainable competitive edge, not recommended as a means of competition – unless you have massive cost advantages.

Case study

In the 1970s the UK daily newspaper *The Times* ran a campaign to sell more by reducing its price to a very low sum (£0.10p). The logic was that it would increase its circulation and thus attract more advertising due to its greater outreach. It later increased its price to a more commensurate level with that of its competitors once it had attained its circulation growth.

◆ **Product** – where customers leave due to product deficiencies or issues it is very hard to rectify for those customers – the damage is probably irretrievable and their decision irreversible. For remaining customers, however, defects can be rectified and then given to existing customers as part of the customer servicing process.

◆ **Market defectors** – are caused by a sea change in the nature of the competition. For example the arrival of new channels allowing greater choice, such as telephone insurance or Internet banking, or by new competitors entering the market from outside – such as non-financial organizations such as stores and utilities. They may also leave you because the market has moved on in terms of what it represents and your marketplace either disappears or you are forced to become a niche player to survive.

◆ **Politics** – customers may leave because they disagree with some aspect of your operations. In the 1970s there was a student boycott of Barclays because of its links with South Africa, since relinquished. There is little that can be done with this type of defector except to send counter information – especially correcting a misapprehension – or by changing the ethos of an organization – a very difficult and long-term ploy.

◆ **Technology** may drive customers to go elsewhere – either by offering what you cannot or because it is better realized, or just 'trendy' to do it. The only way to counter this is to improve your own technology to match – or at least go much of the way towards the competition; the proliferation of on-line and dot-com banks and insurance was a reaction to this type of defection. The perceived strategy was 'clicks' but many have now realized that it is a combination of Internet and branch networks that is the right strategy for them: 'bricks and clicks'. This of course has implications for the cost base as players in both markets must bear both sets of costs.

Any organization therefore must put in place a strategy for dealing with defections and ensuring that there is proper feedback and reappraisal of its operations to minimize such occurrences.

20.6 Measuring service levels and customer satisfaction

One of the key aspects for any organization is to obtain feedback and information from its customers as to how it is really doing. For this to be useful it must be obtained directly from customers. Similarly in order to confirm how customers are serviced it is necessary to test the staff – often by using mystery shoppers. This must be carried out against the backdrop of a well thought through set of measures that reflect the way in which the organization expects to service the customer – and reflect its corporate philosophy.

Measures for customers

Any company that is considered excellent will have a well-established and effective mechanism for measuring how well customers feel that they are serviced. It may consist of several activities, but the main point is that these are collated and that something is done about it where appropriate.

One of the key questions is 'What should you measure?' For many firms the only feedback that they receive is of the negative sort when customers complain about errors or poor service. To improve, however, you not only need to find out where you are failing to delight your customers, but you also need to know where you are managing to achieve this. You need to make sure that you are focusing on the right issues and therefore hitting critical factors for customers, rather than what your organization might assume are the right ones.

The items for measurement must be set not from the organizational point of view – but rather from the customers' perspective - 'How do I feel about my interactions with the organization?'

They might include:

◆ Measures of customer service such as courtesy or promptness in calling back;
◆ Staff knowledge when dealing with customers;
◆ Turnaround in dealing with complaints.

But they should also include some tangible measures that customers are satisfied – such as:

◆ product penetration;
◆ product extension into family;
◆ referrals etc.

Ultimately the only true measure of customers' satisfaction is that they place their business with you. What you are trying to do is pre-empt anything that might stop them from doing this and resolve it before it becomes an issue.

There are a number of methods that can be used to ascertain customer satisfaction:

◆ Focus groups
◆ Questionnaires
◆ One to one interviews
◆ Counter encounters
◆ Exit interviews
◆ Telephone surveys
◆ Market research
◆ Web sites
◆ Mystery customers

Below a brief view of the pros and cons is given. See also the chapter on Market Research which covers many of these in detail.

Focus groups

A small group of people are brought together and discuss issues. This needs facilitation and should be carried out regularly with the same people for consistency's sake.

Pros

 ◆ Detailed views
 ◆ Subjective opinions.

Cons

 ◆ Only a few people involved
 ◆ Takes time
 ◆ Depends on skills of facilitator.

Questionnaires

A series of questions which the respondees complete for later analysis.

Pros

 ◆ Consistent data
 ◆ Cheap to use.

Cons

 ◆ Relies on returns
 ◆ Works best for simple questions
 ◆ Can give skewed or false results if not very well thought through
 ◆ Can take time to analyse – especially if subjective answers sought.

One to one interviews

Customers are interviewed to obtain their views on a range of issues. Ideally should be combined with other events to ensure acquiescence (ie when a new customer is taken on or at account review time).

Pros

 ◆ Detailed views can be obtained
 ◆ Very personal.

Cons

 ◆ People intensive
 ◆ Customers may not want to get involved
 ◆ Depends on skills of interviewer.

Counter encounters

These types of events occur every day in a branch. It is an excellent opportunity for obtaining customer feedback. As the transactions are carried out the cashier or customer manager can ask a series of short questions which enable either some data to be gathered or for a further more detailed encounter – such as a one-to-one to take place later.

Pros

- ◆ Easy to execute
- ◆ Data can be gathered directly relating to services as they are processed.

Cons

- ◆ May be time consuming if not careful – especially if there is a long queue
- ◆ May light a fire if a pet hate subject is touched on.

Exit interviews

A sad event when a customer leaves – but an opportunity to learn. Whenever a customer leaves an interview should be held to try to ascertain why it is that she or he is leaving – what are the reasons – what was done about it? Is it still redeemable?

Pros

- ◆ First hand fresh feedback
- ◆ May get a chance to reverse the situation.

Cons

- ◆ Time consuming
- ◆ May turn into a general 'moaning' session.

Telephone surveys

Customers (and non-customers) are called to elicit their views. In essence an interactive questionnaire.

Pros

- ◆ Easy to carry out
- ◆ Facilitates analysis.

Cons

- ◆ Need good scripts
- ◆ Can be difficult to get responses – especially in business-to-business examples.

Market research

The investigation into customers' needs and wants or views on issues.

Pros

- ◆ Detailed views
- ◆ Subjective opinions.

Cons

◆ Only a few people involved
◆ Takes time
◆ Depends on skills of facilitator.

Websites

An open advertisement for customers to give thoughts – may be initiated by them, or can be directed – eg by letting them know on communications that they can use the website. You can also directly tell them to use it in certain circumstances.

Pros

◆ Cheap as customer does the work
◆ Provides valuable feedback in set format.

Cons

◆ Largely passive
◆ Many customers are web 'inarticulate/illiterate' and cannot express themselves.

Mystery customers

The use of staff and/or outside agencies to test services and processes by posing as a customer and attempting to transact business (eg asking for advice, attempting to open an account, calling and requesting items or information). For example many banks claim to test every branch at least once a month – a considerable undertaking.

Pros

◆ Easy to execute
◆ Consistent comparisons across several sites – by area, by region and nationally.

Cons

◆ People and time intensive
◆ Needs consolidation and follow up in a constructive manner
◆ Must be used to give positive feedback or may be regarded as 'spying'.

Summary

Complaints are a normal feature of business. The key issues are the frequency of complaint and the consequences of customer defections as a result of the issues (which may not always be articulated by leaving customers). It is necessary to put in place a procedure for capturing defections, analysing them and taking steps to make cost-effective changes to retain those the organization wishes to keep.

1 Problems occur in all industry sectors and in all players – the key difference is how they are handled.
2 There are several stages involved when a problem arises. In many cases, which are usually not documented and unrecognized, they are handled successfully and quickly. Sometimes however they are not and a lot of 'noise' can be generated.
   The stages can be thought of by using the acronym 'CREDIT':

   C   **Communication**
   R   **Response**
   E   **Emotion**
   D   **Decision**
   I   **Informs**
   T   **Termination**
3 Complaints cost you money – from two sources: the cost of rectification – which usually increases with time – and the potential business lost from the complainant. It is important therefore to ensure that complaints are handled quickly but sensibly.
4 Negative customer feedback and complaints should always be viewed as an opportunity for improvement.
5 Defections should be analysed and a proper strategy developed to deal with them.

Select bibliography

'An explanation of customer exits in retail banking': K Stewart [*International Journal of Bank Marketing*. Volume 16, No 1 (1998)]

Keep the right customers: Mark Stewart – McGrawHill

Notes

1 Dawn Iacobucci – *FT Mastering Marketing* pp221/222
2 Professor Vikas Mittal, Northwestern University USA (as quoted in *FT Mastering Markleting*)
3 see Robert Lauterborn – 'New Marketing Litany' (article in *Advertising Age*, October 1990)

Twenty-one

Ethical selling

Topics in this chapter

Misleading statements

Purpose

Best advice

Promotion

Money laundering

Consumer sovereignty test

Green issues

Introduction to this chapter

The science of marketing is often ranked low in terms of ethical behaviour, along with politicians, estate agents and second-hand car salesmen. In recent years financial services – especially in the life insurance market – has also suffered due to, *inter alia*, pension mis-selling. The reasons that ethics come into play is that there can sometimes be a conflict between the objectives of the different stakeholders – ie customers may have different objectives from those involved in selling products and services. Frequently they are driven by remuneration policies that require very high or challenging results which force some staff to cut corners to achieve them.

The energy and telecoms sectors, which have recently seen some spectacular failures (Enron etc) have highlighted some suspect practices in as much as some banks have been accused of using their research departments to write 'glowing' reports on clients in order for their corporate finance arms to win deals – were this proven it would indicate a clear moral issue (even if it is legal). In response to these criticisms and without admitting liability some banks have split their research and investment arms off from the main body to allow greater independence.

Ethics is, however, not really about illegality. It is about moral judgements and therefore it is much more subjective because morals differ between people – one man's moral dilemma is common practice to another. In ancient Sparta young boys, as part of their training to be warriors, were encouraged to forage for themselves (stealing) and the only crime there was to be caught. As moral feeling gathers force the issue is increasingly translated into legislation. It is not so long ago that slavery was legal in many places.

Marketing bumps up against ethics all the time- eg truth in advertising (washes whiter!), product descriptions (is it really a top ten investment – they all seem to be in some top ten or other?) or equitable treatment of distributors. Historically it used to be *caveat emptor* but the pendulum has swung quite dramatically towards increasing duties of care (*Donohoe v Stevenson*), consumer protection (CCA) and higher penalties, coupled with an increasing tendency to sue and claim damages. As a result it behoves financial services staff to be aware of the ethical and moral issues that they might encounter.

21.1   Misleading

This is really a lie by omission but it is again not clear cut as a moral issue. It might arise either as carelessness or by a deliberate attempt to deceive, but also many customers mislead themselves by their own intent or perception. This might be because of their preconception or by misreading a document (who reads small print?) and they assume some issues to be facts. Many facts are based on social agreements and not objective truth and are therefore ambiguous – known as ' social facts'.

Purpose

One of the key issues in lending has always been to undertake analysis. In one of the mnemonic aids used by banks (PAPERS) (Purpose, Amount, Period, Earnings, Repayments, Security), the first question is Purpose – ie what is the money to be used for? This allows you to consider whether it is (a) legal and (b) moral, although again that is a subjective judgement. In some countries where prostitution is legal – is it moral for a bank to lend for that purpose?

Some people feel that the arms trade is immoral and the recent FTSE4Good index of ethical companies excludes companies engaged (*inter alia*) in the arms industry.

Those employed directly in the trade, and those in the armed forces, plus the indirectly employed would of course take a completely different view – ie they have a different moral perspective. Similarly local employment may depend on it as may local branch profitability and the arguments for it include: good for balance of payments, jobs, and the value chain (suppliers).

Best advice

This is another good example of a moral situation. What constitutes 'best advice' to a customer? It might be taken as meaning that they have received the best possible advice that they could. To a multi-tied adviser it might mean that they have given the best advice from a range of products similar in nature but from different providers, but to a single tied agent it means that they have given the best advice that they can – usually on one product, or between different types of products.

FSA

Although the FSA is concerned with legal regulation it also looks at ethics. In 2002 the FSA stated that it wished to raise ethical standards in the City and mailed out a laminated sheet to 'remind' staff in the city of (abstract) values such as openness, responsibility and fairness. As an incentive to those who abide by the spirit as well as the letter of the law it is offering the carrot of lighter-touch regulation. It wishes people to think about the implications of their actions as well as whether they comply with the strict legal wordings, and as such is placing a moral burden of judgement on staff.

Promotions

It has long been a well understood legal principle that advertisements must not be taken at their face value because they may contain what is known as 'advertisers' puff'[1]. However, the FSA has recently decided to enforce fairness in financial promotions.[2] These must be 'clear, fair and not misleading' as well as complying with regulation generally, where a promotion is defined as '...an invitation or inducement to engage in a 'controlled activity' relating to a 'controlled investment''. It applies to all forms of communication whether written, verbal or oral, e-mail, Internet website, advertisement or broadcast, and so is of direct relevance to anyone involved in marketing, selling or even customer service.

A very good maxim, used by marketers globally, is '...do unto others as you would have them do unto you...' What this means is that if you feel that what you are doing would not be what you would wish someone else in the same situation to do to you – do not do it.

Money laundering

This is a topic of some currency especially after the events of 11-9-01 highlighted the flows of terrorist funds, and therefore adequate procedures should be in place to deal with it. The practical result of the rules, however, that require amounts over £10,000 to be queried, is that it is viewed by many customers as an unreasonable intrusion. Given that most average house prices are over £200,000, far too many transactions will be caught, resulting in a lot of extra work and disgruntled customers.

Advertising standards

The Advertising Standards Authority (ASA) is an independent, self-regulatory body for non-broadcast advertisements, sales promotions and direct marketing in the UK (ie not TV and radio). It administers the British Code of Advertising, Sales Promotion and Direct Marketing (the CAP Code) to ensure that advertisements are legal, decent, honest and truthful.

Banks and other financial institutions, (in the UK at least) being generally responsible organizations, subscribe to its principles and these must be borne in mind whenever an 'advert' is used. This covers all and any forms of customer communication and, inter alia, includes such items as window posters, leaflets, as well as whiteboards and flipcharts with service details on – often used in branches to get that 'informal' feeling across – and any letters to customers referring to services, as well as Internet adverts and 'pop-ups'.

Customers can complain to the ASA if they feel that an advert – or communication – falls foul of its principles. There many principles and full details can be found on its website. Below the general principles are given:

Principles

'All marketing communications should be legal, decent, honest and truthful.'

'All marketing communications should be prepared with a sense of responsibility to consumers and to society.'

'All marketing communications should respect the principles of fair competition generally accepted in business.'

'No marketing communication should bring advertising into disrepute.'

'Marketing communications must conform with the Code. Primary responsibility for observing the Code falls on marketers. Others involved in

> preparing and publishing marketing communications such as agencies, publishers and other service suppliers also accept an obligation to abide by the Code.'
>
> 'Any unreasonable delay in responding to the ASA's enquiries may be considered a breach of the Code.'
>
> 'The ASA and CAP will, on request, treat in confidence any genuinely private or secret material supplied unless the Courts or officials acting within their statutory powers compel its disclosure.'
>
> 'The Code is applied in the spirit as well as in the letter.'

Note the last point which gives it licence to uphold complaints that are at the margin of acceptability. Financial organizations will not want the adverse publicity attendant on an upheld complaint and will take a dim view of outlets and staff that breach the rules.

Distance selling

For distance selling (eg telephone, fax, Internet) there are additional rules. A summary of general principles is given below but the full rules are available on the website mentioned below:

> 'For the purposes of the Code, distance selling marketing communications are the final written advertised stage in the process that allows consumers to buy products without the buyer and seller meeting face-to-face. Marketers should comply with the Consumer Protection (Distance Selling) Regulations 2000. Guidance on the legislation is available from www.dti.gov.uk. These clauses should be observed in conjunction with the legislation; they do not replace it.'

Staff should familiarize themselves with the provisions, and also with the relevant parts of their handbook covering communications etc.

21.2   Consumer Sovereignty Test

The Consumer Sovereignty Test (CST)[3] can be used to decide the morality of a decision. It is based on an analysis of whether consumers can exercise informed choice. It looks at three dimensions: consumer capability; information available and choice, as shown in Figure 21.1:

Figure 21.1: Consumer sovereignty test

Dimension	Establishing adequacy
Consumer capability	**Vulnerability factors** – age; education; income
Information	**Availability and quality** – sufficient to judge whether expectations at time of purchase will be fulfilled
Choice	**Opportunity to switch** – level of competition; switching costs

For example – should you tell a customer that the current version of the product is about to be replaced by a superior one? Using the CST it can be seen that this dilemma becomes unethical as it violates the second criterion – that of information (insider trading could be seen in the same light prior to the introduction of legislation).

Tobacco marketing is often held up as a prime example of violation of the consumer sovereignty test. Research shows that most people start smoking when they are very young (early teens), and as such it fails the first test of capability because teenagers are very vulnerable to advertising and peer pressure, as well as being less able to decide whether a thing is good or bad.

Due to the addictive nature of nicotine, it fails the third test – of choice – ie it is hard to choose to give up because of the physiological and physical addiction induced by tobacco.

In developing countries the second test is also found wanting because there is a less well-developed caucus of information about the harmful effects and therefore they are making an uninformed decision, whereas in developed countries more and more people are trying to quit (and fewer are smoking in the first place).

Benefits

Ethical conduct can contribute to a company's good reputation and unethical behaviour can destroy it! The largest banks have millions of customers and hardly anything goes wrong for most. However if a lapse receives publicity it has a disproportionate effect on a firm as that instance of bad publicity has far-reaching repercussions because people weigh such lapses heavily.

Key questions

There are a few questions that you must be able to answer – either for yourself or for others (management, auditors, regulators etc):

◆ do you understand your products and do you explain them fully and truthfully?
◆ do you understand you customer base (to spot money laundering)?
◆ does any money come from FAFT (Financial Action Task Force) blacklisted countries?
◆ do you have '…reasonable grounds to know or suspect…' that a customer is engaging in money laundering? (if you do and you do not bring it to the right competent authority then you could be guilty and face jail) then
◆ if you received the same advice in the same circumstances would you feel comfortable (can I sleep at night?)

21.3   Green issues

Environmental or green issues have become an increasingly important item for organizations and indeed political parties over the last few years. This phenomenon has changed fundamentally the way that a bank must look at its activities – both in the way it assesses its own operations and in how it perceives the risks when offering facilities to clients.

> 'from raw materials to waste processing, design to advertising, businesses are now under ever-increasing pressure to take account of the environmental implications of their activities'
>
> Sir Brian Corby, President of the CBI (1993)

There are two main areas of environmental concern for financial organizations:

- ◆ firstly that they give due regard to the environmental impacts of their customers' business; and
- ◆ secondly that they ensure that their own operations are conducted in an environmentally aware manner. It would be embarrassing in the extreme to be telling customers to go green when you yourselves are not!

In addition lenders could be held responsible for any damage caused in lending if their facilities supported these actions. In particular some potential areas are:

- ◆ that banks may not be repaid because customers' cashflow has been depleted by environmental clean up or other related costs;
- ◆ asset values may depreciate due to environmental impacts – eg land values will plummet if the land is contaminated;
- ◆ a bank itself may be held responsible for any clean-up costs (because it is likely to be seen as the one with the deepest pockets) – see United States versus Fleet Factors Corp Case Study below;
- ◆ a bank may be deemed to be a 'shadow director' – ie one in accordance with whose wishes the directors of a company act;
- ◆ failure to comply with relevant legislation (eg the Environmental Protection Act) may result in its licence being revoked.

Case Study

United States versus Fleet Factors Corp (1990) – where the factoring company was deemed to have participated in the management of a company (which had caused environmental damage) following foreclosure on stock and equipment and was held liable for US$400,000 clean-up costs.

Steps to ensure green issues are analysed

- ◆ Review existing portfolio for potential problems – and take action accordingly
- ◆ Take the initiative in green issues – by ensuring that where there is a risk borrowers complete environmental questionnaires
- ◆ Visit potential difficult sites
- ◆ Ensure green issues form part of the normal credit-assessment process
- ◆ Develop green action plans for use with customers – and check compliance with them
- ◆ Ensure insurance is in place and is adequate
- ◆ Ask for copies of green audits. (There are several types of these:

❏ Full audit – looks at organization's full range of activities from an environmental point of view
❏ Compliance audit
❏ Take-over audit – as part of a due diligence
❏ Project audit – assesses the environmental impact of a project (very commonly used by the EBRD) such as establishing a mine or a waste tip
❏ Site audit – looks at a particular location.

That banks take this issue seriously and are also responding to green issues is shown by website extracts:

HSBC

We recognize that companies have a responsibility for the stewardship of the planet, which we all hold in trust for future generations. HSBC has a long record of support for the environment in the countries where it operates. However, recognizing the vital importance of this area we decided to redouble our efforts in order to demonstrate our commitment even more clearly and to make a real and lasting difference.

In February 2002, we launched Investing in Nature, a new US$50 million eco-partnership with Botanic Gardens Conservation International (BGCI), Earthwatch and WWF. The decision to create this unique partnership was driven by some challenging facts. For instance, 1.2 billion people lack access to safe drinking water today, even though water is the essence of life. The world's water supply and freshwater habitats have become increasingly vulnerable. If we do not act now, by 2025 more than 60 per cent of the world's population could face a water shortage, and thousands of species and habitats will be gone forever. Plants provide us with food, fibre, medicine, timber and fuel. They help to regulate our climate, bind soil and provide habitats for the majority of creatures on the planet. Investing in Nature will protect 20,000 plant species from extinction, breathe life into three of the world's major rivers, train scientists from the developing world, and send 2,000 HSBC employees on conservation projects worldwide.

We will keep you informed about our progress with Investing in Nature in the years ahead.

Barclays

We work to develop policies and practices that help preserve the physical environment and we try to influence our business customers to do the same. As well as benefiting the environment, these initiatives often result in cost savings to Barclays.

Contributing to sustainable mining

As a provider of project and corporate finance to the global mining sector, Barclays takes a keen interest in the industry's efforts to improve its corporate social responsibility. We participate in the Mining Minerals and Sustainable Development Project, which brings together individuals, non-governmental organizations, institutions and companies to address critical issues facing the sector. As financiers, we use the World Bank's environmental guidelines both as minimum criteria for lending decisions to the industry and for ongoing loan performance monitoring.

Commercial lending

Objective: Ensure risk and relationship management employees have the awareness, tools and training needed to take due account of environmental risk issues in appraising business lending propositions world-wide.

During 2001, we reviewed and confirmed in the Group Risk Committee the appropriateness of all Barclays environmental risk-management policies relevant to our commercial lending activity. Following recommendations made by PricewaterhouseCoopers last year, management controls surrounding risk policy implementation in Barclays Capital have been developed. Work will continue in 2002 to implement similar controls in Business Banking.

While we are not responsible for our customers' environmental practices, we have a long-standing commitment to managing the environmental risks associated with our lending. Through our Environmental Risk Management Unit (ERMU), environmental risk has become part of our credit assessment process for many business customers' financial propositions. ERMU provides guidance on environmental risk assessment to staff in all of Barclays businesses. The team has gained considerable experience and provides valuable support for our lending managers.

In designing policies and lending processes, ERMU has taken a risk-based approach to assessing both industrial sectors and the business activities within them. The team's expertise is particularly relevant to project financing (in which our Environmental Impact Assessment policy plays an important part), the financing of waste-management concerns and financing involving commercial land development/collateral, where soil contamination is a potential issue. When lending to the waste management sector, where sound environmental management is particularly critical to business viability, relationship managers are required to refer to ERMU for support.

For risks specifically associated with commercial property in the UK, ERMU has developed a land-use questionnaire which is used to identify cases where further environmental risk assessment by external specialists is advisable. During 2001 we issued 6,180 questionnaires, with a growing number of more complex cases (32% compared to 25% in 2000) needing further enquiry.

Governments too are aware of the issues, as this extract from the UK Government's website shows:

Greening Government – good progress but challenges ahead

Committing all Government departments to purchasing 10% of their energy from renewable resources by 2008, and dramatically cutting water usage by 2004 are just two of the 'wins' by Green Ministers last year.

Each Government department has a Green Minister who champions sustainable development and environmental matters in their own department and also work collectively to integrate sustainable development across government and the wider public sector.

The Green Ministers' Third Annual report sets out the contribution all Government Departments have made to achieving sustainable development in the last parliament and also includes Green Ministers' plans for the year ahead.

Banks must therefore be aware of green issues and ensure that they are an integral part of normal procedures.

Summary

Attention to marketing and selling ethics is important because it is generally accepted that we have a duty to live good moral lives and it is just as applicable in business as it is in our personal lives. Similarly green issues are part of the fabric of life and must be taken into consideration by financial services both internally and in dealing with customers.

I Ethics is, however, not really about illegality, it is about moral judgements and therefore it is much more subjective.
2 The Consumer Sovereignty Test (CST) can be used to decide the morality of a decision. It is based on an analysis of whether consumers can exercise informed choice.
3 The Advertising Code covers all customer communications and, therefore, all must conform to the Code.
4 Ethical conduct and concern for green issues can contribute to a company's good reputation and unethical behaviour or disregard for the environment can destroy it!
5 Ethics are just as applicable in business as in our personal lives.

Select bibliography

Mastering Marketing – pp 59-63 and 159-162

Principles of Marketing: Kotler

Notes

I *Carlill v The Carbolic Smoke Ball Co.* (1892)
2 (FSA paper 'FSA's regulatory approach to financial promotion'
3 FT *Mastering Marketing* (page 61)

Section summary

This final section has looked at customer service – that is maintaining the good relationship established during the initial sale. It has also considered ethics, an increasing issue for financial services. Although all three sections have examined separate aspects of persuading customers to take your offerings – they are all interlinked and customer service starts with the first contact, and even before with the marketing planning that establishes the environment for sales.

Twenty-two

Glossary

Benefit: A feature (qv) of an offering translated into what it can do for the customers

Category killer: An organization that focuses on one small segment of product offering that by buying in bulk and trading through large outlets, can take vast market share

CHAPS: Clearing House Automated Payment System

CVP: Customer Value Proposition

Fad: Excessively high demand for an offering that never lasts long because it meets only short-term wants and does not satisfy a long-term need

Feature: A characteristic of an offering

Footfall: The number of people passing by or through a location

HINWIS: High net worth individuals

Intangible: An offering for which there is no physical delivery

RDMS: Relational database management system

Data warehouse: Method of storing information that facilitates analysis

Data mining: Extracting information from masses of data

Latent need: A need that has not been identified nor articulated but which emerges when an offering meets it (eg 'music on the move')

Regulation: Laws governing what an industry can or cannot do

Green: Concerned with the environment

PAPERS: (Purpose, Amount, Period, Earnings, Repayment, Security)

Value proposition: The combination of benefit and price that you are offering to a customer. The customer will choose one that offers the best trade-off between the benefit and costs to them

White labelling: The production of goods or services supplied to a seller which then brands them as its own

White goods: Electrical goods such as washing machines and fridges – so called from the traditional colour

Further reading

Principles of Marketing	Kotler	Prentice-Hall
Value Pricing	Fletcher & Russell-Jones	Kogan Page
Change Management Pocketbook	Russell-Jones	Management Pocketbooks
Pyramid Thinking	Barbara Minto	Pitman
The Whole Business Brain	N Herrmann	McGraw-Hill
Decision Making Pocketbook	Russell-Jones	Management Pocketbooks
Values in Decision Making	R Keaney	Harvard
Strategic Safari	Mintzberg	
Competitive Advantage	Porter	Free Press
Strategic Planning	Anschoff	
FT – Mastering Marketing	many	FT
EVA	Stern, Stewart	
Competitive Targeting		
Value-based Marketing	Peter Doyle	Wiley 2000
Financial Services Marketing	Tina Harrison	FT Prentice Hall
Organizational Behaviour	Huczynski & Buchanan	FT Prentice Hall

Index